HOW WE BECAME
POST-LIBERAL

HOW WE BECAME POST-LIBERAL

The Rise and Fall of Toleration

Russell Blackford

BLOOMSBURY ACADEMIC
LONDON • NEW YORK • OXFORD • NEW DELHI • SYDNEY

BLOOMSBURY ACADEMIC
Bloomsbury Publishing Plc
50 Bedford Square, London, WC1B 3DP, UK
1385 Broadway, New York, NY 10018, USA
29 Earlsfort Terrace, Dublin 2, Ireland

BLOOMSBURY, BLOOMSBURY ACADEMIC and the Diana logo
are trademarks of Bloomsbury Publishing Plc

First published in Great Britain 2024

For legal purposes the Acknowledgements on p. viii constitute an
extension of this copyright page.

Illustration © Annabel Hewitson

Bloomsbury Publishing Plc does not have any control over, or responsibility for,
any third-party websites referred to or in this book. All internet addresses given
in this book were correct at the time of going to press. The author and publisher
regret any inconvenience caused if addresses have changed or sites have
ceased to exist, but can accept no responsibility for any such changes.

A catalogue record for this book is available from the British Library.

A catalog record for this book is available from the Library of Congress.

ISBN: HB: 978-1-3503-2293-6
         PB: 978-1-3503-2294-3
       ePDF: 978-1-3503-2295-0
      eBook: 978-1-3503-2296-7

Typeset by Integra Software Services Pvt. Ltd.

To find out more about our authors and books visit www.bloomsbury.com
and sign up for our newsletters.

In memory of Norman Talbot and Godfrey Tanner – great teachers and wonderful eccentrics.

CONTENTS

ACKNOWLEDGEMENTS

As with every book I've been involved in, I've talked with numerous friends and colleagues, and I appreciate every conversation. Of course, the (somewhat controversial) opinions expressed herein are my own and should not be attributed to anybody else.

My wife, Jenny Blackford, read a late draft of the entire manuscript and gave me detailed, helpful feedback. As always, Jenny's presence in my life kept me sane throughout the exercise. During the time needed to research and write *How We Became Post-Liberal*, I wrestled not only with the complex questions involved, including all their convoluted history, but also with a series of individually small, yet cumulatively distracting, health issues. I couldn't have made it through this period and actually delivered a book manuscript without Jenny's constant help in innumerable ways.

During the same period, I benefitted greatly from the regular meet-ups of the Novocastrian Philosopher group, convened by Joe Mintoff, where topics related to this book often came up in discussion (partly, but not entirely, because of my particular obsessions). I also benefitted in recent times from online meetings of the Law and Philosophy Forum, convened by Jelena Gligorijevic of the Australian National University, and the 2021 online meetings of the Freedom of Speech Reading Group, convened by Adrienne Stone of the University of Melbourne.

A book such as this, covering over two thousand years of historical developments, often in some detail and sometimes venturing beyond the West, is a challenge to research and stitch together. In consulting sources, I've taken all possible care to get my facts straight and my interpretations at least plausible, but there are bound to be some errors and misunderstandings. Whichever they are, I'm entirely to blame for them.

NOTE TO READERS

What follows is a complex story that evolves over the centuries, but I've tried to tell it as clearly as the subject allows. In every age, there's been a logic of persecution. Why tolerate ideas and ways of life that you object to, especially when much is at stake? True, there are often reasons for practices of toleration and an attitude of tolerance. Often, toleration is needed for social peace. Often, people and movements push back against interference, persecution and suppression. But the logic of persecution always lurks as an option.

In an earlier book, *The Tyranny of Opinion* (2019), I identified what might be called our post-liberal situation in today's liberal democracies, though on that occasion, I didn't use the term *post-liberal*. It's a useful term for a situation that arose quite recently, after what had seemed a movement towards liberal societies. There has been a loss of trust in liberal principles, values and language. Conversely, we see new kinds of surveillance and new ways to enforce conformity. How did this come about? In *The Tyranny of Opinion*, I described the outcome as it seemed to me at the time (and since then, the situation has only grown more intense). But how and why did it happen? What steps and motivations were involved?

In researching and writing *How We Became Post-Liberal*, I've tried to answer those questions, hoping the answers might shed light on our current predicament. The result is a kind of companion to *The Tyranny of Opinion*, though the two books can be read separately and a few years have passed in which my thinking has changed a bit.

What follows, then, is a kind of philosophical history. As it's turned out, it's also a legal history. I'm not writing narrowly for legal scholars (one of the tribes that I belong to), but in the end this is a book for them as well. Evolving legal materials, especially outcomes in the courts of law, tell much of the story of social opinion changing over time. I freely discuss cases in a way that is meant to interest general readers while meeting scholarly standards. The scholarly apparatus is lighter than in books aimed more specifically at lawyers and jurists, but I provide enough detail of the cases for those who want to locate them. There are formal legal citations within the text for cases that I actually quote.

I live in hope that better understanding means better self-awareness and better public policy. That remains to be seen, but *How We Became Post-Liberal* is written on an assumption that the game isn't over for liberalism and toleration within Western liberal democracies. There's still some point in advocating secular government, free inquiry and discussion, and the rule of law, and in promoting values such as individuality, spontaneity and original thinking. As I stated in *The Tyranny of Opinion*, liberal ideas can still resonate if only we take some trouble to explain them.

1 MOTIVATION AND OVERVIEW

Not the best of times

It's not the worst of times, but it might have turned out better. As we see in each day's news reports, public disagreements become bitter struggles for survival. Political opponents view each other as corrupt, morally irredeemable, not worth efforts at understanding. The go-to tactic is radical condemnation, and the aim is to triumph, destroy all opposition and salt the earth. In an extended essay published in 2022, the high-profile Australian broadcasters Waleed Aly and Scott Stephens express their fears for civil society if this continues. Such conflict, they warn, forecloses tolerance and compromise. It cannot be reconciled with efforts at 'cultivating a common life even in the presence of disagreement' (Aly and Stephens 2022: 7).

How did it come to this? And once it's happened, why take part in public life? Why not stay safe and cultivate our gardens? At the least, we might hold fast to our particular moral tribes, immerse ourselves in their dogmas and not try to think for ourselves.

We now live – most of us reading these words – in so-called liberal democracies. That idea suggests elections and representative governments, and with them a broader commitment to liberal ideas. Right now, however, that commitment has gone missing. In the chapters that follow, I ask how this came about, I tell the story as best I can and I offer my reflections on our current predicament.

We have never lived in perfectly liberal societies, but not many decades ago we seemed to be well on our way. And then we leapt to something reasonably called post-liberal, beginning around the mid-1970s and intensifying ever since. Partly, there was a backlash from the political Right, and partly there was disillusionment and transformation on the Left. These didn't come out of nowhere; they stemmed from anger, fear and frustration, and from an element of fragile hope. To understand them and their all-too-human causes, we'll need to step into history.

Liberal ideas

As I explained in an earlier book, I wish the word *liberal* (with cognates such as *liberalism*) were clearer, with a commonly agreed meaning (Blackford 2019b: 4). In some contexts, especially in the United States, these words refer more than anything to schemes of public welfare and government intervention in capitalist markets. As we'll see in Chapter 6, this usage dates to the 1930s and the political rhetoric of Franklin D. Roosevelt.

By contrast, I understand liberalism in an older and more international sense: as a political tradition or tendency that values individual freedom – especially freedom of speech, although the meaning of this is open to interpretation. The philosopher Gerald Gaus explains as follows:

> The liberal tradition in politics is, first and foremost, about individual freedom. Although its roots go far back in the history of political thought, liberalism emerged as a distinct political theory as a call for freedom of speech and thought.
>
> (Gaus 2003: 1)

This brief passage is worth a moment's reflection. Gaus refers to a 'liberal tradition' as well to liberalism as a 'political theory', and it's well to emphasize the 'tradition' aspect of this. Liberalism emerged from earlier ideas that were not necessarily a unity. It developed in many different places, sometimes discarded ideas or changed emphases, and repeatedly interrogated and renewed itself. In their 'Liberalism' article for the prestigious *Stanford Encyclopedia of Philosophy*, Shane D. Courtland, Gerald Gaus and David Schmidtz acknowledge that liberalism fractures 'into a range of related but sometimes competing visions', and is not a unified political philosophy (Courtland, Gaus, and Smith 2022: 1).

A good place to start for those interested in liberalism's history and its current challenges is the journalist Edmund Fawcett's superb book on the subject, *Liberalism: The Life of an Idea*. Fawcett attempts to convey the gist of liberal thought with four themes that he refers to as *conflict, power, progress* and *civic respect* (Fawcett 2018: 7–15). As he elaborates on these, they are all complex concepts, and once they're developed and explained there is some overlap. Nonetheless, I find them evocative and useful, and they can be summarized as follows:[1]

- An acceptance of conflicting worldviews and material interests where they exist within the same society, with an implication that the conflict is permanent and that it should be tolerated and managed rather than settled by crushing certain participants.

- Hostility to unchecked power of all kinds, especially, but not solely, arbitrary government power.

- The belief and commitment that the social life of human beings can be improved.

- Acceptance by the legal system and the society as a whole that different people will attempt to flourish in different ways, and that they should be given room to pursue their own projects and plans in life.

These could be relabelled as ideas of *toleration, liberty, meliorism* and *social pluralism*, but in any event they are broad tendencies within liberalism that can be given different emphases in different times and places.

Historically, liberalism arose in the nineteenth century in opposition to the interests of landowning nobles, and in support of free trade, economic modernization and various humanitarian objectives. Liberal thinkers and statesmen valued equality, rather than hierarchies and relationships of domination, but this form of equality – doing away as far as possible with social ranks and inequalities before the law – did not necessarily mean eliminating all inequalities in economic outcomes.

From the beginning, liberals favoured representative democracy (though that is no longer a distinguishing feature), limited and secular government, due process for people accused of wrongdoing and

---

[1]This brief summary is intended to do justice to Fawcett's subtle presentation of his ideas, but it employs my wording rather than his. Accordingly, it may express a certain bias or emphasis of my own.

more generally the rule of law. As to the latter, the broad idea is that constitutional and legal arrangements should restrict the exercise of arbitrary government power. They should give an assurance of how we may plan and live our lives within the scope of the laws so that, as Baron de Montesquieu wrote in the eighteenth century, no one need 'live in [their] society without knowing precisely what engagements one has contracted' (Montesquieu [1748]1989: 158).

Liberals promoted secular government and religious freedom. They resisted the power of established churches, and they favoured conceptions of the state in which individuals were not accountable to the secular authorities for their religious beliefs. To speak more broadly, they favoured individual freedom against the might of the church and state.

The liberty of the moderns

It's worth making explicit that the liberal conception of freedom is what is often called 'the liberty of the moderns' – most closely associated with the French author and statesman Benjamin Constant, though the great Russian British philosopher and public intellectual Isaiah Berlin traced the idea back to the seventeenth century. According to Berlin, it received classic expositions in the work of Constant among others, and perhaps culminated with John Stuart Mill's writings in the middle of the nineteenth century. Berlin explains that this is an essentially *negative* freedom or liberty: the ability for individuals to live their lives as they please *without external restrictions*, enabling them to develop their own individual natures even to the point of eccentricity (see Berlin 2014: 5–6).

This can be contrasted with other conceptions of freedom, such as an individual's status as a free person rather than a slave, the individual's freedom to participate in the institutions of government and political decision-making, or the collective freedom of a people from occupation by a foreign power. Liberalism evolved through the efforts of Constant, Mill and others. As it took form, liberals saw little need for limits to 'negative' or 'modern' freedom. For liberals, the only limits should be whatever is needed to protect the rights or the common security of others (Berlin 2014: 6).

Liberals have, therefore, embraced such values as individuality, spontaneity and original thinking. They inherited the eighteenth-century

Enlightenment's emphasis on reason, social meliorism and progress. In the Enlightenment tradition, liberals have hoped for scientific, philosophical and moral improvement, enabled by a social environment of free inquiry and public discussion. As a corollary of their emphasis on individual freedom, liberal thinkers argued for the broadest practicable toleration of ideas, ways of life, and associated cultures and sub-cultures.

The flipside of liberalism, therefore, is toleration. Conversely, liberalism's enemy is intolerance.[2] At least since Mill's *On Liberty*, published in 1859, liberals have emphasized that governments are not the only threats to individual freedom. Even more important, perhaps, than tyrannical government is the tyranny of the majority, or as Mill famously expressed it, 'the tyranny of the prevailing opinion and feeling' (Mill [1859]1974: 63). If we're going to be free to live our lives with minimal restrictions, growing and flourishing as individuals – perhaps even non-conformist, eccentric ones – we need some space to be left alone. Others might dislike how we live, disagree with our beliefs and ideas, even oppose our goals, but in a liberal society they'll need to show us forbearance.

In a liberal society, therefore, an element of self-restraint will be exercised by citizens for their mutual advantage. This might not keep us from expressing our objections to beliefs, practices, ways of life and other things that we disapprove of. We might be harshly critical or scornful of some of the things that we tolerate, but we'll have reasons for putting up with them, at least to some extent. We'll hold back from trying to suppress whatever thought, speech and action we object to, while our fellow citizens will restrain themselves in the same way. Thus, a liberal society will not only enact liberal laws but will also maintain a liberal *practice of toleration* that extends beyond the law-making process and the formal justice system.

There's a long history of resistance to these ideas, mainly from conservative forces: not least from the Christian churches, and often from governments unwilling to relinquish power. But by the 1950s, liberalism and toleration were starting to dominate law-making and much else in the working of Western societies. This trend accelerated in the Long Sixties: the period from the late 1950s to the early 1970s, dominated

---

[2]In Chapter 2, I'll have much more to say about the particular words *toleration, tolerance* and *intolerance*. Important though they can be, semantic niceties need not concern us for the moment.

by dramatic social revolutions. Governments dropped many controls; censorship and social *mores* loosened; women rebelled against sexist stereotypes and demanded new opportunities; and in many Western nations, the churches lost much of their power. Extrapolating from, say, fifty years ago, we might have predicted the emergence of highly liberal societies by the twenty-first century.

But that was not to be.

We are post-liberal

I am not, by any means, the first person to use the term *post-liberalism* (or alternatively, *postliberalism*). To take a recent example, a 2017 academic article by the political theorist Adrian Pabst identifies 'postliberalism' as a new central ground in British politics. Here, the word seems to be roughly a synonym for *communitarianism*, in that Pabst writes (for example) of a social order shifting towards 'social solidarity and fraternal relations' (Pabst 2017: 501). This is close to what I have in mind, though Pabst's analysis includes what strikes me as a premature claim that Britain was moving beyond identity politics in recent years. In any event, I hope to sharpen up the discussion in my own way, showing how Western liberal democracies have entered an era of eroded support for traditional liberal ideas.

In his 1993 book *Post-Liberalism* (paperback ed. 1996), the political philosopher John Gray argues that liberalism is dead, which seems to be an exaggeration wrapped around a middle-sized grain of truth. Gray identifies four philosophical elements that he thinks constitute liberalism, at least since Mill. These are similar to the liberal themes that I've attributed to Edmund Fawcett and given my endorsement. They are, in senses that Gray defines, *universalism, individualism, egalitarianism* and *meliorism* (Gray 1996: 284–7). For Gray, liberalism is dead because it's committed to defending these values in an absolute and extreme form that is now untenable because we recognize a wider plurality of values that cannot be objectively measured against each other.

However, Gray argues that universalism, individualism, egalitarianism and meliorism (if only in what he considers 'contextualized' forms: Gray 1996: 320) *are*, indeed, the best social and political values for cultures marked by what he calls 'a diversity of incommensurable conceptions of the good' (Gray 1996: 284). He adds that this description is intended to include virtually all modern cultures. He thus defends liberal values – at least the ones that he identifies and summarizes – for the purposes of almost all contemporary nations including all those of the West. Admittedly, the defence relies on historical and pragmatic considerations, rather than on more metaphysical or fundamental grounds. For what it's worth, we can agree on that much.

For three decades now, Gray has appeared increasingly hostile to Mill and the liberal tradition, but his position in 1993 was more like a variation of liberal thought than a genuine post-liberalism. As I see it, he exaggerates the metaphysical commitments in the writings of Mill and most other liberal thinkers, while underestimating the diversity of liberalisms supported in the past by statesmen and public intellectuals in many countries, responding in practical ways to concrete circumstances. That, however, is an argument for another occasion. For now, when I write of post-liberalism, I have something more in mind than a metaphysically modest form of liberalism.

The contemporary problem, as I see it, is that liberal ideas have lost their cachet. Over a few short decades – an eyeblink in historical time – liberal tolerance stopped being seen as a virtue and a valued pro-social option. Instead, tolerance is often regarded as a vice. Accompanying this, we see greatly inflated concepts relating to harm: for example, concepts of hurt, trauma, distress, violence and harm itself. As these concepts expand, they compress the zone of what is seen as tolerable. Some liberal ideas are still given lip service, but they're undermined by new interpretations.

In this sense, then, the social environment of contemporary Western liberal democracies is post-liberal. Part of the story is a resurgence of right-wing viewpoints, often in the form of nostalgic populism. But part of the story is very different. There is now a successor belief system to older styles of left-wing ideology that were often connected to Marxist theory. For want of a better name for it, I'll label this new system or 'successor ideology',[3] or the broadly based movement that promotes it, *the Social Justice Movement*.

---

[3] The idea of a successor belief system is not in itself new – most notoriously, Marxism was viewed by many as a successor belief system to earlier systems of thought such as Christianity. But some credit should go to the essayist Wesley Yang for popularizing the phrase *the successor ideology* in our contemporary context. If we can rely on his Wikipedia biography, he appears to have introduced it to social media in about March 2019.

While not technically a religion, at least by my definition (see Chapter 2), the Social Justice Movement has the superficial trappings of one. For many people, it has become something like a religion. It plays the religion role in their lives.

The road ahead

In the remainder of this book, I trace the history of greater toleration from late antiquity to the Long Sixties, and then its collapse beginning in the mid, and then late, 1970s, and intensifying ever since. Chapter 2 will analyse the idea of toleration, including variations in terms of what is tolerated and *how far* it is tolerated. The concepts introduced here will pay off for the reader in later chapters. Historically, toleration was often the alternative to specifically religious persecution, and Chapter 2 will also discuss the nature of religion. I will comment upon religious pluralism in the ancient world, prior to the rise of Christianity, as well as in non-European civilizations such as those of China, India and the Middle East.

In Chapter 3, I turn to the rise of Christianity in late antiquity. Christianity proved to be an unusually intolerant and even persecutorial religion, qualities that led to deep divisions within Latin Christendom following the Protestant Reformation. The outcomes included persecutions and wars across Europe, but in their turn these produced a need for theological and philosophical ideas to support greater toleration.

Chapter 4 reflects especially on the eighteenth-century Age of Enlightenment. This was an age of new ideas, revolutions and battles over state censorship. It was marked by an ideal of progress and by prototypes of what came to be considered 'liberal' notions, yet it ended with events that suggested, once again, the fragility of toleration if the perceived stakes are high enough.

Chapter 5 covers the 'Long Nineteenth Century' from the final years of the 1700s to the beginning of the First World War. This was a time when liberalism crystallized in Europe as a political movement and the first explicitly named liberal parties were formed, beginning in Spain. It was an era of ideologies and new national states. The Long Nineteenth Century saw increasing toleration in some respects in some societies, but also severely retrograde events such as the beginning of modern antisemitism.

Chapter 6 turns to an intense period of world history: the four decades from the First World War and the Bolshevik Revolution in Russia to the Second World War, the Nazi Holocaust and their immediate aftermath in the late 1940s and the 1950s. This period included the Great Depression and, as one response to it, the beginnings of a distinctively American version of liberalism. The momentous events of these decades had consequences that continue to unfold. Most immediately, they included a post-war arms race and the decades-long Cold War, but they also prompted deeply considered philosophical and political responses to the shocking experiences of total war, totalitarianism and genocide.

During the Long Sixties there were struggles within Western liberal democracies for greater personal freedoms. Chapter 7, the longest in the book, focuses on this period. Left-wing activists obtained important victories, but not the total transformation of society that many hoped for. They increasingly perceived their successes as incomplete and insufficient. This led to internal conflicts within the Left – broadly understood – over values, goals and tactics.

Chapter 8 comments on a retreat from liberalism in the later 1970s, and especially during the 1980s and beyond. The victories obtained during the Long Sixties continued to feel like failures, and something more than liberal ideas seemed required. The 1980s and 1990s saw a rise of identity politics, based partly on a continued sense that the Long Sixties revolutions had fallen short. One sign of the times was the Rushdie Affair in 1989. Many politicians and commentators – including some on the political Left – turned against the award-winning novelist Salman Rushdie, rather than defending his freedom to publish.

In Chapter 9, I examine the emerging situation in the twenty-first century. Post-liberal ideological thinking has evolved, obtained popularity and exerted increasing power and influence. In its popular forms and in the online world, it has become ubiquitous. It works with new harm-related concepts, and follows tactics of surveillance, shaming and career destruction.

In Chapter 10 – the book's final chapter – I reflect upon contemporary challenges to and for liberalism. In the twentieth and twenty-first centuries, we have seen the rise of illiberal ideologies and movements. These provide alternatives to liberalism and set challenges in that sense, but they also provide a more subtle kind of challenge for liberals to respond without losing their liberal credentials.

Stepping into history

If our world were entirely unpredictable and uncontrollable, the study of history might futile – except, perhaps, to prepare us for more surprises. But our situation is not completely hopeless. We cannot predict the future, but sometimes we see, or appear to see, patterns playing out. The study of history might, I think, offer some insight into human responses. It can warn how statesmen, revolutionaries, zealots, opportunists and fearmongers might respond in situations that have happened before. Some kinds of situations do recur, and at least we can see what *might* happen.

The Austrian philosopher Karl Popper was a leading opponent of historicism (as he called it): the idea that there is a 'plot' to history in the sense of a narrative with a foreordained and perhaps foreseeable path. But in a paper entitled 'A Pluralist Approach to the Philosophy of History', even Popper conceded some truth to the idea of a plot discoverable '*in* history' (Popper 1994: 136; Popper's emphasis). That is, we can observe through recent human history – and ultimately through the evolutionary history of life – an incremental growth of knowledge, particularly scientific knowledge.

Popper did not postulate historical laws that could ground predictions about humanity's future, but he saw value in asking questions such as: 'How did the two world wars break out? Were they avoidable?' (Popper 1994: 138). For Popper, such questions, and the efforts to answer them, might increase our understanding. Indeed, without subscribing to any grand narrative of historical events, he often discussed examples that he viewed as illustrative and useful. He affirmed the impact of ideas on events, and at one point drew a comparison between the Russian and French revolutions: for Popper, Vladimir Lenin's seizure of power in 1917 in the name of Karl Marx paralleled Maximilien Robespierre's seizure of power in the name of Jean-Jacques Rousseau more than a century earlier (Popper 1994: 187–8).

I'll return to both sets of events in later chapters. For now, let's acknowledge room for debate about Popper's comparison. We can question just how faithfully Lenin followed the thought of Marx, or how well Robespierre emulated Rousseau. In such cases, we should be alert to differences as well as finding parallels. Nonetheless, studying history tells us something of how statesmen and revolutionaries – and many others – respond to the stresses of their roles. As we learn about the past, and how the present came about, it illuminates our situation – albeit not too brightly. With any luck, it might help us do better.

These are not the best of times, and that especially shows in the standard of public discussion in contemporary Western democracies. Some ideas that were taboo a couple of generations ago are now expressed freely, but new taboos have been established. New threats have arisen to our ability to express ourselves without fear. Punishments take the form of public shaming, online abuse directed at people with unpopular ideas and orchestrated campaigns of varied kinds against disliked speakers. None of this advances what Mill meant by liberty of thought and public discussion.

If we still find value in liberal ideas, we need to understand why so many people have come to disagree. We can then meaningfully consider what should be said and done in response. That is the point of a book like this.

2 RELIGION, TOLERATION AND RELIGIOUS TOLERATION

Toleration and tolerance

The words *toleration* and *tolerance* are a source of endless bafflement in the academic literature, with no end of attempts by historians, philosophers and other scholars to distinguish, define, refine and possibly redefine them.

In one classic discussion, the political scientist Preston King distinguishes between tolerance, as 'enduring some physical discomfort, such as pain', and toleration, as 'putting up with some intellectual discomfort, like a competing doctrine' (King 1976: 12). However, he sees this distinction as pedantic and seldom maintained, and instead he prefers to use the term *toleration* more broadly than *tolerance* – with the latter reserved for minimal kinds of toleration that retain the objection to whatever is tolerated (King 1976: 13; for a similar view, see Balint 2017: 24). But other scholars head in precisely the opposite direction, using the word *tolerance* for something more positive and welcoming than, as they see it, mere toleration (Bejan 2017: 16; Spencer 2018: xiv–xv). To say the least, this is perplexing.

The German political philosopher Rainer Forst, a leading theorist of toleration, views it as a conditional acceptance or non-interference with beliefs, actions or practices that are viewed as wrong (Forst 2017: 1). The political philosopher Andrew Jason Cohen refers to '*an agent's intentional and principled refraining from interfering*' (A. Cohen 2018: 2; Cohen's emphasis). For Cohen, therefore, refraining in a spirit of pragmatic compromise is not toleration: we exercise toleration only when we feel we *should*. Likewise, David Heyd seeks to distinguish between toleration and a pragmatic avoidance of interfering with others' beliefs and practices for the sake of peace, compromise, coexistence or social stability (Heyd 2021: 81).

What if we turn to a dictionary? Dictionary definitions can miss subtleties of meaning that philosophers regard as important and attempt to explain. In this case, though, I see no reason to stray far from the *Oxford English Dictionary* (OED), which provides the following definition of *toleration*: 'The action or practice of tolerating or allowing what is not actually approved; forbearance, sufferance.' *Pace* Forst, we do not need to assess an action or practice as in some sense wrong – as opposed, for example, to annoying or unpleasant – before we can tolerate it.

Likewise, we can have many reasons to refrain from interfering even if they are not especially principled ones. If I exercise self-restraint in a spirit of pragmatic compromise, that is nonetheless acting for a reason, though not one that would satisfy all philosophers as adequately principled. Perhaps, however, not just *any* reason can be consistent with toleration. Consider, for example, a government's strategic decision not to ban an Islamist organization such as Hizb ut Tahrir: that is, it decides not to ban the organization because driving it underground might backfire (for discussion, see Balint 2017: 37, 95; Baumeister 2021: 141). Peter Balint, an expert in politics and international relations with a special interest in issues relating to political toleration, would consider this an example of toleration based on pragmatic reasons. Perhaps so, but it's at least questionable whether it's a *good*, or illustrative, example of toleration if the decision is part of an indirect strategy to frustrate the group's purposes. At best, this seems like a borderline case.

Balint raises another complication that cannot be avoided entirely. In his 2017 book *Respecting Toleration*, he suggests that there is a broader conception of toleration in our everyday thinking and language. Within this conception, forbearance is not involved because there is no objection to whatever is being tolerated. That is, the so-called objection component of toleration (King 1976: 44–51) is not present in these cases. Balint refers to a common usage in which some societies are described as remarkably tolerant, yet this does *not* mean that myriads of objections are constantly being set aside or overcome. Rather, most people and institutions within the society 'do not really care about a great many things to which others would object, and consequently are relatively permissive' (Balint 2017: 6). Accordingly, for Balint, tolerant societies are accommodating societies in which people are relaxed about each other's aspirations and activities, and 'any restriction is properly justified' (Balint 2017: 8).

This usage seems to be genuine, and hence English speakers have a conception of toleration (or at least of tolerance) that involves a disposition towards inaction without the experience of conscious forbearance or deliberate restraint. Even here, however, Balint provides a clue when he refers to people and institutions showing indifference to beliefs, practices and things 'to which others would object'. That is, the objection component seems to remain in a watered-down or ghostly form. What is said to be tolerated is not actually objected to in this society, but there's a hint that the society treats as matters of indifference certain beliefs, actions or practices – or perhaps other things – that, human history being what it is, might be expected to attract objections.

For current purposes, I will avoid these niceties as far as possible. Writing in the 1980s, the philosopher Jay Newman discussed the concepts in a way that I find persuasive. Newman reserved the word *toleration* for instances or practices of tolerating. He distinguished this from *tolerance*, which refers in his usage to something more psychological. Thus, tolerance is a disposition of character that we show when we exercise self-restraint by accepting, enduring or putting up with something towards which we have a negative attitude such as dislike, disrespect or disapproval (for discussion, see Newman 1982: 4–6). This seems about right according to the OED and my own linguistic intuitions.

For the sake of clarity and consistency, then, I will generally use the word *toleration* when referring to acts, courses of conduct, policies or the like, that involve forbearance. Where relevant, I will follow Newman and other scholars for whom *tolerance* refers to a psychological disposition to tolerate, and thus to exercise self-restraint – as when we say of someone who is much put-upon that she is reaching the limit of her tolerance. Unfortunately, the word *intolerance* will have to suffice as an antonym for both *toleration* and *tolerance*. For my purposes in the following chapters, there is no need to refine the concepts any further or to stipulate a definition that departs from common usage.

Dimensions of toleration

Toleration (and indeed, tolerance) can have a number of aspects or dimensions. In one dimension, different kinds of beliefs, activities, practices – and perhaps other things – can meet with objections and become candidates for toleration. There can be different reasons to tolerate something that is nonetheless objected to, and clearly enough toleration can come in different degrees.[1]

In any particular situation, toleration might have limits. For example, the political authorities might dislike a particular religion and not countenance its dissemination to school pupils or to the general public. They might, nonetheless, be willing to allow its adherents to meet among themselves without interference.[2] Even liberal-minded people might tolerate the beliefs and practices of religious minorities only up to a point: perhaps a point where those beliefs and practices start to conflict with major social institutions to which those liberal-minded people are committed. Beyond that point, they might ask 'How much, after all, can fairly be expected of us?' and might think that the people in the religious minority are the ones who 'should have to do the accommodating' (Newman 1982: 15).

In his *Stanford Encyclopedia of Philosophy* article on the topic of toleration, and in his monumental historical and philosophical study, *Toleration in Conflict* (Forst 2016), Rainer Forst sets out what he regards as various conceptions of toleration. These conceptions can also be viewed as varieties of toleration based on different sorts of reasons such as the following: avoiding persecutions in order to preserve civil peace; avoiding oppressive demands (such as requiring groups or individuals to act against conscience or to abandon deeply held beliefs); maintaining peaceful coexistence through mutual forbearance; establishing a framework of mutual respect for each other's rights; or even finding something worthy of esteem in beliefs, activities and practices to which there is, all things considered, some remaining objection.

---

[1]For a different view, however, see A. Cohen (2018: 35–6).
[2]An alternative analysis is that the government tolerates private exercise of the religion but not its public expression. This is logically coherent, but we should be able to ask, non-rhetorically, *how far* a government or a society tolerates a religion that it regards as false or otherwise objectionable.

These rationales – and there are doubtless others – imply different relationships between whoever, or whatever, is tolerated and whoever is doing the tolerating, and those relationships may be reflected in the structures and processes of entire societies.[3]

Some authors who write about toleration (e.g. Kamen 1967: 7) focus on non-persecution over religious differences, but there is a far wider variety of things that a government, local population, organization, group, movement or individual might object to, and which might therefore attract some kind of censorship, restriction or punishment. One important example is toleration (or otherwise) of political dissent. Another example relates to the expression of human sexuality, which has been regulated by lawmakers throughout recorded human history: 'At any given point in time, some forms of sex and sexuality have been encouraged while others have been punished without mercy' (Berkowitz 2012: 7).

All the same, the area of religious disagreement has been enormously important. At least until the eighteenth century, issues relating to religion were the prime mover of debates about toleration. This, however, prompts the question of what counts as religion or religious, or as *a* religion.

Religion

Most of us think we can recognize a religion when we see one – yet the boundaries of religion are difficult to define. Unfortunately, there is no agreed definition among scholars who study religion or religions, and indeed some are sceptical about whether there is a unitary phenomenon of religion at all. There seems to be even more scholarly scepticism about talk of 'religions' or 'the religions of the world', and we can easily wonder whether (for example) Christianity, Daoism and the pagan polytheism of the ancient Graeco-Roman world are all examples of the same kind of thing.[4]

Yet, we do sometimes need to distinguish religion and religions from non-religious beliefs or worldviews. This is often a practical issue for

---

[3]For the full detail of this analysis, see Forst (2016: 26–32).
[4]Here, the classic text is Wilfred Cantwell Smith's *The Meaning and End of Religion* (1963). Notwithstanding the title of his book, Smith argues throughout that the concepts of religion and 'the religions' are deeply misleading. For more, see Blackford (2021: 2–4).

courts of law and similar bodies when they confront the issue of what counts as a religion. For example, Arif A. Jamal (2015) has examined the difficulty in defining *religion* for the purposes of international human rights law. Similar issues frequently appear in interpreting and applying a nation's constitution, which might, for example, provide for freedom of religion or free religious exercise. Alternatively or in addition, it might forbid applying a religious test for political office. Again, the courts might need to deal with a legal document, such as a statute, a contract or a trust deed, that gives 'religious bodies' a tax benefit or provides for certain funds to be set aside to be spent on 'religious purposes'.

One place to turn is the work of Charles Taylor – a distinguished Canadian philosopher – and especially his 2007 book *A Secular Age*. As a caveat, Taylor makes clear that his account of the phenomenon of religion is not meant to be definitive of all beliefs, practices and forms of experience that are commonly regarded as religious. His goals in this particular book lead to a focus on Christianity, and to a lesser extent the other 'Abrahamic' religions (i.e. Judaism and Islam).[5] Nonetheless, he makes interesting comparisons with other traditions – especially Buddhism – and with some of the philosophical systems of classical antiquity.

Taylor invokes the idea of a twofold cosmic order: the natural world known to us through our senses, and a reality or order of things that transcends the natural world. As a further step, he discusses a transcendent dimension to human life as it is seen from a religious standpoint, so that our lives 'extend beyond' our natural lives as creatures that are born, reproduce and die (Taylor 2007: 20). On Taylor's account, then, religions construe the transcendent reality – and with it, the transcendent dimension to human lives – as having a significance for how we ought to live and act within the natural world.

To take this a step further, religions (again, Taylor is especially, but not solely, thinking of Christianity) typically postulate deep, personal transformations to ensure that their goals relating to the transcendent reality can be achieved. Religious adherents associate in likeminded communities in which there is shared adherence to moral norms and

---

[5]In summary, Taylor investigates how the European nations and their offshoots went from being pervasively Christian to being markedly more secular societies where Christianity is merely one of many options.

shared participation in rituals and forms of worship. Moreover, a religion's moral norms are often given some kind of metaphysical explanation. They might, for example, be understood as what is needed to conform to a god's commands, attract the good will of gods or spirits or achieve some kind of favourable life after death.

Similarly to Taylor, the British philosopher Tim Crane defines religion in terms of *the transcendent* and human beings' relationship to it: a religion is thus 'a systematic and practical attempt by human beings to find meaning in the world and their place in it, in terms of their relationship to something transcendent' (Crane 2017: 6). In this passage, Crane portrays religions as coherent systems of belief (or at least of narrative or metaphor) and practice.[6] In addition, he views religions as providing answers to the meaning of life – the question of how to relate to the totality of the things – that involve living in particular ways in awareness of a transcendent order. Crane resists the word *supernatural*, which he understands as presupposing a certain scientific or similar understanding of the operation of laws of nature (Crane 2017: 10), but instead uses the word *transcendent* to capture whatever lies beyond ordinary or natural experience, including the findings of science.

Courts of law have shown some convergence in formulating an understanding of religion for their own purposes. Here, two influential cases are *Church of the New Faith v. Commissioner of Pay-Roll Tax (Vic)* (High Court of Australia; decided 27 October 1983) and *R (on the application of Hodkin and another) v. Registrar General of Births, Deaths and Marriages* (UK Supreme Court; decided 11 December 2013). In these cases, the respective courts needed to determine whether, for particular legal purposes, Scientology had the status of a religion.

Both courts upheld the religious status of Scientology. In the Australian case, the five judges who took part produced three separate judgements, though all agreed in the result. In the UK case, Lord Toulmon handed down a judgement that attracted concurrence from each of the other judges on the bench. Taken broadly, the relevant judgements referred to belief in some kind of supernatural or transcendent being, entity or principle, together with teachings about how to live in alignment with it. Lord Toulmon, who had the benefit of considering the earlier Australian

---

[6]The word *practice* includes rituals and requirements of conduct.

case, expressed a preference not to use the word *supernatural*, since he viewed it as 'a loaded word which can carry a variety of connotations'.[7] In any event, he briefly described religion as follows:

> I would describe religion in summary as a spiritual or non-secular belief system, held by a group of adherents, which claims to explain mankind's place in the universe and relationship with the infinite, and to teach its adherents how they are to live their lives in conformity with the spiritual understanding associated with the belief system. By spiritual or non-secular I mean a belief system which goes beyond that which can be perceived by the senses or ascertained by the application of science.
>
> ([2013] UKSC 77, 18)

All of this suggests some scholarly and judicial convergence on a thick description of the word and concept *religion*. In reflecting on Lord Toulmon's judgement and those of Australia's High Court judges, we might emphasize that modern liberal democracies attempt to allow freedom for their citizens to respond in their own ways to fundamental existential questions that seem to confront humanity. As the Australian court discussed, some of us seek answers in science or philosophy, or in any event some kind of inquiry based on reason and the evidence of nature, whereas others see a relationship between human life and a supernatural, otherworldly, transcendent or spiritual order of things.

Clearly enough, a tolerant approach to each other's beliefs has not always prevailed historically, but the distinction made by the Australian court gives us a workable sense of how religious understandings of the world can be distinguished from others.

---

[7]Tim Crane and Lord Toulmon are not alone in expressing misgivings about the word *supernatural*. For example, the great French sociologist Émile Durkheim made a similar point to Crane's (Durkheim 1915: 24–9). As it happens, I am not convinced that there is any serious problem with the word. It can be traced back to classical Latin and even to an equivalent in ancient Greek. It appears that the idea of beings, entities, places and the like, placed somehow 'above' the observed or everyday order of things, existed well before the modern understanding of scientific laws. But for our purposes, nothing depends on this one way or the other.

Religion and ideology

By contrast with the analysis to this point, some scholars are sceptical about the idea of a twofold cosmic order, which brings a further scepticism about any distinction between religions and 'secular' ideologies. Before going much further, therefore, something needs to be said to address this particular kind of scepticism and consider how much truth it might contain.

First, what exactly are these secular ideologies? Although we can locate other meanings within, for example, Marxist theory, an ideology is, in essence, a system of ideas about society. The most common and recognizable meaning of *ideology* in current usage is captured by the fourth definition in the OED: 'A systematic scheme of ideas, usually relating to politics, economics, or society and forming the basis of action or policy; a set of beliefs governing conduct' or 'the forming or holding of such a scheme of ideas'. It follows that the common meaning of the word *ideological* is – again drawing on the OED – '[o]f or relating to a political, economic, or other ideology … ; based on a principle or set of unshakeable beliefs'.

Like most definitions, these leave an area of uncertainty. For example, how systematic does a body of ideas need to be to count as an ideology? Some ideologies might come in very detailed and systematic forms, but the details might be taught only to a small vanguard of theorists and intellectuals, while other adherents are committed to just a few key ideas. Some ideologies might go beyond political, economic and social analysis to offer comprehensive views of the world, including metaphysical or even religious content. Others might be more restricted in their claims and might be compatible with other ideas – for example, the claims made by some forms of socialism might be compatible with a variety of metaphysical or religious worldviews. Nonetheless, *ideology* and related words are useful in everyday contexts, where ordinary people are able to employ them with familiarity and confidence.

One important and representative figure in the debate about religions and ideologies is the Catholic theologian William T. Cavanaugh. Cavanaugh complains that expressions such as *transcendence, the transcendent, the supernatural* and *an invisible world* are vague and do not clearly establish which systems of belief and practice are or are not religious (Cavanaugh 2009: 102–5, 112–13). Accordingly, these words might be meaningful in certain contexts, such as discussions of the relationship between the Creator God of Christianity and the created world, but they do not apply neatly to systems of belief and practice such as Buddhism and Confucianism.

In particular, Cavanaugh questions the distinction commonly made between religions and the systems of thought that are viewed as secular or political ideologies. At one point, he remarks on how the ex-communist contributors to *The God That Failed* – a 1950 collection of disillusioned reminiscences of communism and the Soviet Union – describe their experiences. These individuals portray Marxism, as they encountered it, in what Cavanaugh describes as religious terms: 'a vision for the destiny of all humanity, unwavering faith in authoritatively promulgated doctrine, communal solidarity and ritual, and so on' (Cavanaugh 2009: 111). In Cavanaugh's favour, each of these elements – a vision of destiny, authoritative doctrine, and the community aspect – might, indeed, be seen as among the trappings of certain religions, especially Christianity.

Cavanaugh goes on to cite numerous other scholars, Marxist and otherwise, to support his view that Marxism appeared to many as a successor belief system to Christianity, and, indeed, as something like a religious creed in its own right. In respect of the contributors to *The God That Failed*, he describes the distinguished Hungarian British author Arthur Koestler as typical in recognizing a similarity between the revolutionary 'faith' of Marxism and a more traditionalist kind of faith (Cavanaugh 2009: 111).

However, a fair reading of *The God That Failed* suggests that things are not so simple. Admittedly, Richard Crossman in his introduction to the volume draws parallels between Christianity and Marxism. Crossman views Marxism as a kind of religion, and to a lesser extent this viewpoint also appears in Koestler's essay. By contrast, some contributors, including Ignazio Silone, Richard Wright and Stephen Spender, appear to have adopted a more critical stance towards Marxism, the Communist Party and goings on in the Soviet Union. Communism never seems to have been a substitute religion for those particular authors. It is not accurate to suggest that all of the contributors to *The God That Failed* were wholehearted and uncritical during their periods of party membership (or of close association with communism) or that communism played in their lives what we might call *the religion role*.

There is, moreover, a notable difference in tone and language between the political utopianism that these authors describe and the language of spiritual salvation in an afterlife that typifies much Christian doctrine and preaching. The contributors to *The God That Failed* portray communism, as they experienced it, as dogmatic, fanatical and intolerant, often led by hypocrites, and sometimes ludicrous in its demands and pretences. It does not follow, however, that it is indistinguishable from a belief system based on claims about a spiritual afterlife.

With those caveats, I don't doubt that Marxism did, for a period, play the religion role as an overall guide to life for many individuals, including numerous Western intellectuals. Perhaps it still plays that role for many people in the remaining countries based on Marxist principles, and even for some theorists and activists in the West.

As a system or set of systems, Marxism is based on this-worldly utopianism, despite Karl Marx's well-known refusal to describe the detailed workings of a post-revolutionary utopia. It can, accordingly, provide goals that make everything other than its political success appear unimportant, since so much is at stake in its ultimate success or failure. Marxism provides a novel, somewhat comprehensive and somewhat esoteric body of revelations about history, human societies and the future – in short, about how the world supposedly works. Such a system of ideas can bring people together in joint activities and produce deep psychological transformations. All of this resembles some of Charles Taylor's remarks about religions.

On a larger scale, committed Marxists plan for the radical transformation of entire societies – if not the entire world and even human nature. With so much at stake, Marxist organizations have often sought to enforce strict controls over the actions and speech of their members, as revealed in *The God That Failed* and in many other memoirs. Likewise, Marxist governments have attempted to exert total control over entire nations, societies and economies.

Cavanaugh has a point insofar as it is difficult to define a clear boundary between what is and is not a 'transcendent' entity, rather than one that is part of the natural world. Furthermore, some belief systems with ancient origins may have been, in their original forms and contexts, more like emerging schools of philosophy or non-Western science, or new approaches to morality and politics, than like the Abrahamic religions with their Creator God. Consider Confucianism for example – this is an example that Cavanaugh himself invokes.

Confucianism first emerged in ancient China during a period of political instability and civil war. Its early sages did not deny the existing background of beliefs in spirits, ancestors and local gods. However, they reinterpreted and rationalized these beliefs, and most importantly they added a body of moral and social ideas that eventually permeated Chinese culture. The overriding aim, responsive to the imperatives of the time, was essentially political: to provide the moral and other foundations for a more stable and harmonious kind of society. In itself, this aim might not appear 'religious', and interestingly Confucianism is not one of the religions officially recognized today within the People's Republic of China, whose ruling regime views it as a body of moral and social thought.

And yet, Confucian ideas have a place within contemporary mainland China as one component of a syncretic practice of religion that includes elements of Daoism, Mahayana Buddhism and service to the spirits of the dead. It is commonplace in China to observe that the traditions of Daoism, Buddhism and Confucianism blend and become one at the level of local practice (Oldstone-Moore 2015: 118–19), and even then they do not exhaust the complexity and subtlety of belief and practice among the Chinese people. For present purposes, it must suffice to observe that much in Chinese religion falls easily within what Western common sense understands as invocation of transcendent beings, entities and principles. This is so, even though the specific body of ideas *added by* Confucianism in ancient times might not be regarded as religious if viewed in isolation.

There is an intuitive distinction to be made between thoughts and worldviews that are confined to this world and those that describe another order of things which cannot be directly observed with the ordinary senses or located within the picture of the universe cumulatively developed by science. Cavanaugh is correct that this distinction cannot be used to draw a line that will satisfy all philosophers. Still, it suffices for many practical purposes such as those of Western law courts.

In the case of Marxism, we see a system of thought that does not aim at salvation in a heavenly afterlife, but at avoiding or overturning what Marx regarded as the inevitable immiseration of the industrial proletariat under capitalism. Marxism does not postulate anything like a twofold cosmic order or a transcendent, or supernatural, dimension to human life. Plausibly or not, Marxist theory claims to be scientific. Marxist scholars strive for political change based on their study of history, economics, political formations and the organizational features of human societies. Even if Marxist accounts of all this are mistaken, a government that acted in accordance with them would not thereby lose its secular credentials.

Indeed, the governments of modern liberal democracies rely on their particular understandings of history, economics, social organization, political formations and so on, in the process of making and justifying their programmes, and in appealing for support at the ballot box. As it is understood today, democracy involves contests between rival understandings of exactly these sorts of topics.

Political religions

It appears, then, that we can distinguish in a practical – but not theoretically sharp – way between religions and secular ideologies that focus on such issues as history, economics and social organization. Nonetheless, wide-ranging and systematic conceptions of the social and economic world, especially where their adherents either seek or fear radical social transformations, can occupy a similar place in an adherent's life to that played by more traditional religions. To take this a step further, it makes sense to regard some of these ideologies as *political religions* – not as systems of belief and practice with all of the characteristics discussed by Charles Taylor (for example), but nonetheless with some of the trappings of historical religions such as Christianity and, moreover, with great explanatory and transformative power.[8] Furthermore, where its goals become all-important to its adherents, such a conception of the social and economic world can be a source of dogmatism and zealotry.

In a discussion of religious violence, partly absolving religion of the charge that it is a uniquely significant cause of wars and atrocities, Tim Crane refers to the death counts of the Third Reich and the communist governments led by Joseph Stalin and Mao Zedong. Surprisingly, I think, he alleges that these totalitarian regimes 'were in no sense religious' (Crane 2017: 125). But were they really religious in *no* sense at all?

Here it is worth referring briefly to the work of Émile Durkheim, a great founding figure of the discipline of sociology who developed an

---

[8]The term *political religion* was popularized in the 1930s and 1940s, especially by the political philosopher Eric Voegelin. It was taken up by the economic historian Karl Polanyi among numerous others. However, the term has a longer history, and related ideas can be found in eighteenth- and nineteenth-century writings by authors such as Jean-Jacques Rousseau, Alexis de Tocqueville, Henri de Saint-Simon and Auguste Comte. Voegelin referred to fascism as a political religion, and as will be discussed in Chapter 6, Benito Mussolini believed that Italian Fascism was religious in some sense.

important theory of religion in *The Elementary Forms of the Religious Life* (first published in French in 1912). It is not my intention here to explicate Durkheim's theoretical approach in its entirety, much less to defend it or the early-twentieth-century ethnography on which it is based. Still, his work contains insights that remain useful today.

For Durkheim, the crucial distinction is not between the immanent (or 'this-worldly') and the transcendent, or between the natural and the supernatural, but between the sacred and the profane. That is, certain 'sacred' practices, objects, items of apparel, symbols, times, places and other things are set apart from the rest of 'profane' life and approached with a special kind of awe, veneration and humility. Sacred things are protected by strong interdictions as to how they can be treated, or how humans can permissibly relate to them.[9] For Durkheim, therefore, religions are unified systems of belief, practice and communal participation that are organized around whatever a society treats as sacred. Furthermore, the system of beliefs and practices that constitute a religion have the effect of uniting its adherents into a single moral community (Durkheim 1915: 42–7).

Durkheim identifies the widespread religious belief in an external moral force as arising from experiences of 'general effervescence' (Durkheim 1915: 210) or 'collective effervescence' (1915: 226): a shared feeling of exaltation, intensity and personal transformation when individuals participate jointly in psychologically powerful rituals or other kinds of fervent activity. The contrast between everyday life – with its regular, mundane tasks – and experiences of this effervescence creates a sense of two separate (profane and sacred) worlds (Durkheim 1915: 218–19). Nonetheless, the symbols of a society can become sacred and even worth dying for, as when a soldier risks his life to retrieve his nation's flag from the hands of the enemy (Durkheim 1915: 220).

Durkheim describes connections or relations between whatever a society regards as sacred and the society's conception of the larger cosmos, which often includes what we would, today, intuitively regard as transcendent beings, entities and principles. In practice, then, his understanding of religion might not be all that remote from those which emphasize belief in transcendent elements and dimensions of the total reality. However, his work has the virtue of helping us to understand

---

[9]Durkheim somewhat deprecates the word *taboos* – borrowed from Polynesian sources – as a synonym for these interdictions (Durkheim 1915: 300).

that a society might approach some practices, objects and so on, with awe, veneration and humility, *even without regarding these things as transcending the natural, material world.* Social practices relating to these things might constitute an important form of solidarity among members of a community, and might provide a source of strength, hope and trust in renewal.

All of this highlights the possibility of belief systems that appear intuitively religion-like but are not likely to be recognized as religions by today's law courts. Nothing in Durkheim's analysis removes the fact that well-known religions such as Christianity, Islam and Hinduism do, indeed, include belief in specific beings, forces, principles, unseen places and so on, that we readily regard as transcendent. Durkheim himself acknowledged that religions have evolved to include such beings and forces. Thus, he need not deny the commonplace observation that religions such as Buddhism and Daoism – which in certain of their expressions look more like systems of philosophy than like theistic religions – have accrued stories and doctrines about divine or spiritual beings.

What I take from Durkheim, then, is not a reliable account of religion's origins, or its essential characteristics, so much as a reminder that what we classify as religions frequently show the features that Durkheim labels with such terms as *the sacred, the profane, interdictions* and *general* (or *collective*) *effervescence.* Furthermore, although it is not Durkheim's emphasis, these features may attach to systems of belief that do not invoke a transcendent reality, or a transcendent dimension to human life, but nonetheless play the religion role. In this sense, *political* religions can, indeed, function for their adherents much like *religions.*

Religious power and religious conflict

Though many of the lines that are drawn in this discussion are frustratingly blurred, it was a significant historical achievement for liberal democracies to get (to a large extent) out of the religion business. That is, they generally do not base or justify their actions on concepts such as salvation, sin and divine providence. To the extent that this development has taken place, it removes a serious source of conflict.

Because they involve metaphysical and moral beliefs, often including beliefs about spiritual salvation or comparable outcomes in a life after death, and because they socialize their adherents to adopt specific values and attitudes, religions strongly *motivate* their adherents. Religions typically include *providential doctrines* (relating to divine assistance for rulers and societies), *soteriological doctrines* (relating to individual salvation or comparable goals) and/or *eschatological doctrines* (involving the fate of the dead, and perhaps the ultimate fate of the world). In all of these cases, much is at stake to override the claims of everyday freedoms. At various points in history, therefore, these sorts of doctrines have provided motives for coercion or violence.

Furthermore, religions often stand as radically opposed alternatives to each other: they offer mutually inconsistent worldviews and prescribe different ideas of how human beings should live their lives – particularly how they should conduct themselves with respect to the transcendent reality. Thus, rival religions can be a source of deep divisions and conflicts within or between societies. Some religions have been unwilling to tolerate either non-belief or rival religions, or have granted only the limited toleration of consigning non-believers and the adherents of other religions to a second-class social standing.

In Graeco-Roman antiquity, there was nothing like a body of sacred and unquestionable scripture, though there were narratives of great cultural and religious importance. No single understanding of the gods and their deeds was enforced, but there were sometimes limits to freedom of religious thought. We can find cases in ancient Greece where especially unorthodox cults, philosophies and naturalistic explanations of the universe, including outright atheism, were not regarded as tolerable (Whitmarsh 2016: 117–24). Nonetheless, many foreign religions, such as the Egyptian cults of Isis and Serapis, were accommodated in the Hellenistic Greek world that arose from the conquests of Alexander the Great, and with some exceptions these cults were also accepted by the rulers of ancient Rome (for discussion of Isis and Serapis, see Rüpke 2018: 264–72).

There was no separation of religion and the state authorities in the Roman Empire, as the latter incorporated an official priesthood that carried on a tradition of festivals, sacrifices and other public rituals. However, the Romans did not suppress the religions of the territories they conquered. No such practice was needed for imperial purposes, and it would have made little sense within the syncretic approach to religion and the gods that the Romans had inherited from earlier empires (see, for example, Johnson 2009: 36–7). A policy of religious persecutions would only have alienated the local elites whose abilities and cooperation were a practical necessity.

The Romans famously identified the Greek gods (among others) with their own: so Zeus was identified with the Roman Jupiter, for example, and Aphrodite with Venus. When the Romans invoked the gods in their imperial rites, the point was not salvation in an afterlife, or anything analogous to it, but divine assistance for the collective purposes of the Empire. For the pragmatic and instinctually syncretic Romans, 'religion was very much a matter of what worked in the everyday world inhabited by gods and humans' (Johnson 2009: 35). Thus, the Romans were tolerant of foreign cults so long as they allowed participation in the imperial rites and did not otherwise seem to challenge the established social order.

One exception to Rome's tolerance occurred long before the Roman Republic morphed into the Roman Empire. This was an attempt by the Roman Senate in 186 BCE to suppress the cult of Bacchus, apparently on grounds relating to public order and safety. The cult survived this attack, however, and it seems to have been an aberration brought on by panic. The Bacchanalian festivals were believed to provide cover for anti-social conspiracies, and respectable Romans' anxieties were heightened by lurid allegations of sexual abuse inflicted on young men (see Berkowitz 2012: 87–90). Much later, Rome's tolerance ran out when it came to Christians, who refused to take part in the rituals of any god but their own and, indeed, 'proclaimed that the pagan gods did not exist or were malevolent demons' (Zagorin 2003: 5; for discussion of Christian attitudes, see Johnson 2009: 1–10). This obstinacy and fanaticism, as the Romans viewed it, led to violent, though sporadic, persecution of Christians, especially in the third century CE.

The civilizations of classical antiquity had notions broadly comparable to our contemporary ideas of freedom and toleration, and many authors have particularly emphasized the Athenian concept of *parrhēsía*: a frankness or boldness in expressing opinions (see, for example, Mchangama 2022: 13). But an outer boundary was reached when novel ideas seemed to threaten the relationship between the state and the gods.

This does not mean that the ancient Greek and Roman civilizations were liberal or tolerant by the standards of modern liberal democracies. They featured inflexible roles for most people and many kinds of subordination to authority that would not be unacceptable today – most prominently, but not only, the brutal institution of slavery. Nonetheless, there was considerable toleration of a wide variety of religious beliefs and practices, made possible by the syncretism of the time and the general disinclination of ancient pagans to deny the existence or capability of each other's gods.

Religious disagreement beyond the West

Other great civilizations, such as those of India and China, have sometimes experienced religious tension and intolerance, and they developed their own approaches to mitigating the effects. We can find mechanisms of syncretism and religious toleration in these civilizations, though with distinctive aspects.

One example is the edicts on religious coexistence issued by the Buddhist emperor Asoka in the third century BCE. These called for free interaction and civility – and indeed, a demanding level of mutual restraint and courtesy – among all religions and sects. Asoka discouraged treating other religions as rivals to one's own or engaging in ostentatious support or advocacy of one's own religion.

Scholars such as Rajeev Bhargava argue that the promulgation of such edicts is itself evidence that they were needed: that is, they suggest a background of conflict whose details are no longer accessible. At this point in Indian history, there may have been tensions between worldviews with contradictory moral, social and soteriological ideas. In particular, fundamental doctrines in Vedic and early Upanishadic religion may have come under challenge from later Upanishadic teachings and from Buddhism (Bhargava 2014: 183; Kaviraj 2014: 236–9). In any event, there is evidence that India's ancient and medieval rulers – not only Asoka as an exceptional case – tended to permit, and indeed give patronage to, a variety of religious groups, sects, ritual practices and philosophical schools. Famously, Akbar the Great came to power in 1556 CE and adopted a policy of religious toleration.

The scholar Sudipta Kaviraj identifies two theoretical strands in the policies of toleration pursued by these rulers. One was a recognition of separate spheres for political action and religious life, enabling 'a kind of self-regulation' for the latter 'without political interference' (Kaviraj

2014: 253). The other – related – strand of toleration distinguished between the ruler's choice of a personal religious/moral path and his public responsibility for the welfare of all religious communities within his territory. Such thinking depended on pragmatic considerations relating to the limits of political power and the difficulty in identifying a single, absolutely correct, body of religious and moral truth.

We can find religious tensions throughout the recorded history of China, including hostility between popular religion (based around the worship of spirits, ancestors and local gods) and proponents of the so-called Three Teachings (Daoism, Buddhism and Confucianism). Folk religion, however, proved resilient, partly from widespread belief in the efficacy of its practices for attracting worldly blessings. This is illustrated by a story connected to the Emperor Wu of Liang – or Liang Wudi – founder of the Liang dynasty, whose long reign covered approximately the first half of the sixth century CE.

Wu was a zealous convert to Buddhism, while also adopting Confucian ideas of governance. He persecuted Daoists, and attempted to reform the traditions associated with the old gods. According to the story, however, he turned to the local god Jiang Ziwen in the face of a disastrous drought. When this failed after one hundred days of prayer, he decided to burn down the god's temple, but before he could light the fire a storm fell – leading the terrified and contrite emperor to embrace Jiang Ziwen and the other local gods (Lagerwey 2019: 59).

China's religious history is also notable for the appearance, from time to time, of militant syncretic cults that were able to mount large-scale rebellions. Among others, these included the fourteenth-century Red Turban Rebellion, which overthrew the Mongol-led Yuan dynasty, the White Lotus Rebellion at the turn of the nineteenth century, which challenged and weakened the ruling Qing dynasty before it was finally crushed, and the Taiping Rebellion of the mid-1800s, which again challenged the Qing dynasty and left a legacy of many millions of deaths. Chinese history also shows occasional efforts to suppress one religion or another. These efforts included anti-Buddhist persecutions by several emperors between the fifth and tenth centuries.

However, the Three Teachings each developed doctrinal resources to justify attitudes of tolerance and practices of toleration. From the beginning, Confucian scholars sought to influence moral feeling and public policy, all in an effort to create a stable, successful, refined society. Yet, Confucian teachings also advocated an environment of general, though not unlimited, toleration. Confucianism encourages openness to ideas and an element of voluntary reticence about pressuring others to conform to our own views of what is best (see generally Yu 2018). Similarly, the texts and traditions of Daoism include the idea of tolerating and accepting what strikes us as bad, and they encourage a wise reluctance to resort to violence or coercion (see generally Liu 2018).

Buddhism has viewed other religious traditions as, to some extent, its rivals, and has understood itself as superior to them as a source of right ideas and a spiritual path to Nirvana. But this is not the same as malice towards followers of other religions. Buddhism has incorporated aspects of other religions' iconography, mythology and rituals, and has sometimes developed concepts of forbearance that resemble Western ideas of principled non-interference with rival religions – ideas that we might find in the work of thinkers such as John Locke (Schonthal 2018: 193).

None of this is intended to idealize Indian and Chinese religious history or the specific religions of India and China. Clearly, these religions were not uniformly tolerant throughout ancient and medieval history. Moreover, we do not have a full and convincing record of their historical interactions with each other and with other religions such as Islam. We could surely find many examples where the adherents of Eastern religions have been less than tolerant, but to the extent that the great civilizations of Asia were able to avoid religious persecutions and warfare; some reasons for this might be found in the traditions of the religions themselves.

The record of Islam deserves particular attention, since it claimed superiority over all other religions within the territories conquered by Muslim rulers. However, Islam also developed an approach to toleration, admittedly of a limited sort. With certain exceptions, such as the intensely persecutorial Almohad Caliphate of the twelfth and thirteenth centuries, which ruled much of northern Africa and the Iberian Peninsula, the medieval Islamic empires tended to be more tolerant than the Christian kingdoms of Europe.

Like their Roman counterparts, Muslim conquerors generally did not seek converts. Nonetheless, they maintained an explicit hierarchy of religions. Among the subordinate religions, Judaism and Christianity were favoured for their monotheism and because of an Islamic belief that Jews and Christians had received genuine revelations from God via prophets such as Moses and Jesus. Jews and Christians were allowed to practise their religions, and under the Islamic *dhimma* system their local communities were granted some autonomy. They were, nonetheless, subordinated and controlled in numerous ways. Above all, Jews and Christians were not free to proselytize, build new places of worship or offer any kind of public challenge to Islamic doctrine.

When Muslim rulers gained control of large areas of the Indian subcontinent, beginning in the thirteenth century, they had little choice but to apply the established Islamic approach to toleration more widely. They found themselves governing territories in which their fellow religionists were greatly outnumbered by Hindus, whose beliefs, traditions and practices were radically alien to those of Islam. The response from medieval Muslim rulers was not necessarily uniform, but the general practice appears to have been one of 'noninterference in the social affairs of their Hindu subjects' (Kaviraj 2014: 247). Rulers of the Mughal Empire during the sixteenth to eighteenth centuries – or at least the more enlightened of them – theorized this on the basis that they had a responsibility for the spiritual security and well-being of their subjects, including their non-Muslim subjects (Kaviraj 2014: 250–1).

The fate of Manichaeism – an example of religious intolerance

As we've seen, some ancient and non-Western civilizations had considerable resources for managing religious disagreement, and they've left valuable – if incomplete – histories of their approaches. But equally, many religions have found reasons to be intolerant, as shown by the consistently hostile treatment of Manichaeism across the land mass of Eurasia.

Manichaeism had its origins in the Sasanian Empire, one of several ancient empires that arose over time in the region of Persia, or what is now Iran. This religion was founded in the third century CE by the prophet Mani, who taught a dualistic cosmology in which the power of light and goodness struggled eternally with that of darkness and evil. Manichaeism thrived for several centuries, becoming one of the great religions of its time, with a following that stretched from the western regions of Europe to the western regions of China. However, it had the misfortune of being persecuted by many of the great empires of late antiquity and the early medieval era.

Manichaeans were persecuted within the religion's original home – the Sasanian Empire – and Mani himself was executed (tradition has it by crucifixion) by Bahram I, the Sasanian King of Kings, in 274 CE. Mani was viewed by the Zoroastrian priests, most notably the ambitious chief priest Kartir, as a threat to their power. Manichaeism also suffered from sporadic persecution in pagan Rome, but this became more determined and intense after Christianity became the official religion of the Empire. Manichaean teachings may or may not have influenced some medieval Christian heresies: the interactions of religious groups in late antiquity and thereafter are complicated and unclear, and any lines of influence from Mani to – say – the Cathars of medieval France are indirect.

During the Tang dynasty, from the early seventh to the early tenth century, Manichaeism spread eastward into China, where, like Buddhism, it took on a distinctive Chinese form. As an example of the phenomenon of syncretism, early Chinese Manichaeism adopted Daoist elements. In the eighth century, however, the Tang emperor Xuanzong forbade his Chinese subjects from converting to Manichaeism, though he did not ban the religion outright. This reflected a common attitude among Chinese officials of suspicion towards religions that were regarded as insufficiently Chinese – a problem that was also encountered by Buddhists around this time. Thus, the issue was more one of cultural xenophobia and an imperative of imperial unity than the soteriological concerns that so often motivated religious persecutions in Western Christendom.

Manichaeans were persecuted in China during the ninth and tenth centuries and thereafter, and the religion was essentially extinguished within China in the fourteenth century. This historical episode illustrates the typical Chinese motivation for religious persecutions: a concern for Chinese unity and purity of Chinese culture. Nonetheless, Chinese Manichaeism outlived its original variants, and its doctrines influenced folk religion and Chinese syncretic cults.

Manichaeism is now virtually, or entirely, extinct, despite the lingering philosophical and theological appeal – at least for some thinkers – of its basic dualism, which at least has the merit of offering a solution to the ancient Problem of Evil.

Religion and persecution

The extent and seriousness of religious conflict can vary, depending on features of the locally dominant religion or religions, as well as the state's understanding of its own role and limits. For example, the state might assume some direct responsibility for saving the souls of its individual citizens. On the other hand, any religious role assumed by the state might be limited to public sacrifices and other rituals aimed at obtaining divine favour for the society's worldly prosperity. Alternatively, the state might see itself as having no role, or only a minimal role, beyond maintaining public order. The role of the state, as locally understood, will affect what is seen to be at stake when the authorities take action or choose not to do so.

The ancient traditions of polytheism and syncretism show how religions can (usually) avoid warring with each other over matters of doctrine. By contrast, the great Abrahamic monotheisms have been more willing to engage in persecutions and forced conversions where the circumstances permitted. In ancient times, even the much-persecuted Jews were not above engaging in this. Notably, Judea became a conquering state under the rule of the Jewish high priest and ethnarch John Hyrcanus in the second century BCE. Hyrcanus required the populations of these conquered territories to convert to Judaism and adopt Jewish laws and customs, including circumcision.[10]

Referencing these events, the Jewish historian Mark R. Cohen concludes: 'It seems … that monotheistic religions in power throughout history have felt it proper, if not obligatory, to persecute non-conforming religions' (M. Cohen 2008: xxiii). To a considerable extent, monotheistic religions have resisted pressures towards syncretism, and even where they have shown a degree of toleration, as with the medieval Islamic empires, they have viewed rival religions as inferior to their own and requiring subordination and control.

In Chapter 3, we'll examine the record of the most successful monotheistic religion of all, at least so far: Christianity.

---

[10]It would take us far afield to discuss other examples of Jewish militant groups or Jewish efforts at persecution of other religions. One notable example from late antiquity is Dhū Nuwās, a Jewish king of Himyar (roughly corresponding with modern-day Yemen), who persecuted Christians during his reign for about a decade early in the sixth century CE.

3 THE RISE AND DIVISION OF CHRISTENDOM

When Christians became persecutors

In Chapter 2, I briefly discussed the syncretism and toleration that characterized the empire of ancient Rome. As we saw, however, there were limits to Rome's tolerance when it came to Christians, who seemed fanatical and intransigent in their refusal to take part in the imperial rites. Even when compromise and clemency were offered, as appears to have been common (see Nixey 2019: 80–4), Christians of the time often refused to accept them and preferred the rewards of martyrdom.

The Romans responded with sporadic persecutions that reached their peak in the third century under the emperors Decius (ruled 249–51 CE) and Diocletian (ruled 284–305 CE). But when Christianity began to obtain secular power, under the reign of the Roman emperor Constantine the Great early in the fourth century,[1] it proved to be more persecutorial than the imperial cult of Rome had ever been.

Constantine began the persecution of Christian heretics in 325 CE, following the Council of Nicea, and thereafter – with little respite – the Church implacably opposed anything that could be construed as heresy. As early as the 340s CE, Christian emperors were issuing anti-pagan edicts. In his 2005 book *There Is No Crime for Those Who Have Christ*, Michael Gaddis examines the violent clashes over religion during the final centuries of the Western Roman Empire up to the Council of Chalcedon in 451. He finds considerable evidence, from multiple sources, of Christian mobs attacking synagogues, pagan temples, sacred

---

[1]Constantine ruled from 306–37 CE, initially as a junior emperor in the Western Empire but eventually as sole imperial ruler.

trees, statues of pagan gods, and other places and objects sacred to non-Christians. Often, it appears, the public destruction of pagan statues and cult objects was intended to demonstrate 'the emptiness of pagan claims regarding their gods' power' (M. Gaddis 2005: 190).[2]

During this period, formal and informal persecutions were directed at Jews, Manichaeans, polytheistic pagans, self-declared or suspected magic workers and astrologers, Christian heretics, and thinkers associated with the Graeco-Roman philosophical schools. Christian scribes and officials censored books containing ideas that were thought to have demonic origins: this included works from important schools of philosophy, as well as books on magic, astrology and divination. As the historian Dirk Rohmann summarizes the Christian viewpoint of the time, '[b]ook-burning could prevent readers from burning in hell' (Rohmann 2016: 298).

The picture that emerges from Rohmann's research is that Christian censorship in late antiquity took place, albeit on a regional rather than imperial scale, at least until the age of the Byzantine emperor Justinian (ruled 527–65 CE). Much in the Greek and Roman traditions was crushed by Christian rulers and populations, and the classical culture of free thought and philosophical debate was decisively rejected. The Christian authorities demanded a total transformation of public and private life in accordance with their exclusivist doctrines and an ascetic morality.[3] Materialist philosophical systems and pagan critiques of Christianity were suppressed for many hundreds of years, and many important texts remain lost.

From the Church's perspective, heretics violated Christian unity and at the same time 'brought damnation on themselves by separating from the church and rebelling against its teachings' (Zagorin 2003: 35). Saint Augustine, the most influential theologian of late antiquity, originally favoured toleration for heretics, based on considerations of charity and respect for conscience. He changed his mind, however, when confronted by the Donatists, a sect of heretics who associated with violent troublemakers known as the Circumcellions and were themselves notably intolerant. During the fourth century CE, in the aftermath of

---

[2]For detailed discussion of archaeological evidence for Christian iconoclasm in late antiquity and the early Middle Ages, see generally Sauer (2003).
[3]For wide-ranging and accessible accounts, see Kirsch (2004), Freeman (2005), Freeman (2008), M. Gaddis (2005), Rohmann (2016) and Nixey (2019).

anti-Christian persecutions under Diocletian, the Donatists refused to accept the authority of priests and bishops who'd saved themselves by symbolically renouncing their faith. Thereafter, they maintained their own church in North Africa, in opposition to the orthodox Church authorities.

Augustine developed an influential defence of coercing heretics, but he never favoured the death penalty for them (see Forst 2016: 47–55). However, hostility to heretics intensified in the eleventh century and thereafter. The Church developed an ideology of heresy-hunting, and the penalty of death became common, accompanied by a succession of definitions, decretals and anathemas. By contrast with the relatively mild attitude of Augustine eight or nine centuries earlier, Saint Thomas Aquinas maintained in his *Summa Theologiae* (written in the 1260s and 1270s) that it was right to kill impenitent heretics for corrupting the faith. Across Europe in the thirteenth, fourteenth and fifteenth centuries, blasphemy laws were promulgated with severe penalties that typically involved bodily mutilations (Nash 2007: 150–1).

During this period, too, Jews came to be regarded by the Christian authorities as children of Satan in human form and as perpetrators of hideous crimes. As with heretics, Augustine had theorized a relatively mild attitude to the Jews, and for several hundred years this largely prevailed, thanks to a belief that biblical authority itself demanded their survival and gave them a purpose in the unfolding of God's plan. In conformity with Augustine's teachings, they were subordinated and persecuted, but were allowed to survive within Christendom. Thus, David Engels states: 'Contrary to a common misconception, the medieval Church leadership did not encourage violence against the Jews. Officially its position was that Jews must be allowed to live among Christians, although their status must be visibly degraded in order to remind Christians of the dire consequences of denying the divinity of Jesus' (Engels 2013: 13).

However, Engels acknowledges the increasing popular, clerical and royal hostility that developed towards the Jews. Unfortunately, 'animosity against the Jews increased over the course of the later Middle Ages' (Arnold 2011: 119) until they were seen as intolerable blasphemers for their rejection of Jesus of Nazareth as the Son of God and saviour of mankind.

One striking incident – often seen by historians as a turning point – took place in 1096 when would-be crusaders heading eastward to liberate Jerusalem from Islamic conquerors carried out massacres of Jews on their way. In the following centuries, thousands of Jews were slaughtered in pogroms, and beginning in the late thirteenth century they were forcibly evicted from most kingdoms and regions of Western Europe. To be fair, the papacy itself often discouraged or attempted to moderate this trend, but in general there was vicious hostility against the Jews throughout the later Middle Ages (for discussion, see W. Laqueur 2006: 52–62).

Sex was mostly sin

All human societies set limits to the expression of sexual desire, but their form and extent vary greatly. The sex laws of ancient societies can appear alien to present-day sentiment, with concepts strikingly different from those employed within twenty-first-century liberal democracies. Most notoriously, perhaps, the *mores* of the ancient Greek city states were permissive of sex between male partners – including between adolescent boys and mature men – but did not use our concept of sexual orientation. There was, for example, no conceptual equivalent of 'a gay man', as we might now say. This does not entail that sex between men was unregulated by moral and legal standards, but only that regulation of sexuality in ancient Greece employed different concepts from ours. For example, it included a hostile attitude to men who were regarded as, in one way or another, feminizing themselves by their sexual behaviour (see Berkowitz 2012: 72–5).

The medieval Catholic Church adopted an especially austere approach to the phenomena of sexual desire and pleasure. The gist of its approach was not original to Christianity, but can be found in some ancient schools of philosophical thought – particularly in some Stoic teachings. However, the Church attained a level of social and political influence far beyond that ever enjoyed by Stoic (or any other) philosophers, and it elaborated at length on the nature and detail of sexual sins. The Church's approach, which provided the basis of traditional Christian morality for many centuries, contrasted with the sexual frankness and relative permissiveness of ancient Rome.

The philosopher and medieval scholar Pierre J. Payer has observed that pre-Christian thought at least allowed some moral room for sexual pleasure and satisfaction as acceptable in themselves (Payer 1993: 182). We have evidence – not least from erotic statues and frescoes that were preserved under the volcano ashes of Pompeii – that Roman society could, and frequently did, glorify sexual love and pleasure, particularly but not solely between husbands and wives (see Nixey 2019: 184–91). By contrast, Payer describes an ascetic view of sex in the writings of Saint Augustine and other Christian authors. According to these authorities, sexual intercourse was morally permitted only between a legitimately married man and woman, and only for the purpose of procreation. It follows that the vast range of human sexual activity lying outside heterosexual marriage was condemned as sinful (Payer 1984: 3–4).

This doctrine persisted throughout the Middle Ages, and it led Church authorities to categorize the particular forms of sexual sin, together with appropriate forms of penance. Payer's research on the confessional manuals – or penitentials – that developed from about the sixth century reveals much fascinating detail. As these manuals evolved and spread, they established 'a virtually all-inclusive register of proscribed sexual acts' that was largely consistent across Western Europe including the British Isles (Payer 1984: 5). Although the meanings of some passages in these manuals are obscure, it is clear that numerous acts were forbidden, often with provision for severe and lengthy penance. Sex was prohibited on many days of the year, and numerous sexual positions were forbidden entirely. As Payer elaborates, the penitentials devote close attention to sexual activities involving priests and others within the service of the Church, and to what we would now think of as lesbianism and male homosexuality.

Strangely, the penitentials make little reference to prostitution, perhaps, as Payer suggests, because they were written for largely rural societies where organized prostitution was not practical. But in any event, the Christian kingdoms of medieval Europe were surprisingly tolerant of prostitution (Berkowitz 2012: 147). Despite sporadic local attempts to stamp out the practice, the tendency was to regard it as a necessary evil. The later Middle Ages, however, was an era of systematization in Christian learning; this was a time of great scholars such as Peter Lombard, Thomas Aquinas and the renowned jurist Gratian. At this point, scholars working in a more sophisticated intellectual milieu were able to give a topic such as prostitution 'ample treatment' (Payer 1984: 117).

Payer observes that the absence of a procreative intention during sex came to be regarded as not, in itself, a serious sin 'unless procreation itself was interfered with through contraceptive methods' (Payer 1984: 115). Moreover, the penitentials devote relatively little attention to heterosexual conduct between unmarried laypersons. It seems that the societies of the Middle Ages showed some tolerance for such 'simple fornication' – indeed, we have evidence from later medieval texts that some people, even some priests, did not regard this as seriously sinful (Payer 1993: 182, 195). Nonetheless, this view was contrary to orthodox teachings, and it was rejected by Aquinas and other authoritative theologians.

Overall, the written sources available to us reveal a hostile attitude on the part of the Church to sexual desire and to the experience of sexual pleasure. The (hetero)sexual act itself was morally justified, and even praiseworthy, for its power to bring children into the world, but only for that reason. Unsurprisingly, we would search in vain for Church documents praising sexual interactions for the ecstasy that they afforded participants. On the contrary, seeking out or luxuriating in sexual pleasure, even in the context of Christian marriage, was condemned as gravely sinful. Virginity was considered 'superior to all other states of life' (Payer 1993: 18), and although procreation was viewed with favour, it was evidently best for sex to take place with as little enjoyment as possible.

Sexual sins were not the most serious recognized by the Church,[4] and of course they had gradations of seriousness among themselves. But in Christian theology, there was a strong connection between sin and sex: 'disordered' desire and 'immoderate' pleasure were viewed as blameworthy. Sexual activity of almost any kind was open to questions about the motivation behind it, and was likely to involve venial or even mortal sin.

During the Middle Ages, sexual offences were typically punished by church courts. For lesser sins such as simple fornication, these courts imposed relatively light sentences – commonly public penance that involved flogging (see Arnold 2011: 105–7). In some localities, however, the Church's code supported extreme punishments for particular sins, such as execution by burning for what was regarded as sodomy (see Berkowitz 2012: 155–71 for gruesome detail).

In practice, there were limits to the ability of medieval clerics to act as moral and theological police. While the power of the Catholic Church was at its height in the Age of Cathedrals – the late centuries of the Middle Ages – Christian practice in Europe also permitted a degree of local variation and flexibility in what was demanded of individuals. The

---

[4]For example, increased economic activity in the twelfth century tended to make the sin of avarice an especially pressing concern (Arnold 2011: 156).

medieval Church did not possess the resources available to a modern state, and even if it wished to, it could not exercise totalitarian surveillance and control in the manner that recent communist and fascist regimes aspired to and achieved to some extent. In some cases, therefore, its efforts to obtain compliance were futile.

Nonetheless, the Church possessed considerable ability to *regulate* society, even if this fell short of *control* (Arnold 2011: 182). Its moral system was substantially accepted by the people at all levels of society – sufficiently to produce considerable self-policing, mutual policing and overall conformity.

To some extent, new attitudes to sexuality arose with the Protestant Reformation of the sixteenth century. The Protestant churches rejected the idea of clerical celibacy, and inclined to a more positive approach to sexual pleasure within marriage. At the same time, they were less inclined to tolerate prostitution than the medieval Church had been: they abandoned the more traditional theory that prostitution at least confined the social and physical location of sexual sin (see Berkowitz 2012: 176–8). In a more general way, moral regulation by the Christian churches attenuated during the centuries of European modernity. Nonetheless, Christian sexual morality was not forcefully challenged until the middle decades of the twentieth century. Indeed, traditional Christian attitudes to sexual desire and pleasure continue to be influential even in today's liberal democracies.

As and where appropriate, I will take up this story in later chapters. At this point, however, I turn to the theological controversies of the late Middle Ages and early modernity, and with them the physical and intellectual struggles for religious toleration in Western Christendom. I will then discuss political dissent in the same centuries, following the rise of the printing press and with it the ability to criticize rulers and governments.

Suppression of heresy

During the later Middle Ages, suppression of heresy was sometimes carried out on a massive scale. Examples include the Albigensian Crusade of the thirteenth century, in which military forces acting for the Catholic Church substantially exterminated the Cathar heretics of Languedoc, and a series of crusades in Bohemia in the fifteenth century, mounted against followers of the reformer Jan Hus – who had been burned at the stake in 1415. The precise number of deaths in the Albigensian Crusade is disputed and impossible to ascertain accurately, but on all accounts hundreds of thousands of Cathars were killed.

However, the immediate background to modern ideas of religious toleration and religious freedom was the Protestant Reformation of the sixteenth century. Martin Luther and other major reformers of the time reacted against aspects of late-medieval doctrine and practice that they viewed as departures from New Testament Christianity. Among other difficulties, the reformers could identify no biblical foundation for the Church's elaborate practices of venerating the saints and seeking their intercession with God. These and other practices of the late medieval Church took their place in a complex theology whose central vision included expiation of sins in Purgatory before the souls of the dead could be admitted into the bliss of Heaven.

Luther's immediate objection in 1517 related to the sale of indulgences: purchasers obtained a document whereby the Church guaranteed intercession for the souls of deceased loved ones and thus remission of their time of purgatorial suffering. The money raised from selling indulgences was then used by the Church for its worldly purposes, most notably the huge expense of building Saint Peter's Basilica in Rome. For Luther, all this fell outside the spiritual authority of the pope or the Church. In the end, of course, the Reformation went far beyond a theological dispute over indulgences, and it shattered the unity of the Latin Christendom.

Luther's revolt took place in an age when the spread of learning was being revolutionized by the invention of the printing press in the middle decades of the 1400s. This created extraordinary opportunities to spread ideas, and in particular it made translations of the Bible widely available. The combination of the printing press and the Reformation made the word of God – as the Bible was understood to be – available to anybody who could read. One result was an amazing hothouse of new Christianities: an assortment of sects and heresies that arose to compete with the Catholic Church and the large Protestant churches.

Though Luther's first instinct was towards toleration of these rivals and variants – at least within certain doctrinal limits – he soon called for suppression of the Catholic Mass, became bitterly hostile to the Jews and refused to tolerate any theological opinions contrary to his own. He took full advantage of the printing press as a tool for theological and political propaganda: with lurid imagery and language, he denounced the Catholic Church and others whom he saw as enemies. This intolerance typified the mentality of other sixteenth-century reformers, including important figures such as Huldrych Zwingli and John Calvin. Zwingli was deeply implicated in the persecution and killing of Anabaptists in Zurich (and later across Europe). Calvin's reputation is especially tainted by his involvement in the heresy trial and subsequent execution of the non-Trinitarian theologian Michael Servetus, who was burned at the stake in Geneva in 1553.

This event, in particular, prompted calls for religious toleration, most prominently from Sebastian Castellio, a Calvinist theologian who became a tireless – and in consequence, hated – critic of Calvin. Castellio's first contribution to the controversy over Servetus, *Concerning Heretics*, was possibly written in collaboration with others. It was published anonymously in 1554, then followed by further publications during the 1550s and early 1560s. Castellio argued on theological and other grounds for toleration of heresy, or at least for mercy and gentleness in the correction of heretics. His books were much anathematized, but were widely read (if only in manuscript form) by leading thinkers in Europe.

For its part, the Catholic Church launched what is often called the Counter-Reformation. It examined and restated its traditional doctrines, particularly through the Council of Trent, which met on and off from 1545 to 1563. It also embarked on large-scale missionary work in Asia and the New World. Across Europe, there was 'a tightening up of definition and control, and a closing down of a certain fuzziness and room for manoeuvre' (Arnold 2011: 231) as the rival churches of the Reformation and Counter-Reformation developed more precise bodies of doctrine and more structured and comprehensive requirements for living Christian lives.

In this unforgiving environment, the Italian philosopher and speculative cosmologist Giordano Bruno was burned at the stake in 1600. Likewise, the great mathematician and natural philosopher Galileo Galilei, one of the most important founders of modern science, was tried by the Roman Inquisition in 1633 for his audacious book on the geocentric and heliocentric systems of astronomy. He was threatened with instruments of torture and eventually subjected to permanent house arrest.

Throughout the sixteenth and seventeenth centuries, Western Christendom was torn apart by religious violence. In France, for example, Roman Catholics and Calvinist Protestants – the Huguenots – were caught up in a devastating civil struggle, the French Wars of Religion, in which millions died from a combination of causes that included famine and disease. The ruinous Thirty Years' War commenced in 1618 and was concluded by the Peace of Westphalia in 1648 – by which time many parts of the continent lay desolate. At this stage, religious wars between sub-components of the Holy Roman Empire in central Europe largely ceased, but they 'continued to flourish elsewhere' (Beales 2000: 135), including warfare between the Turks and the Holy Roman Empire (sometimes supported by other European powers).

In the later seventeenth century and beyond, persecutions intensified in some parts of Europe. This included the violent manifestation of the Counter-Reformation in Poland, where the Socinians – followers of the non-Trinitarian theologian Fausto Sozzini (also known as Faustus Socinus) – were driven from the country, and conversion from Catholicism was made punishable by death. In 1685, the French king Louis XIV revoked the Edict of Nantes, which had granted toleration to the Huguenots.

Religious persecution in England is most vividly symbolized by the infamous fires of Smithfield: the site where numerous so-called heretics were burned, particularly Protestants who were sentenced under the reign of Mary I in the 1550s. Thereafter, public and official sentiment turned against cruel executions and mutilations as punishments, and even against the concept of heresy as a crime so long as the teachings concerned fell roughly within the boundaries of Trinitarian Christianity. Nonetheless, England went through severely persecutorial periods, and even the Toleration Act of 1688 (which received the royal assent and became law in the following year) granted only limited freedoms to non-Anglicans. It exempted some Protestant groups from persecution, but 'Catholics, Jews, Deists, and anti-Trinitarians were still beyond the pale' (Mchangama 2022: 114).

The sixteenth and seventeenth centuries were, too, the peak of the horrific witch trials of late medieval times and early modernity. Beginning in the late fifteenth century and continuing even into the 'enlightened' eighteenth century, many thousands of women were tortured and executed at the behest of the Catholic and Protestant churches. The craze eventually slowed down, country by country – perhaps because, as Eric Berkowitz suggests, 'the elite began to fear for their own hides' (Berkowitz 2012: 229). The Dutch Republic had its last case in 1610, but some countries executed supposed witches as late as the 1780s and 1790s. The last case in England was tried in 1710.

Theorizing toleration

Persecutions of heretics and such episodes as the French Wars of Religion and Thirty Years' War prompted deliberations about a safer way forward. This included far-reaching philosophical reflections on the best attitude to religious dissent and the proper roles of churches and secular governments. During the seventeenth century, Pierre Bayle, Roger Williams, Thomas Hobbes, Baruch Spinoza and John Locke made especially influential contributions to this debate. Here, Bayle is an important and instructive example. He was a French philosopher and a committed adherent to Calvinist doctrine. He fled to the Dutch Republic in 1681, and in his writings advocated a spirit of gentleness and tolerance when dealing with heretics. He suggested that religious violence arose from persecution rather than toleration, and he argued that it was possible to be sincerely and blamelessly mistaken about theological questions.

Of all these thinkers none was more influential in the longer term than Locke, whose short tract *A Letter Concerning Toleration* was originally published in 1689. Locke was admired by leading figures in the eighteenth-century Enlightenment and by key members of the United States' founding generation such as James Madison and Thomas Jefferson (Zagorin 2003: 302). In *A Letter Concerning Toleration*, Locke explains and justifies the apparatus of the state through a version of social contract theory. Here, he follows in a long tradition of political thought most prominently represented by his older contemporary the philosopher Thomas Hobbes.

According to Locke's account of the social contract, men and women enter into social arrangements for mutual assistance and defence. This then provides a legitimate, but relatively narrow, role for a secular magistrate, or ruler, who is charged with protecting the citizens' 'civil interests', defined as 'Life, Liberty, Health, and Indolency of the Body; and the possession of outward things such as Money, Lands, Houses, Furniture, and the like', but not 'the Salvation of Souls' and whatever might be our fate in the afterlife (Locke [1689]1983: 26). Accordingly, the state should not attempt to countermand the spiritual teachings of the various churches. Concomitantly, Locke thought, a church is a free and voluntary society aimed at worship of God and the spiritual salvation of its members. Its only power is of teaching and excommunication, and it has no jurisdiction over those who do not belong to it. Accordingly, the churches should not attempt to impose their doctrines on the people through political power or influence.

The idea of a limited role for the state, focused on protecting the purely worldly, or secular, interests of its citizens, had ancient and medieval predecessors, as well as precursors closer to Locke's own time.[5] But in the 1680s it was still a daring way to think about church–state relations (Zagorin 2003: 265). To support his approach, Locke relied on a mix of theological and secular arguments. From one perspective, he argued that God had not given power over religion to the secular ruler. From the other, he claimed that power over religion was not something that the citizens would give up to a secular ruler – or that they *had* given up – in forming a social contract for their mutual advantage.

Elsewhere, I have defended a modified version of Locke's secular arguments,[6] but they will not convince all comers irrespective of their starting positions. Somebody whose prior assumptions include a theocratic model of state power will reject out of hand Locke's theological and philosophical assumptions. Thus, it might not be possible to persuade such a person to adopt Locke's approach without first persuading her to give up her entire system of theology. Such a person might continue to favour persecutions to whatever extent seems necessary for the purpose of saving souls.

The problem becomes apparent if we turn to Locke's back-and-forth debate with the Anglican clergyman Jonas Proast around the end of the seventeenth century. Proast responded in 1690 to Locke's original *Letter Concerning Toleration*, prompting a second letter from Locke in the same year. Proast replied in 1691, Locke produced a third letter in 1692, and there was then a gap until 1704 when Proast responded yet again. Locke died that year, but left behind a lengthy fourth letter. Throughout the controversy, Proast held his own, and this illustrates the difficulty of shaking anyone who begins with and argues from a set of theological commitments.

Locke placed considerable emphasis on a claim that attempts at religious suppression are futile, since the coercive power of the state is

---

[5]Ancient predecessors included the Church Fathers Lactantius and Tertullian. One important medieval predecessor was Marsilius of Padua, writing in fourteenth-century Italy. See Forst (2016: 42–5, 89–95). For detailed discussion of Locke's immediate precursors, see Forst (2016: 138–208).

[6]See Blackford (2012: 39–46).

not able to compel genuine, inward belief. Here, however, Proast was able to find a potential weakness, since it appears that the state can at least do *something* to alter the spread of beliefs among its citizens: it can, for example, embark on campaigns of propaganda for favoured views and censorship of disfavoured ones, or as Proast insists, it can at least compel citizens to acquaint themselves with the 'true' doctrine. Some of these activities might achieve successes, and so, we might think, Locke at least overstates the case on this point.

But even with that granted, suppression of religious beliefs is no small thing. It can involve wasted resources and incalculable financial and human costs, while proving to be largely futile unless taken to the extreme of mass killings, as with the Albigensian Crusade. In Locke's time – as today – many individuals were prepared to accept martyrdom for the sake of truth or salvation, and it was already politically dangerous to create religious martyrs.

Implications

Even in the sixteenth and seventeenth centuries, some religious groups opposed state interference with religious faith. In particular, Baptist groups in Locke's time, doctrinal descendants of the earlier sixteenth-century Anabaptists, construed religion as 'a private matter between the individual and God' and held that no external authority had the right to 'impose a church or any beliefs upon a Christian' (Levy 1995: 103). Thus, seventeenth-century Baptists advocated all-round free exercise of religion, not only for themselves but for everyone else. The seventeenth-century Socinians, who eventually evolved into today's Unitarian churches, took a similar attitude to religious free exercise. These were not the common views of Christians or the Christian churches in the centuries of early modernity, but that gradually changed.

Many people, whether religious or not, can accept that there's a difference between the goods of this world and those of another world or an afterlife, and they might sense that secular rulers are highly fallible guides in respect of the latter. If so, they might conclude that secular rulers should steer away from essentially religious questions. Depending on our particular starting points, we might come to this view based on theological considerations (whether or not they are the same as Locke's) or a secular theory of the proper limits of state power. We might come to think – based, perhaps, on a mix of considerations – that the point, purpose or function of the state is, indeed, a secular one: restricted to keeping order, solving coordination problems, protecting citizens from everyday harms, providing security from attacks by external and local enemies, and the like.

Whether or not they have considered the arguments, many citizens of today's liberal democracies – whether they are religious or non-religious – are likely to accept the abstract claim that state authorities are not, and do not need to be, competent as arbiters of religion. However, everyday citizens might not understand this idea in a sophisticated way or be prepared to follow its implications wherever they logically lead.

This is important, because views such as Locke's contain the seeds of even more radical ideas, but also the potential for significant exceptions. Locke's analysis could imply that the state, if not Christian society as a whole, should tolerate very much in the way of thought and discussion, extending beyond the area of religious debate, and even much in the way of non-conforming – allegedly sinful – conduct. Once the state is assigned a restricted function of protecting the things of this world, it might reasonably conclude that much 'sinful' speech and conduct has little relevance to others' liberty, property, bodily safety or other civil interests. In that case, it falls outside the state's proper remit even if it endangers spiritual salvation.

Thus, with any approach similar to Locke's, an entire layer of motivations for religious persecution falls away, and with it a layer of motivations for state censorship and more general control by the state of its citizens' lives.

But a Lockean approach can have less libertarian implications. For Locke, the state did not have theological (and specifically soteriological) reasons to impose a preferred set of religious doctrines or to persecute dispreferred sects. This enabled him to argue for the freedom of many religions in addition to the Christian churches. However, he supported persecution of atheists and suppression of atheism as an idea without needing to offer a *theological* rationale. At least for the purposes of *A Letter Concerning Toleration*, he did not even need to demonstrate that atheism was false. Rather, he claimed that some ideas cannot be tolerated because they are too socially and politically dangerous.

Like many of his contemporaries, Locke believed that atheists and other sceptics about the afterlife could not be trusted to honour their 'Promises, Covenants, and Oaths' by which society itself was bound together (Locke [1689]1983: 51). Without an apprehension of divine punishment in a life after death, these sceptics would be willing to do whatever they thought they could get away with in this mortal life. For Locke, therefore, it was socially and politically (rather than theologically) necessary to suppress any denial of an afterlife with divine punishment for sin. The same applied to other doctrines viewed as dangerous to society, such as that faith should not be kept with heretics, that any particular sect has the right to assert political authority or to depose kings, and that joining the true religion requires accepting the authority of a foreign power.

Atheism is still looked on with suspicion in many places and by many people, but Locke's view about the need to suppress it has not prevailed over time. It is, however, important to emphasize that his view was not based on what he regarded as atheism's falsity or its effect on spiritual salvation, but on fears about the social consequences of widespread scepticism about divinely instituted punishment. This highlights the possibility of persecuting disliked religions if, for example, the state officials perceive their activities or doctrines as undermining public order, or if their adherents are assessed as potentially disloyal, or simply because of their dissent during politically stressful times (which in practice can be almost any period in history). Governments can always be tempted to prohibit – or at least control – religious, metaphysical or moral beliefs that they see as a threat to the civil order or to themselves.

A leading example in today's world is the People's Republic of China, whose ruling party imposes extensive social controls, including elaborate bureaucratic control over religion. In principle, Chinese communism is a materialist and atheistic ideology, fundamentally hostile to religious belief. However, the state has long abandoned any ambition of eliminating religion from its territory. On the other hand, the Chinese authorities are also determined to maintain the unity of a vast territory with numerous ethnic groups – some of which could potentially form their own nations – and, as we saw in Chapter 2, a long history of experience with militant cults. As a result, the authorities ruthlessly suppress any groups, whether religious, ethnic or otherwise, that they perceive as threats to their own rule or to the unity of China. The state has built a powerful system of control over the religious traditions that it recognizes or tolerates, requiring them to incorporate Chinese patriotism into their teachings and to join the state-established religious associations (Kuo 2017: 35).

Censorship of the press

By the turn of the sixteenth century, the printing presses of Europe were driving an impressive increase in education and literacy. The new century also saw the beginnings of modern science, including the radically innovative astronomical work of Johannes Copernicus, and it was the first great century of European exploration and colonialism. This brought the cultures of Europe into contact with what seemed like strange – sometimes hostile – environments and peoples. For some intellectuals, this provoked a sense of the historical contingency and precariousness of existing cultures and civilizations. In all, there was a ferment of new ideas and knowledge claims, and new themes for public discussion.

As a result, the possibilities for opinion, discussion and debate began to change, leading to censorship of all kinds from authorities that viewed themselves as threatened. Early modernity was, accordingly, a time of intellectual breakthroughs, but also of book-burnings and lists of prohibited books. Most famously, the Vatican established its *Index Librorum Prohibitorum* (List of Prohibited Books) in 1559. This was modified and updated as needed, and maintained in force until 1966. The *Index* included thousands of works that were viewed as dangerous by the Church, in many cases only because they were written by authors who'd expressed heretical, or otherwise unacceptable, ideas elsewhere.

Like church officials, secular rulers in Europe soon found reason for aggressive censorship. They made concerted efforts to suppress books, pamphlets and any other writings that cast doubt on their rightful authority or how they used it. In extreme cases, the punishment was execution for treason: for example, the republican statesman Algernon Sidney was beheaded in London in 1683 after he was accused and tried for plotting against King Charles II. The evidence was his then-unpublished manuscript *Discourses Concerning Government*, which argued against absolute monarchy and in favour of revolution when necessary to overthrow a corrupt government. *Discourses Concerning Government* was eventually published in 1698 and became, like the works of John Locke, a major influence on the American Revolution.

In this era, too, the legal concept of seditious libel was unleashed on political dissenters. This was the publication of any material in printed form (or later, in any other permanent medium) that tended towards rebellion against the established order. In England, the concept was first delineated by the Court of Star Chamber in a case known as *De Libellis Famosis* (Of Scandalous Libels; decided in 1606). This held that it was a criminal offence to defame John Whitgift – the recently deceased Archbishop of Canterbury – and his successor.

De Libellis Famosis was followed by numerous other prosecutions. According to the Star Chamber doctrine, a libel against a private person could be a crime because it tended to provoke acts of revenge and thus lead to breaches of the peace, while a libel against the government could be a crime for the further reason of causing scandal to the public authorities. Under this approach, truth was no defence, since true statements were at least as capable of false ones as triggering public disorder or insurrection.

The Court of Star Chamber became an infamous forum for persecuting real or imagined opponents of the monarchy and the established English church. William Laud, who became Archbishop of Canterbury in 1633, employed the Court of Star Chamber and the Court of High Commission against his enemies, who would then suffer barbaric punishments. Most famously, perhaps, William Prynne, a Puritan opponent of the established church, was sentenced in 1634 to punishments that included amputation of his ears as the state's response to his thousand-page book *Histriomastix* (published in 1632). This volume was a bizarrely exhaustive denunciation of the sinfulness of acting and the theatre, but it was interpreted as having seditious implications.

In 1637, the indefatigable Prynne was subjected to further punishments that included having his face branded and the remaining stumps of his ears cut off. The Court of Star Chamber was abolished in 1641, and Prynne continued a remarkable career that we needn't follow much beyond this point. During the English Civil War he supported the Puritan side, and he became an important figure working for the prosecution in several major court trials, including that of the once-feared Archbishop Laud, who was executed for treason in 1645.

By the middle decades of the sixteenth century, and into the seventeenth, we can see the beginnings of advocacy for freedom of opinion and 'freedom of the press' as it was understood at this time. This was not freedom for a specialized class of professional journalists but for the operation of the printing presses themselves, whether they were utilized by newspaper editors, book publishers, scurrilous pamphleteers or anyone else seeking to communicate widely. The debate over a 'free press' took place against the background of government control of printing through licensing schemes designed to stifle dangerous ideas.

Such schemes involved official vetting of all material intended for print before it could be printed and thus distributed to the public. This ubiquitous form of censorship targeted anything that could be construed as attacking the secular or ecclesiastical authorities, however indirectly.

By today's standards, even renowned works that criticized these licensing schemes, such as John Milton's polemical tract *Areopagitica* (published in 1644), argued only for limited freedoms. Milton opposed a scheme that had been introduced in England by the Licensing Order of 1643, following the abolition of the Court of Star Chamber and a brief interregnum in systematic censorship. He argued passionately and memorably for the value of books and learning, yet *Areopagitica* readily countenances post-publication punishments for books that are found, on inspection, to be mischievous or libellous. Furthermore, Milton specified that his arguments were not intended to apply to opinions that he viewed as seriously heretical and beyond the pale of toleration – notably Roman Catholic doctrine. The constitutional historian Leonard W. Levy therefore comments: 'In all likelihood Milton never intended that anything but the serious works of intellectuals, chiefly scholars and Protestant divines, should be really free' (Levy 1985: 95).

The licensing scheme became more draconian as a result of the Licensing of the Press Act, which came into force in 1662 and was renewed from time to time before it finally expired in May 1695. It was allowed to expire more because it had become unworkable and economically harmful than out of regard for freedom of opinion.[7] Accordingly, this was far from the end of censorship in Britain, and most importantly the law of seditious libel remained in place to be administered by the royal courts. In addition, each of the Houses of Parliament – the Lords and the Commons – had power to prosecute for contempt of its authority. In practice, this gave them a similar ability to the courts to deal with seditious libels. Once again, truth was not a defence.

This system operated far beyond Britain, applying in the British colonies including those in North America during the lead-up to the American revolutionary war. Here, the popularly elected assemblies – the colonial legislative bodies – proved to be a greater

---

[7]For another view, the historian S. J. Barnett suggests that the Act was allowed to lapse because public opinion was against it, but also because neither side of English politics – Whigs and Tories – trusted the other's use of it when in power (Barnett 2003: 102).

menace to free expression than either the local courts or the royal governors (Levy 1985: 17–18).

The common law crime of seditious libel[8] reflected a policy of favouring uniformity of belief and suppressing any criticism of the king or government officials (Bird 2020: 77–7). Any such criticism or other dissent was feared as a threat to the viability of the state itself. At the high treason trial of John Lilburn, a famous Leveller,[9] in 1649, it was stated that 'the law of England is the law of God', and 'the law of God is the law of England' (Banner 1998: 29).

More famously, John Taylor was convicted of blasphemy in 1676 by the eminent judge Matthew Hale. According to a law report from the time, Hale stated:

> For to say, religion is a cheat, is to dissolve all those obligations whereby the civil societies are preserved, and that Christianity is parcel of the laws of England; and therefore to reproach the Christian religion is to speak in subversion of the law.
>
> (*Taylor's Case*, 1 Vent. 293. Also quoted in Levy 1995: 221)

This was not the first known blasphemy case in the British Isles, though it is the first case from the English courts to be reported formally. The idea that Christianity was part of the English common law was often repeated with, slight variations of wording, until well into the twentieth century, and the common law offence of blasphemy was not finally abolished in England and Wales until 2008.

Throughout the seventeenth century, comparable forms of censorship to the British model applied across the continent of Europe, and although these varied from time to time, between nations, and in their details and their harshness, the general pattern was similar. The state protected Christian doctrines, symbols and organizations, and above all Christian rulers, from any form of criticism or disrespect. As late as the eighteenth century, and sometimes beyond, criticism of religion or the government was assumed to undermine the foundations of society, and so could not be tolerated.

---

[8]And seditious words, i.e. words actually spoken rather than printed.
[9]The Levellers were a radical political movement, most prominent and influential in the 1640s, whose goals included religious toleration and popular representation in government.

Before the dawn

The soteriological and eschatological doctrines of traditional Christianity suggest that we are all in danger of eternal hellfire, while also having a chance of eternal bliss. Here, the word *eternal* conveys the immensity of the stakes for even one soul, and the issue of salvation or damnation depended on the exact formulation of correct doctrines. If the state has a role here, it is surely an urgent one, and it could arguably justify burning books or more extreme actions such as burning heretics. On such assumptions, the logic of persecution is inexorable. Once this point is grasped, it is not surprising that Christianity has tended throughout its history to be an exceptionally intolerant religion whenever it has obtained access to secular power.

Thus, as Perez Zagorin explains in his important volume on the history of religious toleration, the theological quarrels in the centuries of early modernity did not, at the time, seem like obscure, abstract speculations. To those involved, these were genuine issues with enormously high stakes for this world and the afterlife (Zagorin: 164–5). Spiritual salvation was put at risk by heretics, and theological ideas were closely bound up with the ubiquitous authority of Christianity and the churches, and with government, policy and the mechanisms of social control. Paradoxically or not, however, the Christian kingdoms of early Western modernity produced a legacy of rich texts on religious toleration, including 'an array of arguments in behalf of liberty of conscience, mutual tolerance and diversity' (Zagorin 2003: xiii).

At this stage in European history, there remained a background assumption of religious orthodoxy – even though this took different forms across Europe – and a political concept of rulers as the masters rather than servants of their people. There was a continuing entanglement of religious and political questions, so that any criticism of the church or the state was considered dangerous to both (Levy 1985: 5).

During the seventeenth century, more modern conceptions of freedom of speech, including a toleration of all ideas, obtained no purchase. Even the strongest advocates of religious freedom stopped short of condemning restrictions on seditious publication or advocating absolute freedom of political expression. As the century ended, such proposals lay in the future. They started to appear in the eighteenth-century Age of Enlightenment.

4 FROM TOLERATION TO TERROR

Enlightened rulers and the public sphere

At the beginning of the eighteenth century, much of Europe was governed by hereditary rulers who portrayed themselves as wielding absolute power, answerable only to God – though in practice their authority often operated within political and social constraints. By the end of the century, the idea of hereditary absolute monarchies was under challenge. Some of them survived either from social inertia or from the resourcefulness of particular rulers, but even in those cases the nature of European states was transformed, with increased attention given by monarchs to the welfare of their subjects (Swann 2000: 23).

Reforming rulers such as Peter I (Peter the Great) of Russia (reigned 1682–1725), Frederick II (Frederick the Great) of Prussia (reigned 1740–86) and the Holy Roman Emperor Joseph II (reigned 1765–90) set out to modernize and transform their lands, systematize the processes of government and promote the education and welfare of their people. Rulers in this mould widened religious toleration and the scope for acceptable theological scholarship. They were inspired by inputs from natural law theorists, intellectual leaders of the churches and others (see Swann 2000: 23–6). Within the Catholic Church, intellectual leaders at this time included representatives of the Jansenist movement, based on the teachings of Cornelius Jansen, a seventeenth-century Dutch theologian whose teachings bore resemblances to Calvinist doctrines and were declared in the eighteenth century to be heretical.

Although the outcomes were patchy across the continent and between urban centres and rural areas, the eighteenth century was a time of markedly increasingly literacy in Europe. It saw the rise of clubs, coffee houses, literary and intellectual salons, Masonic lodges, and many other forums, as well as newspapers, journals and novels that could engage the reading public. For the wealthier social classes, therefore, there were greatly increased opportunities for exposure to ideas, discussion and debate.

The historian Thomas Munck summarizes the emergence of a distinctive public sphere through the forums and publications that provided a social infrastructure for what could meaningfully be called public opinion. Munck acknowledges that public opinion of some kind had existed in all societies since classical antiquity, but, as he carefully expresses the point, 'it may well be appropriate to regard the eighteenth century, and perhaps particularly the second half, as a time when public opinion acquired a more tangible identity and role' (Munck 2000: 75). He refers to the preeminence of London and Paris in developing a sophisticated public sphere based on all these developments, but he adds that these cities did not lack for imitators.

Despite numerous efforts by government authorities, the eighteenth century was an era when new and unsettling ideas could gain serious attention. The works of Voltaire (pen-name of the philosopher and author François-Marie Arouet), Baron de Montesquieu, Cesare Beccaria, Jeremy Bentham, Adam Smith and others were widely read and obtained social and political influence. Various forms of scepticism arose, most prominently in France, as expressed in Montesquieu's satirical novel *Persian Letters* (1721), the scandalously atheistic *Testament* of Jean Meslier (discovered in manuscript form after its author's death in 1729), and the works of Voltaire.

Towards the end of the century, in 1784, the great German philosopher Immanuel Kant penned an essay on the question 'What is Enlightenment?' In this work, he celebrated living in Prussia under the reign of Frederick the Great, enjoying the intellectual freedom granted by an enlightened ruler. Kant begins by stating: '*Enlightenment is man's emergence from his self-imposed immaturity.*' He immediately explains this 'immaturity' as 'the inability to use one's own understanding without guidance from another'. In other words, it is dependence on others, rather than making use of our own faculty of reason. Kant adds that this immaturity is self-imposed, or self-incurred, if it stems from a lack of resolution or courage. Thus, he challenges his readers with what he calls 'the motto of Enlightenment' – 'Sapere aude! Have courage to use your own understanding!'[1]

Kant was not a radical by temperament: he neither predicted nor sought abrupt social change. He believed that improvement to humanity's condition through the exercise of reason would be gradual and would fall within society's capacity to absorb over time. Nonetheless, he argued for complete freedom in what he called the public use of reason. That is, we might legitimately be restricted in how we employ our reason when carrying out the duties of an appointed post (somewhat confusingly, given our modern distinction between work and private life, Kant labelled this as the *private* use of reason). But, he claimed, there should be no restriction on the use 'which anyone may make of [reason] *as a man of learning* addressing the entire *reading public*' (Kant [1784]1991: 55; italics in the original text).

For Kant – a socially cautious, if philosophically innovative, thinker – free exercise of reason in the public sphere was the true path to an enlightened society. Perhaps presciently, he observed that a revolution might put an end to despotism and oppression, but it could not produce reform in thinking and would only create new prejudices to control the mass population (Kant [1784]1991: 55). In short, Kant's essay encapsulated one version of the eighteenth-century Enlightenment ideal.

The Enlightenment and the *philosophes*

It is notoriously difficult to define the Enlightenment, given its cross-currents of debate and its varied manifestations across the lands of Europe and beyond. Like the sixteenth-century Protestant Reformation, the Enlightenment nurtured strange blooms of thought. It was, to generalize, a rejection of earlier ways of thinking and an effort to develop an alternative.

Enlightenment thinkers rejected what they saw as superstition, dogma and ossified tradition. With various emphases and interpretations of their

---

[1] *Sapere aude* = 'Dare to be wise' or 'Dare to know'. All quotations in this paragraph are from Kant ([1784]1991: 54). In each case, italics are in the original text.

own, they turned instead to progress in science, the arts and education, and in legal and political arrangements. The standard Enlightenment view was that the world could become a better place for human beings through rationally guided reform. Enlightenment thinkers typically attempted to frame universal moral and legal principles, though there were exceptions, including the much-lionized Genevan author Jean-Jacques Rousseau, who was notable for his emphasis on national identity.

One of the great culminating works of the time was the multi-volume *Encyclopédie* (Encyclopaedia) edited by the philosophers Denis Diderot and (initially) Jean Le Rond d'Alembert, with Louis de Jaucourt as its most prolific contributor. The *Encyclopédie* was published in instalments from 1751 to 1765, and thereafter with its full set of accompanying plates until 1772. It was later elaborated upon in revised and expanded editions. The *Encyclopédie* included numerous articles on sensitive topics related to religion, theology and politics. Spread throughout its pages was much sceptical and anti-clerical material.

Eighteenth-century France maintained a regime of pre-publication censorship that only became larger and more bureaucratic over time, as well as more complicated, confusing and corrupt. The politics of censorship were not straightforward, and it was neither possible nor desired to block the entire output of ideas from French intellectuals. The *Encyclopédie* faced on-and-off – and relatively half-hearted – efforts at state censorship, as well as arousing the ire of the Catholic Church and being listed on the *Index Librorum Prohibitorum*.

The Enlightenment philosophers of France – the *philosophes* – developed an attitude that was anti-clerical as well as anti-monarchical. By and large, they rejected traditional Christian theology and saw the Catholic Church as a core component of the oppressive *ancien régime* (old regime). But this is not to say that the Enlightenment direction, even in France, was uniformly atheistic.

Rousseau claimed that atheism was intolerable, and even the iconoclastic Voltaire was apparently sincere in his belief in God. Still, Voltaire was a philosophical deist rather than an orthodox Christian, and he was fiercely opposed not only to the Roman Catholic Church, which he viewed as dogmatic and oppressive, but to Christianity itself. In some publications he expressed hostility to Judaism and to the Jews as a people (though this hostility was somewhat theoretical, as the Jews had long been expelled from Western Europe, including France).

That said, the most radical Enlightenment thinkers – including Julien Offray de La Mettrie, Claude Adrien Helvétius and Baron d'Holbach – were, indeed, atheists who denied even the fundamentals of Christianity, such as the existence of a deity, and rejected all religion on metaphysical, moral and political grounds. In recent times, Rainer Forst has criticized d'Holbach for displaying metaphysical presumption in his trust that religion would inevitably collapse under rational scrutiny, and for a kind of intolerance (or even fanaticism) of his own in his desire to bring about a post-religious society (Forst 2016: 299). But this assessment is itself contestable.

First, it is not clear that philosophical questions relating to the existence of a god or gods must remain forever intractable. Perhaps at the end of the day, there are correct and demonstrable answers to such questions even if they encounter ingenious and persisting kinds of resistance, and even if such questions are best not investigated and answered by the agencies of the state. In that sense, Forst's allegation of metaphysical presumption is at least premature. Second, d'Holbach's efforts to rid the world of religion were limited to analysis and persuasion rather than practices of punishment or suppression.

Many of the great philosophical writers of France suffered at the hands of the censors, and some were imprisoned for periods, including such luminaries as Diderot and Voltaire. In 1748, La Mettrie, the most philosophically radical French author, notable for his analysis of human beings as complex machines, was driven out of France and the Netherlands, and given refuge in King Frederick's Prussia. In 1759, Helvétius ran into trouble for his philosophical work *De l'esprit* (On Mind), published in the preceding year. This had originally been given approval for publication, but it then attracted unfavourable attention for its atheistic and heretical message. Helvétius was forced to make a series of public recantations and was dismissed from his office at court.

The late Gertrude Himmelfarb (d. 2019), a conservative political historian, highlighted what she saw as the elitist character of French Enlightenment philosophy, in that the *philosophes* often seemed to regard the general populace as separated from their ideas 'by the chasm not only of poverty but, more crucially, of superstition and ignorance' (Himmelfarb 2004: 156). As she elaborates in her critique, the *philosophes* showed little interest in schemes for education of the masses, and we should acknowledge her point that the tenor of their writing was not democratic in our current sense. Likewise, the French Revolution, when it burst out near the century's end, was not about democracy as we know it today, but was a revolt against aristocratic and clerical privilege as these were understood at the time.

That said, the spirit of the Enlightenment was generally liberal-minded. The *philosophes* favoured religious toleration and humane law reform. The latter included more restrained punishment in general and abolishing crimes related to blasphemy, heresy and homosexuality. The *philosophes* opposed, or were critical of, the slave trade, though many of them might have spoken more clearly and passionately on the subject.[2] To the *Encyclopédist* Louis de Jaucourt's credit, his article on slavery in the *Encyclopédie* was a straightforward, plainly worded denunciation.

Perhaps the most powerful repudiation of slavery and its effects appeared in Abbé Guillaume Raynal's *Philosophical and Political History of the Two Indies*, an encyclopaedic volume first published in 1770, with numerous contributors including Diderot and d'Holbach. This work underwent further editions in 1774 and 1780 – the latter was banned in 1781 and prompted Raynal's flight to Prussia to escape arrest.

Rousseau versus the Enlightenment

Enlightenment authors took pride in the advance of their civilization, though there was also disagreement, most notably from Rousseau. Despite its progress in many domains, European society – including France, where Rousseau made his home – was still largely a feudal order marked by great inequalities of privilege and wealth. Rousseau had no wish to defend or preserve this, but he was nonetheless hostile towards the typical values of the Enlightenment.

By contrast with the general view of the *philosophes*, Rousseau criticized all human progress beyond a very early historical stage. He saw humanity in his time as in a miserable situation that was only being made worse by advances in the arts and sciences. He claimed that this was a process of corruption: it created new luxuries and desires for them, new

---

[2]What follows in the remainder of this section draws on the discussion in Munck (2000: 186–92).

kinds of inequality, and new forms of dependence, dissatisfaction, envy, inauthenticity and even cruelty.

For Rousseau, human beings had lost a fundamental and natural freedom that had – conjecturally – once been theirs. This freedom took the form of radical independence from social life, and it was not something that Rousseau thought could be regained on any large scale. But he mourned its loss and also the loss of something rather different from a later period of history: the civil and moral liberty that he associated with the world of classical antiquity, based on social engagement and participation in shaping the polity's laws to further its people's common interest. He was aware, however, that his picture of ancient liberty was, like his picture of even more ancient *natural* liberty, idealized and largely fictional (Wokler 2012: 182). In particular, the political practices of the ancient world were built on social institutions that included slavery.

In one of his most famous works, *The Social Contract*, first published in 1762, Rousseau followed earlier thinkers such as John Locke in affirming that the individual citizen's fate in the afterlife was no concern of the sovereign, who should therefore tolerate most religious views. Nonetheless, on Rousseau's account, the sovereign of an ideal state should require that all citizens acquiesce in a core of shared beliefs constituting a civic religion. Anyone refusing to embrace this should be exiled – or even executed if hypocritically professing to accept the religion's doctrines while acting inconsistently with them (Rousseau [1762]1968: 185–7).

The content of Rousseu's proposed civic religion was not extensive, but nor was it undemanding. In the main, it consisted of belief in a benevolent and providential deity who would reward or punish humans after their deaths. Rousseau made two significant additions: first, a commitment to the sanctity of the social contract and the laws, and second, toleration of others who also acquiesced in the core of common beliefs. While this sounds anodyne, Rousseau demanded a remarkably high level of toleration (and indeed, tolerance). He required not merely abstention from persecutions but, beyond this, that citizens not even privately view each other as excluded from salvation.

From this combination of doctrines, it follows that atheists – along with many religious citizens who believe in only one path to spiritual salvation – would *not* be tolerated in Rousseau's ideal republic. They would face exile or possibly execution.

Steps to toleration

Munck observes that the relatively moderate official response that the *Encyclopédie* received from 1765 suggests 'that attitudes to religious beliefs amongst a significant part of the French elite were becoming quite relaxed', although 'actual toleration' did not come about 'naturally or amicably' anywhere in Europe (Munck 2000: 134–5). Rather, steps towards religious toleration took the form of limited compromises, and in many locales there remained much popular hostility towards non-conformists. In some cases, formal doctrines, and hence theological disputes, became more moderate, but without ending all sources of sectarian hostility. Concessions towards toleration came about through a slow process with numerous setbacks.

Intellectual interest in this issue continued throughout the century, with prominent contributions including Montesquieu's *Persian Letters*, and his great work *The Spirit of the Laws* in 1748, Voltaire's *Treatise on Tolerance* in 1763 and Gotthold Lessing's play *Nathan the Wise* in 1789. While religious persecutions and discrimination did not cease in the eighteenth century, they eventually tended towards moderation.

We may follow the French scholar Pierre Manent in viewing *The Spirit of the Laws* as an essential contribution to the development of liberal thought, perhaps even, as Manent suggests, the contribution that 'determines the definitive language of liberalism' (Manent 1995: 55). Montesquieu set out for the first time an analysis of governmental powers as falling into legislative, executive and judicial categories, with a hope and expectation that these would tend to balance each other to the benefit of the liberty (or 'independence' as Montesquieu thought of it) of the individual citizen. He defined political liberty as the freedom to do whatever the law permits, which mirrors the principle of legality (the maxims *nullum crimen sine lege* and *nulla poena sine lege*): one may not be punished for an act that is not a crime known to the law.

Political liberty in Montesquieu's sense is a protection against arbitrary government power, but not a guarantee against oppression via harsh, yet properly made, laws. However, Montesquieu believed that a legal system designed along his proposed lines would tend to protect the independence of the citizens by generating a body of laws that allowed them broad freedom of action (see Manent 1995: 60).

In France, the eighteenth century commenced amid ongoing persecution of Protestants: Louis XIV had intensified these persecutions after he revoked the Edict of Nantes in 1685. Many Huguenots fled the country, although attempts to flee were themselves harshly punished. The Camisard Revolt, in the kingdom's south, began in 1702 and continued until 1704 – with some fighting for years thereafter. Although the revolt was suppressed, it led to a more conciliatory policy from the government, which sought to avoid further such outbreaks.

A more substantial freedom of religion was not, however, established in France until Article X of the Declaration of the Rights of Man and the Citizen, signed by Louis XVI in October 1789. Meanwhile, occasional outbreaks of persecution provoked an anti-clerical backlash, much of it aimed at the Church's wealth and its ineffectiveness in providing pastoral care.

One notorious incident was the trial and execution of Jean Calas, a Huguenot from Toulouse who was dubiously convicted of the murder of his son after the latter converted to Catholicism. In March 1762, Calas was broken on the wheel and then strangled. His case inspired Voltaire to indignation: he campaigned to clear the man's name and to argue more broadly for religious toleration in France. In his *Treatise on Tolerance*, published in 1763, Voltaire advocated for toleration of all religions and sects provided only that they were themselves willing to abjure religious violence. Calas was posthumously exonerated, and the entire incident, including Voltaire's effective and influential intervention, contributed to the long process through which greater religious toleration came about in France and more broadly across Europe.

The historian Derek Beales comments: 'For the history of religion and culture, the period before the [French] Revolution needs to be divided into two, roughly in the middle of the century' (Beales 2000: 132). That is, Beales identifies a period to at least the 1740s when Christianity pervaded and influenced European society as much as – if not more than – ever, despite the Catholic/Protestant divide. In each European state, there was an established church, with limited, if any, civil and religious rights for followers of rival churches. At this point, the ideas of Pierre Bayle and other great European thinkers of the previous century had little impact on the situation in most of the Catholic countries of Europe. By comparison, Britain and the Dutch Republic were isolated 'havens of religious toleration and of relatively free speech and expression' (Beales 2000: 147).

The situation changed from about the middle of the eighteenth century as the established churches 'were thrown onto the defensive intellectually, politically, and culturally' (Beales 2000: 132). During this later period, the role of the aristocracy also came under question – and following the French Revolution, the monarchy, court and aristocracy were abolished. Under French influence, similar changes occurred in other European countries, though the French Revolution also prompted a backlash.

British and American developments

Once free of the burden of licensing laws in 1695, Britain and its colonies developed a thriving sphere of publication, debate and commentary. However, it was still dangerous to criticize the governmental or religious authorities. Throughout the eighteenth century, the British Crown continued to charge opponents with seditious libel or even treason. This included the prolific author, pamphleteer, freethinker and political radical Thomas Paine, who fled to revolutionary France in September 1792 – out of the frying pan into the fire!

A legal doctrine of freedom of the press developed during the eighteenth century, but it was derisory by today's standards. The idea was that people could write and publish without first obtaining government permission, but they could then be convicted of seditious libel for criticizing the government and failing to show a due spirit of subordination to its authority. There was no defence for publishing material that – as viewed by the royal courts – undermined the social and political order. The official doctrine, furthermore, was that juries were responsible only for finding the facts of publication, while judges had the task of deciding whether the material published was illegal. That said, there were sometimes tussles between judges and juries when the latter asserted a right to judge the entire issue of guilt and innocence.

From about the mid-1760s, British books, pamphlets, newspapers and magazines became overwhelmingly critical of the law relating to seditious libel, seeing it as inimical to freedom of the press (Bird 2020: 195–218). These publications – and presumably their audiences – relied on a broader understanding of press freedom than the doctrine maintained at the time by the courts.

In the colonies that eventually became the United States of America, colonial governors and assemblies responded with intolerance to any printed matter that appeared to criticize them or challenge their actions. They relied only in part on the law of seditious libel, but there were enough such cases to underline the risks of engaging in outspoken political speech. This made the courtroom victory of John Peter Zenger and his attorney, Andrew Hamilton, in 1735 all the more symbolic and important. Zenger was the printer of the *New-York Weekly Journal*, which had published articles highly critical of William Cosby, the New York colony's Crown-appointed governor. He was charged with the crime of seditious libel, but ably defended by Hamilton, a celebrated Philadelphia lawyer who'd held high offices in the colony of Pennsylvania.

In his address to the New York jury, Hamilton argued that truth was a complete defence to a claim of libel against a public official in respect of performance of his official duties, and that the jury was legally able to decide the entire question of guilt and innocence. In response, the judge directed the jury to convict if it was satisfied that Zenger had printed the stories – something that was not doubted or disputed. The jury nonetheless returned a verdict of not guilty, apparently satisfied that the allegations against the unpopular governor were true and that this was enough for Zenger to go free.

Zenger's Case manifested the hostility of American jurors to what they saw as government power and its abuse. The case established a new standard for freedom of the press whereby truth was a defence and the jury was empowered to decide the entire issue. This was not universally embraced even in the American colonies, but *Zenger's Case* weakened the hold of the official legal view.

On the other hand, Andrew Hamilton did not argue for a general freedom to publish political comment, even if it might be inaccurate or debatable. Indeed, many British and American thinkers of the eighteenth century who argued for some form of free opinion and discussion had only a limited freedom in mind. For example, the British deists Matthew Tindal, John Toland and Anthony Collins – in some ways the immediate successors to John Locke – focused on freedom of religious speech and did not expressly critique the doctrine of seditious libel.

Collins' *A Discourse of Free-Thinking*, published in 1723, defended freedom of inquiry in the face of what its author depicts as endless disputation and confusion over matters of Christian doctrine. However, as Leonard W. Levy observes, the freedom that Collins espoused was seemingly limited to the works of scholars and to speculative topics of theology and philosophy, and he left room for suppression of views that might disturb society (Levy 1985: 108). This was only a small advance on John Milton's views in the previous century.

We can, however, find a full-scale defence of freedom of speech published in the 1720s. This appeared in the form of a series of articles, or 'letters', in British newspapers, composed by two authors – John Trenchard and Thomas Gordon – who used the pseudonym *Cato*. Cato's letters were subsequently collected and republished in four volumes, becoming widely read and influential in the American colonies as well as Britain.

Later in the eighteenth century, some authors, including Montesquieu, rejected the idea of punishment for expression with pernicious tendencies. Montesquieu argued that sanctions must be reserved for speakers who incite particular overt acts of violence or criminality, while some thinkers went so far as to argue for punishment only for the acts themselves. Levy identifies the British utilitarian Jeremy Bentham as one of the first thinkers to adopt an 'ultralibertarian' position on free speech, indeed, one that appeared to condone many crimes so long as they fell 'short of actual revolt' (Levy 1985: 167–8). Bentham's comment appeared in chapter IV of his 1776 work, *A Fragment on Government*, which was his searching and sarcastic critique of the jurist William Blackstone's views on law and government.

In chapter IV, Bentham sets out a list of criteria to distinguish between a despotic government and one permissive of freedom (Bentham [1776]1948: 94–5). These can be taken as an early statement of liberal principles. They include the sharing of political power through the ranks of society, the ability to change governments, a responsibility lying on governments to explain their actions, freedom of the press in the form of freedom to publish political grievances to the wider community and freedom of association to oppose those wielding power. Bentham emphasizes the freedom of malcontents to make plans, carry out activities and publish their views. However, *A Fragment on Government* does not develop this idea in detail or with examples and caveats; in particular, the passage does not discuss, or appear to contemplate, incitements to political violence or to ordinary crimes such as theft or murder.

Bentham helped lay the foundations for nineteenth-century liberalism. His writings supported individual freedom, freedom of the press, a rationalization of government power and a radical programme of law reform. It is doubtful, however, that he had a fully formed theory of maximal freedom of speech.

Revolution in America

By the 1770s, prior restraints on publication were a thing of the past in the British colonies of North America, but revolutionary leaders were faced with threats and prosecutions for seditious libel (Bird 2020: 344). With that memory fresh in mind, the founders ultimately inserted freedom of speech and the press into the US Constitution.

It is not surprising that the fathers of the American Revolution are venerated in modern-day America as statesmen and warriors in the cause of freedom, but the revolutionary years also had a darker side for freedom of speech. What seems shocking to today's sensibilities is the extent to which revolutionary leaders resorted to their own illiberal measures against local opponents. They concluded that no serious political dissent on the question of American independence was tolerable, and endorsed free speech only for 'patriotic', that is, revolutionary, contributors to public discussion (Levy 1985: 173–81). In the climate of urgency and fear, unpatriotic speakers were (literally!) tarred and feathered, printing presses were destroyed and critics of the revolutionary war were accused of treason. The American states introduced loyalty tests, interred persons who were suspected of disloyalty and enacted legislation to repress what they regarded as erroneous opinion.

The US Constitution prohibits the passage of bills of attainder by either the states or the federal Congress, so it can be disappointing when we learn that colonial statesmen such as Thomas Jefferson were prepared to use bills of attainder during the revolutionary period. A bill of attainder is a legislative, rather than judicial, finding that a named or identifiable person 'is guilty of a crime and must suffer death as a punishment', while a bill of pains and penalties imposes a punishment that falls short of death (Levy 2001: 68). Bills of attainder or pains and penalties circumvent the processes of the criminal justice system, and in some situations they might be regarded as constitutionally impermissible usurpations of judicial power by the legislature.[3]

Historically the Westminster Parliament used bills of attainder as a weapon against the king's, or its own, political enemies. But during the

---

[3]This is the likely outcome whenever a nation (or a sub-component such as a state or province) has a constitution with an entrenched separation of legislative and judicial powers.

American Revolution, several states enacted bills of attainder or bills of pains and penalties against actual or suspected British sympathizers. The most notorious of these was enacted in May 1778 by the assembly of the state of Virginia at Jefferson's behest (see Levy 2001: 72–4). The target in this instance was one Josiah Philips, who was pronounced to be guilty of treason and other crimes. He and his accomplices were legislatively outlawed, meaning that it was legally permitted to kill them.

As it happened, Philips and several of his associates were captured before the date when the bill was scheduled to come into effect. Philips was tried for the crime of robbery under the ordinary law, found guilty and subsequently executed as a convicted robber. Harsh as this might now seem, it met the standards of justice at the time.

As is well known, the state legislatures of the newly formed United States of America gave approval in 1791 to a Bill of Rights consisting of ten amendments to the US Constitution. These provided for extensive freedoms from actions by the federal legislature – a potentially powerful body that attracted much suspicion, even if its creation was necessary after a period of post-revolutionary chaos.[4] The First Amendment – and thus the first item of the Bill of Rights – includes religious freedoms as well as a prohibition on enacting federal laws 'abridging the freedom of speech, or of the press'. Unfortunately we have little historical indication of what the drafters had in mind by these expressions *circa* 1790, or how they were understood by legislatures that subsequently ratified them.

For example, 'the freedom of ... the press' could have been accorded its established legal meaning in England of no more than a freedom from pre-publication censorship. It could have been interpreted as requiring, in addition, that truth be a complete defence to charges of seditious libel arising from printed material, with the entire question of guilt or innocence in such cases to be decided by a jury. This would have reflected the outcome in *Zenger's Case*. Or it could have been interpreted as abolishing the entire crime of seditious libel, or as possessing some even broader meaning.

---

[4] We can mercifully skip over the mess created by the Articles of Confederation – the loose cooperative arrangement among the states prior to the US Constitution and the creation of the United States as a single nation.

Revolution in France

The French Revolution began in 1789 after King Louis XVI revived and convened an archaic consultative assembly, the Estates General, in a bid to obtain approval for new taxes. The Estates General consisted of representatives of the three estates of the realm: the clergy (the First Estate); the nobles (the Second Estate); and the commoners (the Third Estate).

At this point, the country's finances were suffering from the expense of warfare, including recent support for the American revolutionaries. In the mood of the time, however, the Estates General proved to be resistant. At the behest of the Abbé Sieyès, a clergyman and author who became the theorist of the revolution, the commoners of the Third Estate withdrew from the Estates General and succeeded in establishing a new political order. In the early stages of the revolution, this took the form of a constitutional monarchy and a body called the National Constituent Assembly. The latter moved quickly against the Catholic Church in granting religious toleration, refusing to affirm Roman Catholicism as the religion of France, abolishing the Church's privileges and raiding its lands and property to create a government resource.

With assistance from Thomas Jefferson (by this time, the American ambassador to France), the National Constituent Assembly prepared the Declaration of the Rights of Man and the Citizen, which was promulgated in August 1789. This document has influenced statements of human rights and freedoms ever since. It declared that social distinctions could be based only on public utility – thus attacking any aristocracy of birth – and it guaranteed numerous strongly worded rights. It is worth noting, however, that the Declaration's rights of citizenship applied to only a limited subset of the French population, essentially male property owners over the age of twenty-five. This was a much larger group than the nobles, but it left out the vast majority of the French people.

Furthermore, Articles X and XI, which provided respectively for freedom of opinion (including religious opinion) and freedom of communication, contained potentially significant exceptions. According to Article X the exception for free opinion was when its manifestation might violate the order established by the law. Similarly, Article XI permitted all citizens to speak, write and print freely – except to answer for cases of abuse of this liberty, as determined by the law. If interpreted in good faith, in accordance with the Declaration's historical context and intention, these Articles might have allowed little in the way of censorship or religious intolerance. But a vast range of opinion and discussion can be labelled as harmful to public order, or else as abusive, by those who are hostile to it. The effectiveness of all such documents, therefore, depends on who has the authority to interpret and apply them.

As it happened, the revolutionary governments of France imposed draconian censorship regimes that often included the death penalty. The revolution began, in part, with rejection of the *ancien régime*'s enforcement of orthodoxies, yet revolutionary leaders soon became persecutorial. From a twenty-first-century perspective, this looks like a re-run of the persecutions by Christians once they gained power within the late Roman Empire. Eric Berkowitz comments: 'In addition to persecution for political speech, the Revolution sparked explosions of iconoclasm and book burning, driven mainly by the urge to strike at symbols of the ancien régime and the Catholic Church' (Berkowitz 2021: 106). Revolutionary hatred of everything that had gone before in the governance and control of France led to cultural vandalism on a wide scale.

Louis XVI never accepted the legitimacy of the revolution or his own limited role as a constitutional monarch, and he plotted unsuccessfully to foment a counter-revolution. In June 1791, he attempted to escape from his home in the Tuileries Palace in Paris with hopes of obtaining support in the countryside – this was the farcically managed and humiliating 'Flight to Varennes', which quickly resulted in his capture and return to Paris. Not long after, the National Constituent Assembly voted to dissolve itself and was replaced from the beginning of October 1791 by the Legislative Assembly, which lasted in its turn for about a year. On 20 September 1792, the Legislative Assembly was replaced by a National Convention designed to represent the common people of the nation.

When foreign armies attacked France in 1792 in the hope of restoring the king's powers, the revolutionary leaders found themselves caught in an emergency situation. Louis was arrested and imprisoned in August 1792, and on 21 September the newly established National Convention declared France to be a republic and formally stripped the king of all power. Thereafter, he was executed by beheading in January 1793. During this period in the early 1790s, the nation's problems included rampant inflation; resistance to the nationalization of the Catholic Church; food shortages and associated riots; and war with its enemies.

The National Convention created a powerful new body, the Committee of Public Safety, headed by Maximilien Robespierre. This came into existence in April 1793 with a mandate to identify and punish France's enemies. It soon embarked on the infamous Reign of Terror (*la Terreur*) of 1793 and 1794.

From the beginning, leaders of the revolution engaged in processes of accusation and denunciation aimed at identifying and destroying opponents. Under the Committee of Public Safety, this process became far more systematic and powerful. Robespierre and his close associates did away with anything resembling the rule of law – so nothing was retained that resembled adequate procedures and evidential standards to protect individuals accused of crimes. The justification was that it was a time of emergency, and such actions were needed to ensure the unity of the new state. During this period, too, France introduced mass conscription in response to invasion from its foreign enemies – the innovation of the *levée en masse* – which created an immense conscript army that needed organized civilian efforts for its support.

The Reign of Terror makes for a heart-breaking story. While it lasted, its victims included scientists, feminists and actual or alleged atheists. On 8 August 1793, all of the French learned societies were suppressed, and the great chemist Antoine Lavoisier was executed on 8 May 1794. Feminist groups were suppressed, and the remarkable feminist author and activist Olympe de Gouges was executed on 3 November 1793. Members of the allegedly atheistic faction of Hébertistes (followers of Jacques Hébert, also known as Père Duchesne) were sent to the guillotine in March 1794. Thomas Paine, who had fled to France in 1792, was arrested and imprisoned at the end that year, and he only narrowly escaped execution before being released after the fall of Robespierre. The philosopher and statesman Nicolas de Condorcet died in prison in March 1794 while under arrest as a supposed traitor.

But in July 1794, Robespierre himself went to the guillotine, having aroused fear in too many people, and with his death the executions declined and eventually ceased.

The revolutionary government turned at an early stage to the ideas of anti-clerical radicals and adopted a programme of dechristianization of France. It abolished the old calendar and introduced weeks of ten days, new names for the months and a system of counting years from the foundation of the Republic rather than the traditional birth of Jesus of Nazareth. The revolutionaries originally attempted to institutionalize an anti-Catholic Cult of Reason, beginning in 1792, but the Committee of Public Safety introduced a new cult of worshipping the Supreme Being.

This was a non-Christian Creator God that had no connection to the Catholic Church or its scriptures and traditions, but nonetheless oversaw human actions and handed out eternal rewards and punishments.

Here, Robespierre followed Rousseau, who had clung to the existence of an all-good, though non-Christian, deity based on his own longings and feelings of uplift rather than on deference to sacred teachings or philosophical argument. In following Rousseau, Robespierre repudiated the anti-religious, sometimes atheistic, tradition of the *philosophes*, whom he contrived in his rhetoric to link with the monarchy and the *ancien régime*. He did, however, prudently depart from Rousseau's idea that all who do not believe in God must be banished from an ideal republic. Even Robespierre, who was willing to unleash social convulsions, could see that this would cause widespread fear in the circumstances of revolutionary France (Blum 1986: 247).

Rousseau and the Reign of Terror

A large body of scholarly literature over many years has debated how far Rousseau deserves blame for the Reign of Terror or the French Revolution itself.

The revolutionary pamphlet by Sieyès – *What Is the Third Estate?* (1789) – and the Declaration of the Rights of Man and the Citizen were influenced by Rousseau's *The Social Contract*, and Rousseau was a revered figure in the early days of the revolution. Revolutionary leaders treated *The Social Contract* almost as a holy text as they sought the spiritual regeneration of their country (Wokler 2012: 113, 204–5). These leaders sought to reform family and sexual relations, religion, French culture, and even aspects of the French language in an effort to introduce complete social change.

Despite all the talk of freedom, such grand ambitions entailed intrusive efforts to control the lives of individuals. Anyone who had ever criticized or quarrelled with Rousseau during his lifetime was treated as an enemy of the people and the state – this included almost everybody still alive who had associated with the *Encyclopédists* or who continued to embrace their spirit of intellectual scepticism and scientific progress. Great but deceased *philosophes* such as Helvétius, Voltaire, Diderot and Honoré Gabriel Mirabeau were vilified.

Something of a cult of hero worship grew up around Rousseau after his death in 1778, and Robespierre contributed to this. In his speeches and writings, however, he made almost no detailed references to Rousseau's specifically political works (see Blum 1986: 155), and he may not have known them intimately. He appears to have been more inspired by reading Rousseau's posthumously published *Confessions* (1782), and by an image of Rousseau himself as a paragon of virtue, unjustly persecuted by others who should have treasured and revered him.

However, one of Rousseau's key ideas – that of the general will – can be interpreted as a defence of state power over the individual and hence as a precursor of twentieth-century totalitarianisms. Within Rousseau's thought, the general will is a will devoted to the common good of the community. In Isaiah Berlin's interpretation, for example, such ideas were closely entwined with Rousseau's conception of freedom, and this made Rousseau a formidable enemy of liberty (Berlin 2014: 52). When we act in accordance with the general will, it appears, we thereby express our better, more real selves. When we depart from the general will, we also depart also from *our own true will* (Berlin 2014: 49).

Berlin argues that this leaves no room for legitimate diversity of thoughts, desires or policy preferences, and hence it plays into the hands of autocrats who claim to know our true will better than we know it ourselves. Compare an observation by Charles Taylor (1994: 51), who views Rousseau's idea of common dependence on the general will and participation in a 'tight common purpose' as having been 'the formula for the most terrible forms of homogenizing tyranny' (Taylor 1994: 51).

Rousseau himself was under no illusions about the difficulties of establishing an ideal republic such as described in *The Social Contract*, and he believed it was possible, if at all, only within a small polity such as Geneva or Corsica. He never proposed that his principles be extended to a large and populous nation such as France. We might, therefore, speculate that he would not have advocated something like the French Revolution and that he might have recoiled from the Reign of Terror if he'd lived to see it. But even his pocket-sized ideal republic would have had no place for either atheists or evangelical Christians with a mission of saving souls. Many people with commonplace opinions would, for one reason or another, have found themselves excluded by Rousseau's civic religion, and so be at risk of exile or worse.

Furthermore, a doctrine such as the general will, once it becomes available to a fanatic such as Robespierre, readily lends itself to sacrifice of individuals to collective interests – however these are imagined by whoever holds power. Robespierre need not be viewed as a faithful disciple of Rousseau – he probably wasn't – but Rousseau's theory of the general will can be dangerous in the hands of a demagogue who sees no room for political visions other than his own. At a time of national emergency, such as France genuinely experienced in the early 1790s, any such theory supports persecutions and fanaticism.

The religion of the French Revolution?

Writing in the nineteenth century, several decades after the French Revolution, Alexis de Tocqueville saw its historical role as destroying Europe's moribund feudal order. In that sense, it was a large-scale social and political revolution. Beyond this, however, Tocqueville compared it to momentous religious revolutions such as the Protestant Reformation and the rise of Christianity in the ancient world. He went so far as to portray the revolution as 'itself ... a new kind of religion', albeit 'without God, cult, or afterlife' (Tocqueville [1856]2011: 21).

For many people, revolutionary ideas, with the commitments and practices that they support, do – as Tocqueville perceived – take on something of the character of a religion. According to Tocqueville, the ideas of French revolutionary leaders implied the need for thoroughgoing social transformation, not only in France but more widely, aiming at 'the regeneration of the human race' (Tocqueville [1856]2011: 21).

In his classic reflection on the Age of Enlightenment, *The Heavenly City of the Eighteenth-Century Philosophers*, first published in 1932, the historian Carl L. Becker took Tocqueville's reflection a step further. He insisted that the French Revolution – especially in its later stages – was closer to being a traditional religion than Tocqueville acknowledged (Becker [1932]2003: 154–61). For Becker, the revolution had its own sacred doctrines and its own equivalents of God, worship and immortality – with contributions to posterity and humanity's revival acting as a substitute for Christianity's spiritual afterlife.

Becker distils a set of doctrines that he sees as 'the religion of the Enlightenment': these include faith in humanity's essential goodness; the goal of a good life on earth rather than a spiritual life after death;

the possibility of perfecting life on earth through the exercise of reason; and the necessity of freeing human minds from 'ignorance and superstition' and freeing human bodies from 'the arbitrary oppression of the constituted social authorities' (Becker [1932]2003: 102–3). Given the varied writings of the French *philosophes* and other Enlightenment figures, this is somewhat Procrustean, but it seems a reasonable summary of much eighteenth-century philosophy, especially within the milieu of the Parisian salons.

Ideas such as these are emotionally powerful, and they can form an ideology that plays the religion role in adherents' lives, without being religious in any stricter sense such as I discussed in Chapter 2. The Enlightenment's distinctive ideas are incompatible with the *ancien régime* as it operated in France or with the general assumptions of Western Christendom. They might well provide the basis for revolution against, as Kant wrote, despotism and oppression. But must they provide a new foundation for persecutions and oppression if their adherents obtain political power?

Not necessarily. They might, rather, provide the basis for public discussion and the cautious process of social enlightenment projected by Kant in his 1784 essay. In the hands of introspective and liberal-minded people, they might support toleration, discussion and innovative thinking. But at times of crisis, when much is at stake, a belief system such as this can be wielded by fanatics who preach submission to what they call the general will.

5 THE LONG NINETEENTH CENTURY

Themes

The Long Nineteenth Century, roughly from the beginning of the French Revolution in 1789 to the beginning of the First World War in 1914, was a complex and paradoxical period in world history. It included great wars and revolutions, but also a long period of relative peace: the so-called Age of Metternich from the end of the Napoleonic Wars to a wave of revolutions in Europe and Latin America in and around 1848.

European societies and their offshoots were transformed by the First and then the Second Industrial Revolution – the first based on steam, and the second on newer technologies that included electrification, advances in the science of chemistry, the invention and improvement of the internal combustion engine and large, increasingly sophisticated factories. Immense expansion in the productivity of industrial economies enabled population growth of a kind never seen before: as it is often expressed, humanity escaped the Malthusian trap whereby limits to productivity had constrained increases in population.

The American Revolution, French Revolution and Napoleonic Wars encouraged some inheritors of Enlightenment thought to renew their efforts for what they saw as freedom and reason, but others sought to restore order and tradition. In France itself, as we've seen, some revolutionary leaders in the 1790s ruled through terror, and once Napoleon Bonaparte gained control in 1799 he censored internal opposition.

The Long Nineteenth Century was a period of nationalism and nation-building, new empires and new ideologies – socialism, communism, positivism, nationalism, antisemitism and others. From the 1840s, Karl Marx developed his ideas of alienation, class struggle and the inexorable exploitation and impoverishment of the working class. This was caused,

Marx argued, not by the personal malice or moral corruption of the property owners who employed workers, but by structural features of the capitalist economic system. Eventually, on the Marxist account, the workers would have no alternative but to unite and rise up in rebellion against their oppressors. This would produce a new form of society that, unlike its predecessors, would have no internal contradictions needing resolution.

After the failed revolutions of 1848, Marx was sufficiently disillusioned to conclude that the revolutionary path would be much longer than he'd expected. He turned to a deeper study of economics and especially the mechanisms of capitalist exploitation. Nonetheless, he remained convinced of the inevitability of a workers' revolution and a communist society.

In the mid to late nineteenth century, the European nations engaged in a revival of nationalist feeling that came to include renewed eagerness to establish far-flung empires. The geopolitical rivals were soon caught up in a struggle for supremacy and in their own internal debates over national identity. This contributed to ideas of racial pride and purity, including the theory and practice of antisemitism, which took a form rather different from older expressions of anti-Jewish sentiment based largely on religion.

The term *antisemitismus* (which becomes an English cognate, *antisemitism*) first appeared in Germany in 1860 to criticize anti-Jewish racism. Beginning in the late 1870s, however, it was popularized by individuals, such as the journalist Wilhelm Marr, who were ideologically hostile to the Jews and their culture (Marcus 2015: 57–9).[1] Marr claimed that the Jews were 'fundamentally different from others' and so could not be truly assimilated – the only alternative was their defeat by the Christian societies in which they existed as an alien and dangerous presence (Kenez 2013: 5). For Marr and his allies, *antisemitismus* was meant to convey an ideological position analogous to nationalism or socialism for example. The intent was to suggest an ideology of opposition to and hatred of the Jews and whatever they were taken to stand for, while attempting to sound principled or even scientific (Marcus 2015: 9–10).

---

[1] Although the term existed prior to the 1870s, it became popular as a result of efforts by Marr and others with similar views (see W. Laqueur 2006: 21). By this point, following the French Revolution and other developments, large numbers of Jews had returned to Western Europe after their expulsions from most of its kingdoms in earlier centuries.

Jews were not, of course, the only 'Semitic' people, but they were the ones who were represented in Europe, and the word was aimed squarely at them. Historically, individuals such as Marr incited hatred and opposition to Jews based on their imagined racial characteristics (Marcus 2015: 10, 59–61). More broadly, the term *antisemitism* now refers to the full range of anti-Jewish bigotries, whether or not based on late-nineteenth-century racial pseudoscience.

In the 1860s, the United States was torn by a catastrophic civil war fought over abolition or continuation of slavery. Despite the victory for Union forces over the rebel Confederacy, the white majority in the South resisted equality for the freed slaves. Immediately after the end of the Civil War, racist groups such as the Ku Klux Klan began to form, mobilized against black Americans, and sought through intimidation and murderous violence to restore white supremacy in the South. The later decades of the nineteenth century saw the enactment in the southern states of the first 'Jim Crow' laws – enforcing a policy of racial segregation that remained in place until the first successful constitutional challenges in the 1950s.

Initially in Germany, universities took something like their current form during the Long Nineteenth Century. They became bastions of specialized study and (sometimes, but not always) free inquiry. Drawing on themes from the Enlightenment and the French Revolution, liberalism appeared and grew as a political tradition that valued individual freedom. There were new challenges to religious claims, but also new kinds of religiosity. All of this and much more represent an age of variety and seeming contradictions.

For current purposes, we can deal with only a few themes and with events in even fewer countries. This chapter concentrates on issues relating to individual freedom, set against the norms and institutions that continued to shape how men and women thought, spoke and lived their lives.

Dangerous ideas

Outside of France, the French Revolution provoked a reaction in the major countries of Europe: they were horrified and fearful 'that the contagion might spread' (Beales 2000: 174). Governments developed extensive laws restricting discussion of revolutionary ideas, critiques of religion and other topics that were viewed as dangerous. Political leaders were especially concerned to keep what they regarded as subversive ideas away from consideration by women, younger people and the working classes – as opposed to educated bourgeois men. In all countries concerned, censorship extended beyond printed material to theatrical performances, images and new communications media as they were invented.

Specific responses included a crackdown in England on allegedly seditious speech and writing. Fox's Libel Act of 1792 gave English juries the right to render general verdicts, including on the libelousness of published matter, but this was a limited victory for freedom of the press. Against the backdrop of the French Revolution and the Reign of Terror, juries of this time tended to support prosecutors (Bird 2020: 198).

As Britain and France went to war in the 1790s and beyond, American political parties struggled over which side their country should take. Under the political system of the time, John Adams, from the Federalist Party, became America's president in 1797, while Thomas Jefferson, from the Democratic-Republican Party, was its vice-president. The Federalists sided with Britain and were suspicious of the French Revolution, whereas their opponents were sympathetic to the Revolution and to France.

Despite the ringing words contained in the First Amendment, it was not long before the US Congress enacted new laws restricting individual liberty. At a time of political panic over issues of national security, the Federalists were able to enact the Alien and Sedition Acts of 1798. The Sedition Act criminalized numerous activities aimed at frustrating government actions or encouraging insurrection. It included criminal penalties for 'false, scandalous, and malicious' writings that brought the government, either house of the federal Congress, or the president 'into contempt or disrepute'.

The Sedition Act included no provisions for pre-publication censorship, and it provided for trial by jury and a defence of truth. On paper, therefore, its relevant provisions were less draconian than the common law doctrine of seditious libel, which still applied at state level. But it became clear that these innovations were of little avail when the alleged libel was the expression of a locally unpopular political opinion that could not by any means be proved true. Moreover, the legislation was blatantly partisan in its drafting and implementation: it specifically protected the (Federalist) president but not the Democratic-Republican vice-president, and it expired at the end of President Adams' term of office.

In 1800, Jefferson won the presidential election, partly thanks to the unpopularity of the Sedition Act, which duly expired at the same time as Adams' presidency. Under Jefferson's administration, presidential pardons were granted for individuals who had been convicted of sedition. The validity of the Sedition Act was never tested in the US Supreme Court, but it is now considered unconstitutional, and its very enactment prompted a valuable debate about what limits to political speech could be accepted in democratic societies.

One result was the publication of cogent defences of freedom of the press – freedom not only from prior restraint but also from subsequent prosecution – by James Madison, St. George Tucker and Tunis Wortman, among others (Levy 1985: 309–49). A common theme in these publications was that criminal legislation such as the Sedition Act made no principled sense in a newly established democratic nation where federal elections were written into the constitution and robust criticism of elected officials and candidates for office was inevitable and expected. Wortman's book entitled *A Treatise, Concerning Political Inquiry, and the Liberty of the Press*, published in 1800, picked up threads from earlier authors, but wove them into an imaginative synthesis that foreshadowed John Stuart Mill's classic *On Liberty* some sixty years later.

Thus, the crisis brought on by the Sedition Act forced more concerted efforts in the United States to define the meaning of, and the rationale for, freedom of speech and the press in the circumstances of the newly formed republic. One outcome was a body of relatively libertarian political and legal theory. A darker side of the debate, however, is that even Thomas Jefferson was not above encouraging lawsuits against his political enemies using state rather than federal law (Levy 1985: 340–1; Berkowitz 2021: 118).

Later in the nineteenth century, the French author Alexis de Tocqueville studied the development of American democracy, viewing it with much sympathy and seeing in it the future of his own country, but also questioning what happens to minorities, and to their aspirations and viewpoints, in a country where the majority rules. Tocqueville admired the growth of a free and vigorous press with no government censorship or involvement, and with numerous sources of news and information for the public. At the same time, he understood that this did not entail freedom of opinion.

In the first volume of his two-part work *Democracy in America* (volume 1, originally published in 1835), Tocqueville laments, 'I know of no country where, in general, there reigns less independence of mind and true freedom of discussion than in America' (Tocqueville

[1835–1840]2012: 417). He attributed this not to any formal inquisition into heresy but to the informal tyranny of the majority, and particularly to the opprobrium suffered by anybody openly dissenting from established majority opinion. Such a person could expect to be 'exposed to all types of distasteful things and to everyday persecutions', being openly attacked by those who disagreed while any who agreed kept silent and distanced themselves ([1835–1840]2012: 418).

Thus, dissenting voices could be silenced – and apparently were, if we credit Tocqueville's impressions – without any need for state censorship.

Discursive religiosity

As portrayed by the distinguished Scottish historian Callum G. Brown, one legacy of the Enlightenment was a new Christian culture in Britain (and elsewhere) based on individual spiritual experience as an alternative to the established authority of the churches and the routines of weekly worship. Brown points to a 'fading of coercive religion', but also to the rise of an 'overwhelmingly discursive' religiosity (Brown 2009: 195) that informed national and personal identities.

The general culture in streets and workplaces, in popular entertainment, and even in public houses, was saturated with Christian music, language and iconography. From about 1800 until deep into the twentieth century, therefore, religion's social authority was not enforced by state coercion to attend church but via a socially pervasive system of discourse. Without recourse to fire or sword, it required certain forms of behaviour, while it condemned others and stigmatized anyone who failed to conform. Most people reflected this in their own manner of speaking, and few could resist its pressure.

Brown describes large-scale and multifaceted missionary efforts that were organized in Britain during the nineteenth century, especially led by the Methodists. At the grassroots level of evangelism, the Christian churches found common cause. Their efforts were aimed, in part, at the populations of foreign colonies but also at the British population itself, especially at the poor and the urban working class, who were likely to find themselves visited by enthusiastic home missionaries.

All this organization and zeal to bring souls to Christ, and to personal salvation, was accompanied by efforts to puritanize society. That is, there were efforts to demonize and suppress alcohol, gambling, dancing, horse racing, breaking the Sabbath and sexual activities of every kind outside the bond of marriage (or in some cases even within it). As we will see, there was a particular emphasis on the alleged harms of masturbation. The list of sins extended more widely, but these were the most central.

A notable development of the 1800s was that the modes of socially enforced religiosity were strongly differentiated between the respective ideals set for men and women. Piety was increasingly feminized, with a concomitant shift in the social understanding of femininity. The religiosity of women was viewed as 'privileged and pivotal': as paramount to evangelical ideas of morality and the sanctity of the family (Brown 2009: 59). Within this system of understanding the world and society, women were almost worshipped as long as they kept their place and were not 'fallen' from grace and social respectability. Middle-class women were confined to the home and a narrow set of activities, and were saddled with a role of gentle moral police within the family unit. To a considerable extent, then, an ideology of chastity, temperance and women's domesticity became dominant – and almost the official interpretation of Christianity.

Men enjoyed far greater freedoms than women, but they were often portrayed as needing control. As Brown elaborates, masculinity was understood as inherently turbulent, intemperate and dangerous, an ever-present threat to Christian piety and good morals. Many stereotypically masculine activities – particularly, but not only, those involving alcohol and gambling – became targets of moral campaigns for their suppression.

As a system for ordering society, therefore, nineteenth-century discursive Christianity could be oppressive to men as well as women. Some authors and thinkers of the time examined its downsides, and a small minority of dissenters responded with alternative libertine or decadent moralities. Others produced radical critiques of Christianity itself, even if (as most did) they accepted the morality of their time.

Challenges to Christianity

During the centuries of early modernity, rival Christian denominations disputed about doctrine, but some events had the potential to undermine Christianity more generally. Central to Christianity since its rise to power in ancient Rome was its insistence that the Bible is the revealed word of God, and is thus a source of divinely guaranteed knowledge.

But the boldest scholars began to challenge this claim in the seventeenth century, when the traditional attribution of the first five books of the Old Testament or Hebrew Bible began to appear doubtful. If, as close textual examination suggested, these books were not authored by Moses, their authority was shaken – at least according to the era's theological understanding.

By the early decades of the nineteenth century, continuing scholarship relating to Christian texts tended to undermine long-established understandings of the Bible's authority and its basis, creating a threat to the credibility of Christianity itself. This does not mean that the European masses simply withdrew from their faith. However, there is a complex story to be told about the scholars, scientists and intellectuals who questioned the truth claims of Christianity – and religion more generally – during the Long Nineteenth Century. Some of them developed alternative, non-religious understandings of the universe and humanity's place in it.

In England, satirical newspapers, pamphlets and books often challenged the claims and the authority of religion and thereby brought their authors into trouble with the law. Prosecutions during the early nineteenth century typically involved allegations of blasphemy rather than – or in addition to – seditious libel. High-profile prosecutions included three separate (each unsuccessful) trials of the satirist and bookseller William Hone, all conducted in 1817. Most famously, perhaps, Hone's pamphlet *The Late John Wilkes's Catechism of a Ministerial Member* parodied the Catechism, the Lord's Prayer and the Ten Commandments, while including satirical barbs aimed at government figures.

By contrast to Hone's astonishing success in escaping punishment, the radical publisher and activist – and high-profile public atheist – Richard Carlile ended up spending many years in prison, largely for his efforts in selling editions of Thomas Paine's *The Age of Reason*. This was an irreverent manifesto of philosophical deism – and in particular a satirical rejection of Christianity – originally published as a series of pamphlets in 1794, 1795 and 1807. Carlile also advocated women's equality and access to contraception, and criticized the ideals of Christian monogamy and feminine modesty – thus submitting to the public a cluster of ideas that caused friction even with other radicals.

Attacks on religion were seen as tolerable to a certain degree – provided they maintained some minimal level of civility, and unless they appeared in cheap editions available to a wide audience. Any work that treated Christian doctrine with scepticism was seen as dangerous if it undermined the faith, and hence, it was thought, the obedience of the lower classes (Levy 1995: 365).

By the 1840s, blasphemy laws in England had proved counterproductive for suppressing atheist publications, though successful in creating martyrs out of activists such as Richard Carlile and his family and supporters. Blasphemy prosecutions lapsed for a time, only to be revived by events in the 1880s. In the interim, one high point was the founding of a new movement under the label *Secularism* (with a capital *S*) around the beginning of the 1850s and under the leadership of George Holyoake. Holyoake was himself imprisoned for blasphemy in 1842–3, arising from what now seems a mild answer to a question about God that he was asked during a public lecture delivered at the Cheltenham Mechanics' Institute.

Secularism, as Holyoake developed the idea, took a welcoming stance towards moderate or liberal-minded Christians, and despite his socialist commitments Holyoake did not choose inflammatory rhetoric. In this sense, he was a different sort of thinker from Carlile, who died in his early fifties in 1843, or the radical journalist Charles Southwell, who also spent time in prison for blasphemy. Likewise, Holyoake was a more conciliatory figure than his younger contemporary Charles Bradlaugh, who founded the National Secular Society in 1866 as an organization devoted to separation of church and state.

In addition to the term *secularism* (or *Secularism*), Holyoake promoted *naturalism* in its use as, to some extent, a euphemism for *atheism*. This meaning for the word had precedents dating back as far as the mid-eighteenth century, but Holyoake may have been the first thinker and activist to make it a central element of his agenda.[2]

For his part, Charles Bradlaugh stood for parliament unsuccessfully in 1868 and 1874, but was then successful in 1880, winning the seat of Northampton. This led to a farcical saga over whether an avowed atheist could be allowed to swear an oath or affirmation of allegiance to the British Crown, as was required to take up a parliamentary seat. An outcome was not reached until 1886, when Bradlaugh was finally permitted to swear the oath and formally take his place in the parliament. In 1888, new

---

[2]Talk of 'naturalism' and how it should best be understood has long been a topic of philosophical controversy, but an investigation of this issue would take us far afield into philosophy of religion and philosophy of science. One place to begin is Blackford and Schüklenk (2013: 149–53).

legislation was enacted, permitting the use of an affirmation by members of the Houses of Parliament and reforming the existing provisions for affirmations in the civil and criminal courts.

When blasphemy trials resumed in the 1880s, the targets were individuals involved with a new, and assertively anti-Christian, journal – *The Freethinker*. Importantly, one trial associated with *The Freethinker* led to a softening of the legal doctrine of blasphemy: in *Reg. v. Ramsay and Foote* (decided 24 April 1883), Lord Chief Justice Coleridge instructed a jury that Christianity's truth-claims were not beyond criticism, and that 'if the decencies of controversy are observed, even the fundamentals of religion may be attacked without the writer being guilty of blasphemy' ((1883) 15 Cox CC 231, 238). Thus, something more scurrilous or insulting was required than mere disagreement or dissent (for discussion, see Berkowitz 2021: 129–30). In this case, the jury failed to reach a verdict and the authorities did not take further action against the defendants.

For the next two decades, there was a lull in English blasphemy trials, but events early in the twentieth century led to further controversy. Beginning in about 1903, numerous prosecutions were brought against John W. Gott – editor of a magazine called *The Truthseeker* – and an activist named Thomas W. Stewart. Over the next decade or so, both endured guilty verdicts and periods of imprisonment. A 1914 case that culminated in Stewart's conviction 'produced an uproar of protest and renewed efforts to nullify blasphemy laws' (Levy 1995: 498).

Subsequently, a 1917 case at the highest level of the English legal system, *Bowman v. Secular Society* (decided 14 May 1917), moulded the civil (rather than criminal) law to benefit opponents and critics of Christianity. It overruled earlier cases that had potentially restricted their rights in many circumstances. For example, the previous law had arguably rendered void, or voidable, any legal instruments such as wills, trust deeds and contracts, if they 'promoted blasphemy or irreligion' (Levy 1995: 499). *Bowman v. Secular Society* had the effect that legal disabilities befell non-Christians, including critics of foundational Christian doctrines, only when their speech or activities were blasphemous under the criminal law.

This, however, gave no new relief to individuals charged with criminal blasphemy, notably Gott, who ended up being the last individual in Britain to be imprisoned for the crime. He was convicted in 1921 and jailed for nine months. Efforts at further law reform in the early twentieth century produced no agreement among interested parties and came to nothing at the time.

Sex and obscenity in the Long Nineteenth Century

The seventeenth and eighteenth centuries saw impressive scientific breakthroughs, but scientific understanding remained rudimentary in many respects. Indeed, trust in scientific claims was often ill-advised, as with a social panic over masturbation that seems to have started in the early eighteenth century (T. Laqueur 2003: 13–20, 174–9). It reached its height with the work of a Swiss physician, Samuel Tissot. In 1759, Tissot published the Latin version of a book that he subsequently translated into French with extensive additions. This version, *L'Onanisme; ou, Dissertation physique sur les malades produites par la masturabation*, appeared in 1760, followed by its English translation in 1761 (T. Laqueur 2003: 38, 428). Tissot blamed masturbation for numerous diseases of the body and mind, amounting to 'a form of slow suicide' (Berkowitz 2012: 274).

For the next 150 years or more, this idea prevailed in Europe. Major Enlightenment figures such as Voltaire, Rousseau and Kant condemned the practice of masturbation on various grounds that were not necessarily medical (see T. Laqueur 2003: 41–4, 58–60). Educators, governments and moral crusaders campaigned to prevent masturbation, with its imagined deadly effects. Some organized schemes to discourage adolescent boys from ruining their health, while others tried surgical techniques or patented strange inventions. And so, the stumbling medical science of the Age of Enlightenment and the Long Nineteenth Century was used 'to justify old-time sexual repression' (Berkowitz 2012: 275).

Sex began to be viewed in more worldly terms during the eighteenth and nineteenth centuries, with a retreat from the harshest theological attitudes to erotic desire and pleasure. However, the 1800s saw new laws against abortion, a less tolerant attitude to prostitution, and intensifying hostility towards homosexuality. As with masturbation, though admittedly with more credible empirical evidence, prostitution was increasingly seen as a problem of public health. Prompted by fears of venereal diseases, draconian new systems of inspection and regulation were introduced in many European countries, beginning in France, and later in the United States (for detail, see Berkowitz 2012: 341–55).

Oddly enough, given the long history of Christian sexual morality and the invention of the printing press as early as the mid-fifteenth century, obscene publications in the sense known today appear to have become illegal in England only in the 1720s. In 1727 and again in 1728, a publisher and bookseller called Edmund Curll[3] was successfully prosecuted in the law courts (for discussion, see Levy 1995: 306–9). The rationale was evidently that Christian morality, no less than Christianity itself, was, at the time, considered part of the law of England – and hence whatever struck at it could not be tolerated.

However, the first half of the nineteenth century saw a proliferation of erotic literature and art that became widely available even to the less moneyed classes – to the dismay of many wealthy and/or powerful people who feared what passions might be stirred up, and how personal character could be corrupted, by exposure to such 'filth'. The perceived need to act more decisively in suppressing this material led in England to the passage of the Obscene Publications Act – known as Lord Campbell's Act – in 1857, and then to the 1868 case *Reg. v. Hicklin*.

In this case, the Court of Queen's Bench held that a publication was legally obscene if it tended 'to deprave and corrupt those whose minds are open to such immoral influences, and into whose hands a publication of this sort may fall' (LR 3 QB 360, 371 (1868)). It followed that the material caught by Lord Campbell's Act and the *Hicklin* test for obscenity did not line up with what might be regarded as obscene or pornographic today: all that was required was some subversion of morals, not necessarily of a sexual nature.

In *Reg. v. Hicklin*, the material at issue was a sensational anti-Catholic pamphlet entitled *The Confessional Unmasked; Shewing the Depravity of the Romish priesthood, the Iniquity of the Confessional, and the Questions put to Females in Confession*. The judges were not averse to criticism of Roman Catholicism (a rival denomination to England's established church, after all) or the confessional, but much of the pamphlet's content was considered gratuitously sexual and coarse – more than was needed to attack its permissible targets.

In 1877, two leading freethinkers of the time, Charles Bradlaugh – prior to his parliamentary career – and Annie Besant, were arrested and charged under Lord Campbell's Act. Their alleged crime was republication of a pamphlet that had first appeared in the United States in 1832: *Fruits of Philosophy, or the Private Companion of Young Married*

---

[3]I have followed Levy in the spelling of this individual's name. At least one law report from the time has it as 'Edmond Curl'.

People. Fruits of Philosophy was the work of a Massachusetts physician, Charles Knowlton, who had argued on Malthusian grounds for the development of better methods of contraception. Knowlton viewed sexual pleasure as something good in itself, when sought and indulged with moderation, and he offered advice on existing methods of contraception and treatments for impotence. For his pains, he was fined for distributing copies of the book to his patients, then later imprisoned for three months over a second edition with wider distribution.

Fruits of Philosophy appeared in Britain in various editions, including one published by the secularist Charles Watts, who pleaded guilty of printing and publishing an obscene work when charged 1877. In response, Bradlaugh and Besant published their own version with updating and new material to reflect developments in medicine since the 1830s.

When the case came to trial, the prosecution, led by the Solicitor General, Sir Hardinge Giffard, argued that *Fruits of Philosophy* was likely to deprave and corrupt readers' minds by encouraging them to enjoy the pleasures of sex without undertaking what were said to be the natural and God-given responsibilities of marriage – that is, having children. Giffard submitted to the court that this idea would be 'most mischievous' even if the message were conveyed only to married people 'unable to bear the burden of too many children' (quoted in Manvell 1976: 67). Throughout the trial, however, he went further in his allegations against the book. He argued that its natural tendency would be to place in the minds even of young unmarried people the idea of sex without the consequence of children.

Besant and Bradlaugh represented themselves, and they delivered long opening addresses before they called their witnesses. Besant argued that it was in both the public interest and the interest of the individuals concerned for men and women to marry while still young, but to take steps, based on the best available knowledge of physiology, to limit their number of children. When she finished, Bradlaugh argued that the physiological detail contained in *Fruits of Philosophy* was no more than reasonably required to achieve its educational purpose. He demonstrated that works with as much or more detail were freely available, not only to medical doctors and students but to anyone from the higher social classes. Some were even used in public schools to teach the children of the wealthy, but they were not within reach of ordinary working people.

As the transcript shows, the presiding judge, Sir Alexander Cockburn, treated Besant and Bradlaugh with courtesy and respect. Nonetheless, he insisted that Besant's and Bradlaugh's subjective motives in publishing the book were irrelevant if its actual tendency was 'subversive of the morals of society' (Manvell 1976: 151). Conversely, he asked the jury to take into account whether the content of the *Fruits of Philosophy* was a legitimate contribution to public discussion and inquiry. The jury then caused confusion by returning a verdict that was something of an each-way bet: the book was 'calculated to deprave public morals' but Besant and Bradlaugh had published it without corrupt motives (Manvell 1976: 152).

Since the judge had determined as a matter of law that the subjective motivations of Besant and Bradlaugh were not relevant, he ruled that on this basis the jury must find the defendants guilty. Accordingly, Bradlaugh and Besant were handed prison sentences of six months, plus large fines. They were, however, allowed to go free pending an appeal of the verdict, which they ultimately won on a technical ground in the Court of Appeal – *Bradlaugh and Besant v. Reg* (decided 12 February 1878). Theoretically, they could have been charged a second time, with a reworded indictment, but this never eventuated. Nonetheless, the publicity from the case was a factor when Besant's estranged husband gained legal custody of their daughter, Mabel, contrary to the terms of a deed of separation that the couple had signed in 1873.[4]

After the prosecution of Besant and Bradlaugh, and despite its eventual failure, Lord Campbell's Act and the associated *Hicklin* test continued to be employed in Britain to censor art, literature and public discussion of sensitive topics such as Malthusian ideas.

Obscenity in American law

The concept of 'obscenity' attracted only sporadic interest in the American courts for much of the nineteenth century. Stray cases from the time include *Commonwealth v. Sharpless*, decided in 1815 by the Supreme of Court of Pennsylvania, and *Bell v. State*, decided by the Supreme Court of Tennessee in 1851. The former dealt with an erotic or suggestive painting of a man and woman, while the latter involved what seem to have been public rantings by the defendant, heard by others in the town of Louisville. Using colourful and vulgar language, he described his

---

[4]The primary argument related to Annie Besant's atheism, and the judge held that her refusal to give Mabel religious instruction was itself sufficient to decide the case.

sexual adventures and misadventures with the wife and daughters of one Abraham Hartsell.

Over time, and especially after the Civil War, isolated cases such as this developed into relentless suppression of allegedly obscene literature. That, in turn, prompted the use of mail, rather than bookshops, to distribute and sell the material. This background shaped the campaigns of the anti-vice crusader Anthony Comstock, who led the attack against any such literature, along with much else that he and his supporters deemed contrary to Christian sexual morals. In 1873, the federal Congress enacted a statute entitled an Act for the Suppression of Trade in, and Circulation of, Obscene Literature and Articles of Immoral Use, which became known as the Comstock Act. It enabled the seizure of 'indecent' materials sent via the postal service. These materials extended far beyond anything that would be regarded today as pornography to include, for example, advocacy of free love and references to contraceptive methods.

The Comstock Act was supported by other statutes with similar intent, aimed, for example, at criminalizing delivery of the same items by means other than the postal service, and at preventing their importation into the United States. All of this represented a concerted effort to impose Comstock's ideas of morality on the American citizenry, backed by the threat of savage legal penalties. Like any legal document, the Comstock Act and related statutes required interpretation, and here the *Hicklin* test was imported from Britain for use in cases involving alleged obscenity. The *Hicklin* test was first applied in the United States in a case from 1879, *United States v. Bennett*, and although the test was increasingly questioned and modified in the twentieth century, it was not authoritatively overruled until 1957.

The rise of modern universities

The first universities, beginning with the University of Bologna in the eleventh century, were essentially religious institutions. During the centuries of European modernity, however, universities evolved to meet perceived social needs, reaching something recognizably like their modern form in nineteenth-century Germany, where they underwent a shift from pursuing entirely pedagogical goals to a union of teaching and research. As they continued to evolve, the major German universities converged on a model that was often followed elsewhere – partly by deliberate imitation and partly by independent discovery of its advantages. This model is associated with the idealist philosopher Johann Gottlieb Fichte, the great liberal theologian Friedrich Schleiermacher, and especially with the Prussian philosopher, diplomat and official Wilhelm von Humboldt. It is worth recording, however, that these individuals did not entirely agree among themselves and did not, as a group, have everything their own way in the evolution of the German universities.

During the nineteenth century, the German universities developed an ever-increasing disciplinary specialization, which 'occurred almost in geometric progression in the late nineteenth and early twentieth centuries' (McClelland 1980: 87). They became more secular – less dominated by the objectives of the churches and by their own faculties of theology – and they emphasized high standards of research and publication. In short, universities based on the German or 'Humboldtian' model evolved into institutions of rigorous and free inquiry. During the later decades of the nineteenth century, universities in English-speaking countries shifted towards their own versions of this model.

In the event, however, there have often been tensions. On the one hand, the scholars and scientists employed by modern Humboldtian universities tend to assert considerable intellectual freedoms. On the other hand, they encounter individuals or organizations – often outside the universities, but sometimes on the inside – who wish to curtail sensitive lines of inquiry. These lines of inquiry at any particular time in history give an indication of which ideas were viewed as dangerous in the wider society and which were seen by powerful individuals and institutions as beyond criticism.

In his 1995 book *Zealotry and Academic Freedom*, reprinted in 2017, Neil Hamilton examines the influence of ideology, dogmatism and zealotry in American universities since the Humboldtian model began to dominate in the United States after the Civil War. In that respect, he traces 'several waves of zealotry' (Hamilton [1995]2017: 1), corresponding to an ebb and flow of ideas. He identifies two early waves that fall within the scope of this chapter: a form of fundamentalist religiosity in the late nineteenth century, and somewhat later, a hardcore insistence on capitalist theory and practice.

Through the 1870s and 1880s, and even into the 1890s, American universities and colleges, including many institutions that are revered today such as Columbia, Yale and Princeton, identified the mission of higher education as one of inculcating religiosity, belief in biblical authority and a commitment to Christian morals. Individual academics who cast doubt on any of this were likely to experience stunted careers. Students as well as their teachers were closely scrutinized for religious orthodoxy and what the churches regarded as moral virtue.

From about the late 1880s, higher education institutions in the United States became, in many cases, dependent on gifts from wealthy businessmen who tended to promote a political and moral doctrine of unfettered capitalist competition. This doctrine was inconsistent with much research at the time by economists and other social scientists, many of whom advocated reforms to the social and economic status quo. During this era, there were numerous clashes between the economic views of benefactors and those of academic staff, with the latter often dismissed from employment or forced to resign. This inevitably created a pressure for others to keep silent.

The modern idea of academic freedom grew in reaction to events such as these. While the idea had a much longer prehistory, it took the form that we know today as recently as the late nineteenth and early twentieth centuries. In the United States, for example, the first efforts to define and promote academic freedom were made in the years leading up America's entry into the First World War. But as we will see in Chapter 6, the war brought its own pressures for conformity in the academy and elsewhere.

Liberalism in theory and practice

Though liberalism has roots in the European Enlightenment and even in sixteenth- and seventeenth-century debates over religious toleration, it arose as a distinct way of thinking and form of political practice in the nineteenth century, responding to the needs and anxieties of the time (Fawcett 2018: 1–7). It responded, that is, to a new social world of innovation and change, marked, for example, by population growth, political revolutions and the beginning of modern industrial capitalism.

Liberalism developed as a theory of freedom from many constraints, primarily from those imposed by governments, but also those required by a society's prevailing attitudes and moral beliefs. Liberals sought to reserve a space of freedom for ideas and opinions, particularly, but by no means solely, those about humanity's existential questions. In practice, this included freedom to express religious commitments through language or action, but also to criticize or oppose religion.

The first people to label themselves as liberals, or the equivalent in their own language, seem to have been members of a Spanish political party, the *Liberales*, who were one of the groups formed in response to the Napoleonic invasion of Spain in 1808. In the following years, versions of liberalism found their way to Portugal, Italy, France and elsewhere in Europe. Throughout the nineteenth century, and into the early decades of the twentieth, varied conceptions of liberalism also became prominent in the emerging Spanish- and Portuguese-speaking nations of Latin America. The word *libéralisme* entered French around 1816–18, providing one obvious source for an equivalent in English. The first written appearance of *liberalism* identified by the OED was in 1816, but this was in reference to events at the time in Spain.

One leading figure in developing, inspiring and advocating liberalism during its early decades was the Swiss-French author and statesman Benjamin Constant, who in turn was influenced by Locke, Montesquieu and the early ideals of the French Revolution. Today, he is most remembered for his distinction between the liberty of the ancients and that of the moderns, whereby a 'modern' conception of liberty involves individual freedom from the demands of others, including the state.

Constant developed this idea in his essay 'The Liberty of the Ancients Compared with That of the Moderns', first published in 1820 and based on a lecture that he'd delivered to the Athénée Royal in Paris the previous year. For Constant, the liberty of the moderns included freedom from arbitrary government power, freedom of speech, freedom of religion and a general freedom to choose a profession and how we live our lives, to come and go as we please and to associate with whomever we wish for our own reasons (but also to have some influence on the administration of government) (Constant [1820]1988: 310–11).

Constant contrasted this with liberty as he believed it was understood in classical antiquity: a liberty to participate directly and collectively in the administration of the state, which was, however, consistent with unremitting surveillance of the individual by the group and a thoroughgoing subjection of the individual to the group's wishes. Constant argued that the rise of large nations – and of large-scale trade and commerce – had rendered direct participation in government impracticable and encouraged citizens to seek instead a broad zone of independence and privacy. Irrespective of its historical accuracy in describing the Greek and Roman worlds, Constant's essay can be seen as a powerful manifesto of liberal freedoms.

Notably, Constant did not simply denounce the liberty of the ancients or recommend withdrawal from the political sphere. Rather, he encouraged participation in government through public discussion of political issues and involvement in the processes of representative democracy. His proposal was 'to learn to combine the two [liberties] together' (Constant [1820]1988: 327). Nonetheless, he criticized thinkers who'd failed, in his estimation, to understand the difference between the liberties, namely Jean-Jacques Rousseau and especially the eighteenth-century author Abbé de Mably (Constant [1820]1988: 318).

When he was a young man – before his distinguished public career – Wilhelm von Humboldt wrote *The Limits of State Action*, which was not finally published as a complete work until 1852 (long after its author's death in 1835). An English translation became available in 1854, under the title *The Sphere and Duties of Government*, and this influenced the philosopher John Stuart Mill. However, Humboldt's emphasis was on the freedom of individuals to develop their particular faculties without hindrance, rather than on collective intellectual progress. By contrast, both of these concerns informed Mill's thinking. In *The Limits of State Action*, Humboldt was an ancestor of modern libertarian theorists in arguing that the proper functions of the state should be restricted to what he characterized as the negative welfare of its people: that is, security from foreign enemies and 'the aggressive spirit of fellow-citizens' (Humboldt [1852]1969: 82).

In Britain, the word *liberal* and its close relatives, such as *liberals* and *liberalism*, initially referred to the more radical parliamentary opponents of the ruling Conservative Party (Adcock 2013: 17). During the nineteenth century, pro-reform elements in British politics joined to support common goals: the left wing of the Whig party combined with philosophical radicals and business interests to argue for reforms that included extension of the franchise. The landed gentry and the Tory party branded their reformist opponents as liberals in an effort to suggest the radicalism and anti-clericalism of liberal groups elsewhere in Europe (Rotunda 1986: 20; Fawcett 2018: 16–7). However, the word *liberal* and its relatives easily acquired positive connotations because of the non-political meaning of the word when used as an adjective, with its suggestions of tolerance and generosity.

As it took form, British liberalism was not the product of a single coherent political ideology. It originally contained three ideological sub-groups: philosophical radicals who espoused the moral and political ideas of Jeremy Bentham; free market economists such as Richard Cobden, whose thinking descended from that of Adam Smith; and religious nonconformists who favoured religious tolerance and humanitarian projects (Rotunda 1986: 22–5). An informal Liberal Party – really an alliance of Whigs and Radicals – came into existence in the late 1830s, and eventually became formalized twenty years later, achieving electoral success under Lord Palmerston and then William Gladstone. The Liberal Party was a political behemoth until the 1920s. Much later – when it was remarkably diminished – it became part of the Liberal Democrats when it merged with the Social Democratic Party in 1988.

In its 'classical' form, from the 1830s to at least the 1860s, British liberalism was associated with *laissez-faire* economics, but all sub-groups within British liberalism had humanitarian impulses. Some of its leading figures – Herbert Spencer is the best-known example – were implacably opposed to social spending by the state or to state intervention in capitalist markets. Yet, even Spencer's work contains a strong emphasis on self-restraint and benevolence, enabling and assisting the flourishing of others. For Spencer, these were private virtues, not to be coerced and regulated by the state, but that made them no less important.

The humanitarian thread in British liberalism led to a changing emphasis in the 1870s, and especially from the early 1880s when Gladstone became prime minister for the second time. British liberalism increasingly accommodated the views of workers and their trade unions, and successive governments developed welfare programmes and shouldered other responsibilities that were inevitably funded through taxes. The resulting 'welfare liberalism' or 'New Liberalism' became dominant in Britain during the final decades of the nineteenth century and the opening decades of the twentieth, though it maintained some continuity with liberalism's origins and did not abandon the principle of individual liberty or the right to hold property (Rotunda 1986: 14).

Such welfare liberalism can be seen, for example, in the writings of L. T. Hobhouse, a sociologist who became a leading liberal theorist of this period – at least in Britain – or the political practice of H. H. Asquith (British prime minister 1908–16), who can be credited as the father of the British welfare state.

John Stuart Mill and the liberty of discussion

Today, Mill is regarded by supporters and opponents alike as the most representative liberal philosopher and statesman. Indeed, his 1859 book, *On Liberty*, can be viewed as a summary or manifesto containing the essence of liberal thought. Here, he examines a single key issue: the proper limits of political and (importantly) social power over individuals. He argues for broad toleration of others' opinions and ways of life, including those of mavericks and eccentrics, and not confined only to religious differences. Mill places great emphasis on values such as individuality, spontaneity, creativity and original thinking, and free inquiry, and he is not primarily concerned with prohibitions and censorship by the state. He is, rather, concerned about the *many* pressures to conform, emanating from numerous sources.

At one point, Mill distinguishes between legal prohibition of heretical ideas and what he calls 'merely social intolerance' of them (Mill [1859]1974: 94). The latter entails that no one is actually punished by law – as the early Christians were under the rule of Diocletian, for example – but it also means that almost everyone keeps any unorthodox ideas that they might have within a narrow circle, making no serious attempt to spread them further. Mill describes such 'intellectual pacification' as coming with a price – what he calls 'the sacrifice of the entire moral courage of the human mind' (Mill [1859]1974: 94).

In *On Liberty*, Mill is especially concerned with the value of a diversity of opinions, whether they are true or false, to current generations and to posterity. His emphasis is on the free discussion of general topics, such as those to do with natural philosophy (i.e. science) and especially with 'morals, religion, politics, social relations, and the business of life' (Mill [1859]1974: 98). Thus, he does not attempt to defend lying imputations about individuals, or the exposure of individuals' private lives to the intolerant gaze of the public. At least on Mill's approach, liberty of thought and public discussion is not inconsistent with effective laws against defamation and serious invasions of privacy.

Thus, Mill did not argue, either as a public philosopher or during his career as a Member of Parliament, against laws protecting individual reputation and privacy. Rather, he was interested in freedom of opinion on wider topics – the same freedom that Tocqueville had identified as not existing in the United States – and the value of opinions to those who hear them or, conversely, are deprived of opportunities to hear them.

On Mill's account, intellectual progress is most likely where there is freedom to criticize popular opinions and espouse alternatives, and something is lost whenever an opinion is suppressed. In the most common sort of situation, rival disputants each grasp elements of the truth, and while the currently popular opinion may be true, it will seldom be the whole truth. Furthermore, Mill argues, there is wisdom in constantly testing our own opinions against counterarguments and alternative viewpoints, partly because this is necessary to hold our opinions with proper understanding and a warranted kind of confidence.

Unlike Kant in his famous essay on the nature of enlightenment, Mill did not seek to defend only the activities of scholars and intellectuals. *On Liberty* defends the freedom of thought and public discussion for anyone who cares to participate. However, it's worth emphasizing that the main direction of *On Liberty* is to advance arguments against legal or social suppression of unpopular or heretical *opinions* on general issues – and in this respect Mill's view does resemble Kant's. Thus, *On Liberty* does not focus on censorship of cultural products such as paintings and narratives. Mill wrote well before the twentieth-century disputes about censorship of major literary and artistic works, such as the novels of James Joyce and D. H. Lawrence, so *On Liberty* does not need to deal with these issues in any concerted way.

That said, Mill was conscious of the power of creative literature to open our minds and appeal to our imaginations and sympathies (and there is no reason why he would not apply this to contemporary media such as cinema and television). His approach could be expanded to include almost any art and literature with serious thematic content, and it's no surprise when liberal thinkers writing in the same tradition tend to support artistic freedom.[5]

At the end of chapter II of *On Liberty*, Mill considers the idea that free expression of opinion should be limited to speech expressed in a *temperate tone*. On its face, this seems to have merit, but Mill recognizes that strong commitments and emotions make a certain amount of

---

[5]Moreover, liberal-minded thinkers wishing to protect serious art and literature from formal or informal censorship will find much assistance from chapter III of *On Liberty*, which relates to the value of individuality as a source of well-being.

intemperance, unfairness and vituperation almost inevitable as part of public debate. There are, he acknowledges, undesirable ways to express an opinion, but they consist not so much in an intemperate tone as in suppressing facts and arguments and in misrepresenting opponents. But, he notes, these are 'continually done in perfect good faith by persons who are not considered, and in many other respects may not deserve to be considered, ignorant or incompetent' (Mill [1859]1974: 117).

For Mill, the worst wrongdoing in the cut and thrust of public discussion is stigmatizing opponents – merely because of their ideas – as 'bad and immoral men' (Mill [1859]1974: 117). He proposes that we condemn such things as intellectual dishonesty, malice, dogmatism and intolerance when we see them from anyone, on whichever side of an argument. But we should not infer intellectual dishonesty and the rest simply from the substantive position the person is advocating. Conversely, we should honour people who scrupulously report the arguments of opponents without attempting to undermine them by concealing their strengths or exaggerating their weaknesses (Mill [1859]1974: 118).

Thus, *On Liberty* offers a view of how public discussion should be conducted, as opposed to Mill's unwillingness to censor or deter the expression of substantive opinions. Importantly, though, Mill encouraged a *voluntary* commitment to 'the real morality of public discussion' (Mill [1859]1974: 118), rather than recourse to legal sanctions.

The harm principle

Mill's version of liberalism does not deny the benefits of social living or that we are inherently social animals, but throughout *On Liberty* Mill strongly emphasizes the value of individuality. The question then arises: When can we reasonably hold this in check?

In response, Mill defends a broad freedom to live as we wish, and he introduces what is now known as the harm principle. This is intended to apply to all social control over individuals, 'whether the means used be physical force in the form of legal penalties or the moral coercion of public opinion' ([1859]1974: 68). In summary, the harm principle sets a default of political and social toleration even of conduct that might be unusual, self-destructive or capable of causing remote and indirect harms. It justifies suppression only of conduct that causes significant, direct and secular (rather than spiritual) harm to non-consenting others. It rules out punishing someone because her action is imprudent or viewed as morally wrong

In defence of an approach similar to Mill's, the philosopher Andrew Jason Cohen has vividly described the enormous variety of experiences and opportunities that open up once modern societies act with toleration towards a multiplicity of ideas, cultures, personal eccentricities and ways of life (A. Cohen 2018: 72–80). A society that permits these can, as Cohen emphasizes, greatly expand the kinds of art and music that we appreciate, the kinds of food we enjoy, the ways of living our lives that are practical possibilities for us, the people who can become our friends, lovers or spouses, and so on. All of this is greatly beneficial, and should not be restricted lightly by state action or the impact of social intolerance.

Some authors, including Cohen, wish to interpret the word *harm* so that it refers only to *immoral* or *wrongful* hurts, losses, setbacks and the like.[6] To be more exact, Cohen defines harms as *actions* that wrongfully set back someone's interests (A. Cohen 2018: 53–6), but this is not Mill's account and nor is it consistent with everyday usage in which a harm is a kind of *bad outcome* for somebody as the result of an event. Thus, if you break my leg I have suffered a harm in the sense that I have experienced (and continue to experience) pain, that I'm unable to walk (except perhaps with crutches) and that I am otherwise worse off. But I might suffer the same harm if I accidentally fell down a flight of stairs. Exactly how bad an outcome has to be before it counts as harm is somewhat indeterminate, but it flies in the face of everyday English usage to use the word *harm* to refer to the *action* that broke my leg. (On the other hand, it is ordinary usage to say that – barring odd cases – someone *harms* me if they break my leg.)

Ordinarily, an action might be categorized as immoral or wrongful precisely because it causes harm, but there are numerous cases where, according to our ordinary thinking, the infliction of harms can be excusable or justifiable. *On Liberty* does not contain any systematic analysis of excuses and justifications, but it is at least clear that Mill sees some bad outcomes for individuals as justified: that is, if they result from routine participation in social practices that we believe to be beneficial or acceptable overall. In cases of this kind, such as whatever harm is suffered

---

[6]In fairness, Cohen states that he is not attempting to interpret Mill (A. Cohen 2018: 65, 120). But the result is that his defence of 'the harm principle' is not, in fact, a defence of the principle that Mill advanced and developed.

by an individual who misses out on obtaining a job because someone else submitted a more impressive application, no legal or social punishment is justified.

All that said, Mill acknowledges that actions cannot be as free as opinions, and he adds, '[E]ven opinions lose their immunity when the circumstances in which they are expressed are such as to constitute their expression a positive instigation to some mischievous act' (Mill [1859]1974: 119). On Mill's approach, therefore, potentially inflammatory opinions, such as that private property is robbery or that corn dealers are starvers of the poor, should be permitted publication in, say, a newspaper. But it might be legitimate to censure their presentation to an angry mob gathered outside the house of a particular corn dealer. In some cases, it might be justified to go beyond social censure and to provide for official punishment.

Mill justifies his approach to liberty and toleration in consequentialist terms, but in a specific way. For Mill, 'individual spontaneity' ([1859]1974: 70) is not only of value to the individual – something that it would be tyrannical to suppress without a compelling reason – but also of long-term value to society in generating new ideas and ways of living. Likewise, Mill defends liberty of thought and discussion as a requirement 'that human beings should be free to form opinions and to express opinions without reserve' justified by 'the baneful consequences to the intellectual, and through that to the moral nature of man' if this liberty is not asserted ([1859]1974: 119).

Less stable than they thought

The radicals from one period of history may seem moderate or conservative from the perspective of a later period. For example, Annie Besant and Charles Bradlaugh supported the availability of contraception to young married couples to help them control the number of their children. They argued more generally against what they saw as the evils of overpopulation, and that it should be possible to discuss these issues in public, informed by detailed physiological – as well as social and economic – information freely available to all classes of society. They did not, however, argue for the moral or legal permissibility of sex outside of marriage or for abortion as a way to avoid unwanted children – at all points, they appear to have been sincere in regarding these as social evils.

More radical views than theirs were known and proposed in the nineteenth century. They were, however, in the minority even within the free-thought movement, which testifies to the continuing power of discursive Christianity at a time when Christian theology was under challenge. But this situation was not stable.

Many years later, at the first dawn of the 1960s sexual revolution, the Scottish psychiatrist Eustace Chesser made a similar observation. Chesser duly noted that even the great rationalists and agnostics of the Victorian era, questioners of Christian doctrines in general, were at pains not to question Christian sexual ethics. Indeed, they seemed desperate to show that their religious scepticism left existing morality untouched (Chesser 1960: 96). But he also observed that rational criticism of orthodox religious belief would inevitably turn against orthodox Christian morals.

That became part of the story of the twentieth century. It saw a significant weakening of discursive Christianity, including traditional Christian morality, though Christian ideas also showed much resilience in the face of challenges. At the same time, new ideologies, neither Christian nor liberal – and in many cases brutal – arose to challenge Christianity and liberalism alike.

6 TOTAL WAR AND TOTAL GOVERNMENT

Liberalism in a new century

During the nineteenth century, varieties of liberalism were influential across Europe and Latin America. In particular, the concept was central to politics in the UK (Green 1987: 79). There has not been a prime minister from Britain's Liberal Party since the 1920s, but throughout the twentieth century broadly liberal ideas continued to exert influence in, for example, public debates in Britain over literary censorship, abortion and gay rights.

By contrast with British and European experience, the term *liberalism* was little known in American politics until the 1930s. This is not to deny the influence of Enlightenment thinking in the United States or, indeed, on the US Constitution, but everyday American political discussion in the nineteenth century and beyond included words such as *progressive* rather than *liberal* or *liberalism*. Woodrow Wilson introduced references to liberalism during the First World War, and Herbert Hoover adopted this terminology in the 1920s to signify resistance to coercive government action. However, the central distinction between 'liberal' and 'conservative' candidates for American public office emerged only with the rise of Franklin D. Roosevelt as a presidential candidate – and thereafter as president – during the years of the Great Depression.

In the 1930s, political rivals Hoover and Roosevelt each claimed to be the true liberal (Rotunda 1986: 4). Roosevelt succeeded in redefining the word *liberal* – for the purposes of American politics – as indicating a willingness to find 'new remedies', that is, new kinds of government intervention to solve problems. There was a suggestion here of 'governmental generosity' (see Green 1987: 119–24).

As events turned out, therefore, American liberalism came to be associated with the 1930s New Deal advanced by Roosevelt, whose reforms included mortgage relief, social security and support for trade unions. In this respect, American liberalism mimicked British welfare liberalism. Indeed, in the United States the term *liberalism* even came to *mean*, in large part, policies of economic intervention.

We should, I think, conclude that British welfare liberalism and the American liberal tradition that began in the 1930s were revisionary compared to the classical liberalism of the middle decades of the nineteenth century. In general, however, both retained a place in their respective systems of values for individual freedom and unrestricted public discussion. But since the 1910s and 1920s, liberalism has faced numerous challenges. It was placed under pressure by the exigencies of war, and its vision of individual freedom was rejected by a wide variety of socialist, Marxist, fascist, communitarian, conservative, populist, positivist, theocratic and other ideologies. At the same time, liberal ideas continued to run up against religious and otherwise traditional conservatism.

Wars of societies

Over the long sweep of history, wars were typically between entire societies and not just struggles between armies – and as the sociologists Miguel A. Centeno and Elaine Enriquez point out, the survival of societies was not certain (Centeno and Enriquez 2016: 90). In that respect, the more limited 'wars of armies' fought in Europe from the centuries of early modernity until the total wars of the twentieth century were the historical anomaly, resulting from specific military technologies and social forms (Centeno and Enriquez 2016: 90–1).

Precursors of twentieth-century 'wars of societies' (Centeno and Enriquez 2016: 91) can be found in the *levée en masse* adopted by the revolutionary government of France in the 1790s, in the subsequent Napoleonic Wars, and especially in the American Civil War. However, the two world wars introduced new levels of organized violence based on the technologies of the Second Industrial Revolution in the late nineteenth and early twentieth centuries.

Such wars pit entire societies against each other because military performance requires actions on the home front to supply ammunition, equipment, food and a flow of personnel. Unfortunately, this blurs the line between military and civilian targets. It returns us to earlier times when the aim was not only success on the battlefield but the devastation, alteration, displacement or outright destruction of an enemy people (Centeno and Enriquez 2016: 91). One prominent consequence in the twentieth century, especially during the Second World War, was the use of strategic bombing: the large-scale bombardment of civilian populations, with an aim 'to destroy the will of a society to wage war' (Centeno and Enriquez 2016: 110). This had been theorized in earlier decades, but the Second World War antagonists implemented it on a massive scale. It culminated in the use of atomic bombs by the US military to destroy the Japanese cities of Hiroshima and Nagasaki in August 1945.

In wars of societies, the productive power of the entire society is all-important. States engaged in this form of warfare bring every possible element of production and consumption under their control in a search for advantage (Morris 2015: 248). Warfare and sacrifice affect everyone, even children far from the field of battle, who may be caught up in training, rationing and other civilian aspects of the conflict. Equally important is the civilian population's sense of the war's legitimacy: propaganda for the home front becomes a crucial tool. Each antagonist employs narratives and imagery that portray the justice of the cause, the purity of those who fight for it, and the beastly or demonic nature of the enemy.[1]

Controlling the wartime narrative

During the First World War, the imperative to control narratives and images extended to efforts to suppress the horrific facts about experiences and outcomes on the vast new industrialized battlefields of Europe. News came under government control. Art and literature were subjected to strict censorship for the least sign of a subversive message. In perilous circumstances such as these, emotional manipulation becomes a virtue. Honesty and truth are seen as vices.

Amidst ever-present fears of calamity – after the first foolish waves of enthusiasm for fighting and glory – governments on both sides of the First

---

[1]To obviate the need for a swarm of specific citations in this paragraph, allow me to express a general debt to Centeno and Enriquez (2016) and Morris (2015).

World War had no wish to tolerate anything that resembled disloyalty or dissent. The war was also an opportunity for anti-vice campaigners, since a time of societal engagement in warfare seemed unsuitable for anything unwholesome in the public sphere. Irrelevant as it might now seem to the exigencies of armed combat, governments cracked down harder on novels or films with any erotic elements (Berkowitz 2021: 65–70).

Immediately upon entering the war, the UK passed the Defence of the Realm Act 1914, which gave its government authoritarian powers over everyday life and speech. As originally enacted, this Act was very brief. It gave the executive government sweeping powers to issue regulations for public safety and defence, with particular attention to preventing spying/communication with the enemy, and protecting communications and transport infrastructure. In practice, this involved suppressing or restricting everything from kite flying to keeping homing pigeons. The Act was amended several times in late 1914 before being replaced by a consolidated version in November of that year.

Most importantly, the Act granted the government extensive censorship powers, enabling it to take punitive actions to suppress dissent, including the viewpoints of pacifists. Perhaps most prominent of the victims of state intolerance in the UK was the distinguished philosopher Bertrand Russell, who was fined in 1916 for his authorship of a pacifist leaflet. In 1918, he was jailed in Brixton prison for six months – this time for publicly opposing entry into the war by the United States.[2]

In an article published in 2005 in the *Journal of Contemporary History*, Brock Millman describes the increasing practices of suppressing dissent and maintaining surveillance over anyone who came under suspicion for expressing unpatriotic ideas or for inadequate expressions of patriotism. While Millman seems dismayed at this direction in British policy during the First World War, he concludes that the approach was effective and 'perhaps even necessary' for the purposes of sustaining the home front

---

[2]Bertrand Russell got into hot water again in 1940 when he was appointed to a professorial post at the City College of New York, scheduled to commence at the beginning of February the following year. The problem this time stemmed from his writings about nudity, homosexuality, sex outside of marriage and other issues related to human sexuality and sexual morality. His views prompted a furious campaign against his appointment, led by high-ranking church officials and culminating in a successful lawsuit against him in the New York Supreme Court.

(Millman 2005: 440). This highlights the importance of a contest of propaganda as one aspect of modern-day total war. In twentieth-century wars of societies (and continuing into the new millennium), there is an almost irresistible pressure to engage in strategies of propaganda, surveillance and intolerance of any dissent from the government's message. This pressure will be felt even by political leaders with genuinely liberal instincts.

Throughout the war, there was also social panic about an alleged drink crisis, and the voices of prohibitionists and temperance advocates were greatly amplified. Even so much as drinking a glass or two of beer was viewed by many influential people, among them senior figures in the Liberal Party, as degenerate, unpatriotic and subversive of the nation's war effort (see generally Duncan 2013). In response, the British government created a powerful agency, the Central Control Board, with broad powers to regulate and reduce the consumption of alcohol (Duncan 2013: 93). This led to harsh measures to limit the national production of alcoholic beverages, curtail drinking hours and control patrons' drinking practices.

In the United States, brutal action was taken against anyone caught speaking German. Many German-born Americans were sent to internment camps. German-language newspapers were suppressed, and German art and music were treated as if tainted. During and after the war, the culture retained by large numbers of German Americans was discouraged and largely destroyed (Baritz 1989: 51; see also Berkowitz 2021: 175–6).

Neil Hamilton identifies a wave of zealotry affecting American colleges and universities at this time, with victimization of academic staff who opposed American participation in the war, or who merely displayed what was regarded as insufficient enthusiasm. Among many other examples, Hamilton discusses Columbia University's withdrawal of academic freedom for the duration of the war, and beyond this, a general trend across the United States for administrators to ascertain whether any faculty members taught or otherwise promulgated supposedly disloyal or subversive opinions (Hamilton [1995]2017: 15). This attitude continued even after the war's conclusion: it remained unsafe to advocate pacifist ideas or – in response to the 1917 revolution in Russia – any political doctrine that could be associated even distantly with communism.

Between world wars

Some morals campaigns receded after the war, with, for example, increasing legal and social acceptance of drinking and gambling in the UK. Nonetheless, the allied victory in the First World War did not entail the end of wartime controls. The UK maintained an active and comprehensive programme of censorship, even extending to scrutiny and censorship of private postcards and letters.

The British Board of Film Censors, an ostensibly non-government organization that had been founded in 1912,[3] maintained a comprehensive programme of censorship that included bans on films with erotic or socialist content and extended during the 1930s to prohibiting material that criticized the Nazi regime, which attracted establishment support in Britain at the time (compare Berkowitz 2021: 190–1). Anti-Nazi cinema became acceptable only after the German invasion of Poland in September 1939, and Britain's consequent declaration of war against the Reich.

During the years between the wars, British society was also confronted by the question of what to do about literary works with depictions of overt sexuality or eroticism. James Joyce's great stream-of-consciousness novel *Ulysses* (1922) was immediately prohibited, and remained so until the 1930s, while an uncensored edition of D. H. Lawrence's *Lady Chatterley's Lover* (1928) was not openly and legally available for three decades. Legal reforms relating to obscenity, enacted at the end of the 1950s, led Penguin Books to publish a full, unbutchered version of Lawrence's novel in 1960. The publisher was then prosecuted under the Obscene Publications Act 1959, but prevailed in a famous trial where several distinguished literary and cultural scholars gave evidence of the book's merit.

In the United States, the *Hicklin* test was applied in modified form to *Ulysses*, which was held not to be obscene in a 1933 case decided by a US district court judge. This outcome was upheld on appeal in the following year: *United States v. One Book Entitled Ulysses by James Joyce* (decided 7 August 1934).

The affluent 1920s – prior to the financial crash of 1929 – were a period of youthful rebellion on a scale, and with panache and confidence, perhaps never seen before. Yet this was also the decade of Prohibition – a

---

[3]Known today as the British Board of Film Classification.

ban on alcoholic beverages – in the United States. This followed decades of lobbying efforts (and scattered successes) by temperance campaigners. Prohibition was not ultimately repealed until 1933, but there was much non-compliance. Gangsters of the era made large profits by smuggling alcohol from Canada. Nonetheless, the image of Jazz Age America, or the Roaring Twenties, is one of softening moral norms, jazz music (of course) and new efforts at liberation from established social conventions. A vigorous culture established itself around the illegal, but often tolerated, 'speakeasies' where alcoholic drinks were sold.

Meanwhile, the 1917 Bolshevik Revolution in Russia inspired some individuals in the West and struck fear in many others. As well as intervening in the civil war underway in Russian territory, Western governments demonized communist revolutionaries as the new internal enemy. In this environment, political censorship thrived, leading, in the United States, to a series of important cases that found their way to the level of the nation's Supreme Court.

In the first of these, *Schenck v. United States* (decided 3 March 1919), the court upheld the convictions of two executive committee members of the Socialist Party of America, Charles Schenck and Elizabeth Baer, for distributing pamphlets opposing conscription. Schenck and Baer were tried and convicted for obstructing the draft, under the Espionage Act of 1917. They appealed to the Supreme Court, relying on the guarantees provided in the First Amendment. The court unanimously rejected the appeal in an opinion written by Justice Oliver Wendell Holmes, Jr., which included the much-quoted words that even stringent free speech protections 'would not protect a man in falsely shouting fire in a theatre and causing a panic' and that the question is always whether the words are used in circumstances where they 'cause a clear and present danger' of whatever evils the legislature seeks to prevent (249 US 47, 52 (1919)). As the outcome of the case tends to confirm, any such 'clear and present danger' test accommodates censorship of an indefinitely wide range of speech, since legislatures that engage in censorship invariably perceive *some* kind of imminent danger – whether physical, cultural, psychological or spiritual.

More troubling than the *Schenck* outcome, however, was that in *Debs v. United States* (decided 10 March 1919), which related to the conviction of the socialist leader Eugene Debs for sedition. This followed a speech that Debs had delivered in June 2018, towards the end of the First World War. The speech was couched in more circumspect terms than those in the pamphlet that caused trouble for Schenck and Baer, but it used forceful rhetoric to praise some individuals who'd resisted the draft and been punished for it. This was enough for the Supreme Court to uphold his conviction and sustain his sentence of ten years in prison.

In *Abrams v. United States* (decided 10 November 1919), the court upheld the convictions of five Russian Jews who'd distributed so-called seditious pamphlets during the final months of the war. The pamphlets denounced American military interference in events in Russia following the Bolshevik Revolution, and they called for cessation of the manufacture of armaments for use against the Soviet regime if necessary by a general strike of munitions workers.

While the majority of the court upheld the sedition statute under which the defendants were charged, as well as the convictions themselves, Justice Holmes drew a distinction between this case and *Schenck*, which he continued to explain as involving an attempt to commit a crime (i.e. obstructing the draft). His Honour warned against the persecuting tendency in human nature, noting its seductive internal logic, and he introduced into American jurisprudence the concept of a marketplace of ideas – though without yet coining the actual phrase. He stated that the best test of truth was 'free trade in ideas' and 'the power of the thought to get itself accepted in the competition of the market' (250 US 616, 630 (1919)).[4]

A repressive approach from American legislatures and courts continued for many decades in response to fears of communism. In particular, *Whitney v. California* (decided 16 May 1927) resulted in a unanimous decision of the Supreme Court to uphold Charlotte Whitney's conviction under a Californian criminal syndicalism law for her role as a founder of the Communist Labor Party of America.

In *Gitlow v. People of New York* (decided 8 June 1925), the Supreme Court was, for the first time, willing to assume for the sake of argument that the First Amendment guarantee of free speech applied not only to the federal government but also to the states. This is an aspect of the constitutional doctrine of 'incorporation', whereby at least some of the rights and freedoms in the Bill of Rights fall within the 'liberty' mentioned in the Fourteenth Amendment to the US Constitution.

---

[4]The specific wording, 'the market place [sic] of ideas', first appeared many years later in a concurring opinion by Justice William O. Douglas in *United States v. Rumely* (decided 9 March 1953). See 345 U.S. 41, 56 (1953).

Among other things, the Fourteenth Amendment requires: '[N]or shall any State deprive any person of … liberty … without due process of law.' Whatever this originally conveyed when the Fourteenth Amendment was adopted in 1868, it is now interpreted as providing considerable substantive limits, as well as procedural constraints, on any exercise of governmental power by the American states.

The defendant in this case was Benjamin Gitlow, a socialist politician and journalist who had published a manifesto in the left-wing newspaper *The Revolutionary Age*. In classic Marxist fashion, the manifesto called for class struggle, organization of the industrial proletariat, and a communist revolution against the existing economic and political system. Unfortunately for Gitlow, the court found that it was possible to prohibit speech that advocated even a long-term and general goal of overthrowing the government. Despite his conviction, however, the case opened up the possibility for challenges to state-level laws restricting free speech.

Free speech in the United States

The general direction in the United States from the 1930s was towards greater freedom of speech and toleration for unpopular groups and viewpoints, though communists and communism were frequently the exception. The opening of expressive freedoms emerged largely from litigation over the doctrines and actions of the Jehovah's Witnesses, a group that, at the time, was notable for its zealotry, rigid policing of its members' doctrinal purity, and hostility to other religious groups, especially the Roman Catholic Church. In a series of important cases beginning in 1938, the Jehovah's Witnesses won increasing, and increasingly clear, freedoms of speech, assembly and religious exercise.

The key development was the outcome of a US Supreme Court case, *Cantwell v. Connecticut* (decided 20 May 1940), that involved three Jehovah's Witnesses who'd preached in a Roman Catholic neighbourhood and played a highly provocative anti-Catholic phonograph recording. They were convicted of disturbing the peace, but this was ultimately overturned on the basis that it was in breach of the constitutional guarantee of free exercise of religion. In the process, the court held for the first time that this freedom applied to action by the states via the doctrine of incorporation.

The Jehovah's Witnesses did not have everything their own way. In particular, they suffered an important loss in *Chaplinsky v. New Hampshire* (decided 9 March 1942). In this case, Walter Chaplinsky, a proselytizing Jehovah's Witness, was charged with calling a police officer 'a God-damned racketeer' and 'a damned Fascist' during a public altercation with a hostile crowd. This led to his arrest and subsequent conviction under a public order statute. Chaplinsky admitted to using the words alleged, save for the word *God* (315 US 568, 569–570 (1942)). His conviction was upheld by the Supreme Court, which announced for the first time a 'fighting words' doctrine whereby severely insulting words that 'by their very utterance inflict injury or tend to incite an immediate breach of the peace' fall outside of the constitutional protection of free speech (315 US 568, 572 (1942)). In this case, the words *racketeer* and *Fascist* were provocative enough for the purpose.

As well as cases involving their own aggressive proselytizing, the Jehovah's Witnesses became caught up in a series of flag-salute cases. Here, the issue was their unwillingness to salute the American flag, even when compelled by governmental authority. The key outcome was in *West Virginia State Board of Education v. Barnette* (decided 14 June 1943). Here, the Supreme Court struck down a school board's requirement that all teachers and students engage in a joint activity of saluting the flag (using, at the relevant time, the 'Bellamy salute' with the right arm outstretched and the palm upward). For the majority of the court, this was an impermissible action by the government to attempt the unification of opinion and coerce its insincere expression. And so, the Supreme Court initiated a line of cases relating to coerced, rather than prohibited, speech.

Notwithstanding these developments, however, Neil Hamilton identifies a new and separate wave of anti-communist zealotry in the American universities (and by implication, American society more generally) in the mid-to-late 1930s. The result was something like the atmosphere and processes of a witch hunt, characterized by 'public accusations, investigations, threats, and dismissals' (Hamilton [1995]2017: 19).

There was an attempt at this time to address totalitarian ideologies through the activities of the House Un-American Activities Committee. The first iterations of this body, in 1934 and 1938, respectively, were established to investigate local fascist groups, but the 1938 committee soon turned its attention to communists, alleged communists, and the American version of liberalism or left-wing thought more generally, and this became the trend.

Soviet developments

When they obtained power in Russia in 1917, the major Bolshevik leaders were contemptuous of any idea of freedom of the press. They immediately commenced a brutal and increasingly comprehensive effort to halt non-Bolshevik expression in the public sphere (for discussion, including the absurd lengths adopted by the censorship bureaucracy, see Mchangama 2022: 259–68). Over time, the Soviet regime consistently rejected what it regarded as bourgeois rights – that is, the fundamental freedoms supported by liberal thinkers, such as freedom of religion, freedom of speech, freedom of the press and freedom of association. The regime maintained that these freedoms were 'a danger to struggling people's republics' (Glendon 2001: 184).

Like their predecessors in France in the 1790s, the Russian revolutionaries saw themselves as caught in a life-or-death struggle against powerful, malicious opponents. At the same time, they had near-apocalyptic ambitions. During the early period of the revolution, their thought was that socialism would not be confined to one country, but would spread internationally. They imagined themselves lighting a flame, perhaps beginning in Germany and Eastern Europe, that would burn across the entire human world, transforming social and even psychological life (Black 2015: 9).

In fact, the initial dangers to the Bolshevik regime were real. After the revolution, Russia immediately plunged into political chaos, with rival factions building their armies in an effort to take decisive control. The resulting civil war was fought mainly between the Workers' and Peasants' Red Army, which sought to secure the new regime, and the so-called White Army, which built its strength in the Cossack-controlled regions of the south and fought on behalf of an alliance of ideologically divided but in all cases anti-communist groups.

The outcome was clear enough by 1920, and the last interventionist forces were driven out in 1922. However, this did not end the paranoid and authoritarian mentality of communist leaders. Nor did it check the incremental development of Russia – later the Union of Soviet Socialist

Republics, abbreviated as the USSR or the Soviet Union – as a totalitarian state. Like their Tsarist predecessors, the secret police organizations established under communist rule employed brutal methods such as arbitrary arrest, torture and extra-judicial execution. By the late 1920s and early 1930s, the regime had established a comprehensive grip on power in the vast, unruly Russian countryside.

Joseph Stalin and his cadres now asserted command over the population of peasants, who had their own customs and ideas and had previously been largely unaffected by the revolution. The Stalinist regime introduced systems designed to transform the country. Discussing the Soviet Union under Stalin, the historian Peter Kenez observes: 'The totalitarian state claimed authority over all aspects of human life – political, economic, social, and cultural – and in the process did great harm to each' (Kenez 2017: 126). In part, this reflected Stalin's unique – and somewhat inscrutable – personality. Much of what he carried out, beginning in the late 1920s and continuing into the 1950s, seems irrational and inexplicable, so we might speculate that the USSR would have been a somewhat less dystopian place under a different leader, or perhaps if led by a collective of talented individuals. Nonetheless, the basic mechanisms of repression and terror began long prior to his dictatorship.

Stalin ramped up the existing process of show trials and associated purges, particularly after he began an ambitious campaign of forced collectivization and industrialization (in its earliest manifestations in the late 1920s). Most notorious was the Great Purge in the mid-1930s. Here, Kenez (2017: 108) estimates that approximately 1 million people were executed and perhaps 10 million sent to forced labour camps. Whatever the exact figures, Stalin eliminated a huge number of people, including his remaining comrades from the original revolutionary leadership.

The situation of ordinary Russian people was worsened by the collectivization and industrialization programmes. Under the new policies, the peasants were forced to join collective farms. Resistance was not tolerated, and at the same time, the regime came down heavily on so-called kulaks: those peasants who'd been most successful under the Tsarist regime and/or during the early years of the revolution, and who'd acquired a degree of wealth. The definition of a kulak was sufficiently flexible to include anyone in the countryside who could be classified for one reason or another as an opponent of the regime. This included anybody who dissented from the collectivization programme. Ultimately, several million Soviet citizens were classified as kulaks and subjected to varying degrees of persecution ranging from oppressive taxes to outright execution.

The years from the end of the Second World War until Stalin's death in 1953 were perhaps the most repressive of all. Art and literature of all kinds were scrutinized and censored, so that any innovation in these areas was effectively stopped. Soviet authors, artists and intellectuals were required to conform to the party line, and any who resisted could have their careers destroyed, or worse. Thus, prominent contributors to the culture, including the great Russian poet Anna Akhmatova and the popular author and satirist Mikhail Zoshchenk, found their work denounced (for discussion, see Kenez 2017: 176–83).

Despite adjustments made between different phases – with different leaders in charge or different crises requiring responses – the Soviet regime was always brutal. However, things improved somewhat after Stalin's death. Within a couple of years, Nikita Krushchev emerged as the undisputed leader and embarked on a campaign of de-Stalinization. This was carried forward – and especially symbolized – by the 'Secret Speech' that he delivered in February 1956 at the Twentieth Party Congress, denouncing Stalin's cult of personality. Under Krushchev, there was a revival of Soviet cinema, and important novels with political dimensions were soon published. However, severe limits remained as to how much satire or dissent would be tolerated. In late 1956, moreover, the Soviet military crushed a revolution in the Hungarian People's Republic. The violent fate of the Hungarian Revolution, in the same year as Krushchev's Secret Speech, illustrates the very limited exercise of toleration even after Stalin was gone.

Exactly what was tolerated from time to time depended on who was in power, what degree of authority the Soviet leaders actually possessed at particular points during the seventy-odd years of the Soviet Union's existence, and what ideas, expressed by whom, seemed like genuine threats. In its early years, for example, the revolutionary regime was relatively tolerant of the ideas of Russian intellectuals. The concern was not to censor absolutely everything that might be inconvenient to, or inconsistent with, Bolshevik ideology. It was sufficient to focus on expressions of dissent that might persuade the mass of the people. Thus, it was one thing to permit the highly abstract opinions of elite artists and philosophers with little popular reach. It was another to tolerate a 'bourgeois press' with a more realistic prospect of influencing public opinion.

As we saw with the French Revolution, however, there's a more general lesson: an authoritarian mentality can easily take hold among activists with revolutionary aims. From their viewpoint, much is at stake, and this can lead to ruthless suppression of real or imaginary dissent once revolutionaries obtain power. It also prompts stringent policing of conformity among followers and allies.

Fascists and totalitarians

The word *totalitarianism* (or its Italian equivalent, *totalitario*) appears to have been coined in 1923 by the journalist and statesman Giovanni Amendola, a trenchant critic of the Fascist movement in Italy. Amendola rebuked the regime of Benito Mussolini for its unprecedented efforts at control of all aspects of public and private life. For his opposition to the Fascist regime, he was murdered three years later – dying from his injuries after a beating by fifteen Blackshirts armed with clubs.

What one man or woman intends as critique, others might see as vindication. In this case, Amendola condemned the totalitarian nature of the Fascist state, but the leading Fascist philosopher, Giovanni Gentile, saw things very differently, as of course did Mussolini himself. In 1925, Gentile drafted a document entitled *Manifesto of the Fascist Intellectuals to the Intellectuals of Other Nations*, which was signed by many leading intellectual figures in 1920s Italy. This explicitly depicted Fascism as a religious idea: it demanded the sacrifice of the individual to the interests of the Italian fatherland, required a total commitment similar to religious zeal and rejected ideas of individuality or compromise. Whether or not Gentile had a sophisticated understanding of the concept of religion, the manifesto demanded (in its own terminology, of course) that Fascism play the religion role in the lives of Italians. The *Manifesto of the Fascist Intellectuals* defended violence for the purposes of creating and sustaining the Fascist state. Though the word *totalitarianism* does not appear in the manifesto, Gentile and Mussolini soon appropriated it for their own purposes, treating the concept behind it as something positive.

These capital-F Fascists[5] sought to create a regime of total subordination – and indeed, total psychological reconstruction – of the individual in the service of the state. This was a leading theme of Mussolini's 1932 book *The Doctrine of Fascism*, part of which was written by Gentile. Thereafter, the word *totalitararianism* appeared, again as representing something positive, in the propaganda of the National Socialist German Workers' Party – the Nazi Party – led by Adolf Hitler. Irrespective of who was willing to embrace the actual word and apply it to themselves, numerous regimes across Europe, not least the Soviet Union under Stalin, aspired to an environment of total control.

In Germany, the Weimar Republic, which lasted from 1918 to early 1933 when the Nazis came to power, originally adopted an anti-censorship policy. As Eric Berkowitz notes, Germany at this time 'hosted one of history's most astonishing outpourings of creative and intellectual energy' (Berkowitz 2021: 183). This took place during a period of political and economic chaos, and the cessation of censorship did not last long in the face of objections to films with controversial sexual, moral and especially political content.

Germany underwent an economic crisis in the period after its defeat in the First World War; even when this was brought under control in the mid-1920s, unemployment was still high and much social instability remained. With the Great Depression, instability developed into a situation of extreme socioeconomic crisis. In the background was wounded German pride from the outcome of the war and the humiliating terms imposed by its victors in the Treaty of Versailles. For many Germans, democracy itself was seen as an un-German innovation imposed by its triumphant enemies. There was, moreover, a fear of communism and the growing power of the Soviet Union. In this environment, many Germans were open to undemocratic and extremist parties, and to the idea of a strong leader who would take decisive action to solve their country's problems.

Adolf Hitler, a forceful and charismatic public speaker, was able to play that role. Within Hitler's worldview we find an ideology of racial hierarchy and race hate. A supposed 'Aryan master race' was at the top of the hierarchy and had the right to rule. By contrast, the Jews were an evil

---

[5] I reserve the capital F in *Fascism* and its cognates for the specific movement led by Mussolini. The word *fascism* is in lower case when referring to the wider concept of violent, totalitarian, ultra-nationalist and militarist ideologies comparable to Mussolini's.

race lying below or outside all other racial types. Hitler and his cohorts regarded the Jews as immutably vicious and destructive, threatening to tear down everything created by Aryans and admired and preserved by some other races. Within this worldview, all of Germany's problems, and everything that the Nazis despised, could be blamed on the Jews.

Insane as Nazi race theory now appears, it took to extremes a kind of thinking that pervaded much of European society at the time. It was common to think in racial terms and even to imagine a hierarchy of races. But Hitler and the Nazis incorporated such ideas in a totalitarian ideology, obsessed about the Jews in particular and acted upon their racist madness with a new level of organized violence (Kenez 2013: 71–102).

The Nazis carried out large-scale public book burnings throughout Germany in May 1933, and later in Poland and other lands conquered by the military of the Third Reich. Nazi officials took over the operations of the news media and the entire sphere of art and culture. They relentlessly crushed opposition and conducted programmes aimed at destroying the Jewish people. Until Germany's eventual defeat in the Second World War, Nazi organizations and publications, such as the viciously anti-Semitic newspaper *Der Stürmer*, continued to extol the activities and ideology of the regime.

Totalitarianism and the limits of toleration

Since the 1930s and 1940s, many Western intellectuals have criticized liberalism for its apparent weakness in preventing the collapse of the Weimar Republic, the rise of fascist and communist totalitarianisms in Europe, the Nazis' atrocities before and especially during the Second World War, and the frightening emergence of paramilitary fascist groups across mainland Europe and even in the United States and the UK. In response, some political theorists began to suggest that democracies should be a bit more authoritarian in guiding their populations away from totalitarianism and its associated forms of racial and other bigotry. This became a crucial question confronting the new international order after the Second World War.

An early argument for setting an outer limit to toleration of the intolerant came from the German philosopher and political scientist

Karl Loewenstein, who fled from Germany to the United States when the Nazis gained power. In 1937, Loewenstein published an important two-part article in successive issues of *American Political Science Review* (Loewenstein 1937a,b), arguing against democratic rights (including freedom of speech) for fascists. On Loewenstein's approach, it seemed self-destructive for liberal democracies to tolerate the speech of radical authoritarians who would, if permitted, dismantle democracy itself and suppress all speech contrary to their own agenda. For Loewenstein, democratic nations had no choice but to take strong action to preserve democracy.

A few years later, the legal scholar, prominent sociologist and public intellectual David Riesman presented a similar analysis to Loewenstein's in a series of articles in the *Columbia Law Review* (Riesman 1942a,b,c).[6] He emphasized the vulnerability of public opinion to manipulation by propagandists with access to the mass media and a willingness to engage in extreme kinds of vilification and libel as shown by the *modus operandi* of fascist groups in Europe.

In his monumental two-volume work *The Open Society and Its Enemies*, first published in 1945, the Austrian philosopher Karl Popper gave expression to a similar idea with his warning about 'the paradox of tolerance'. He dealt with this in an extensive note questioning how far liberal or 'open' societies could tolerate the most intolerant, would-be persecutorial movements and organizations (see Popper [1945]2011: 581–2). Like Loewenstein and Riesman, he was thinking of political groups that would undoubtedly introduce totalitarian regimes and eliminate democratic and liberal freedoms if they somehow came to power. In *The Open Society and Its Enemies*, Popper suggested that radically intolerant movements should be placed outside the law, which would seem to entail banning at least the most blatantly totalitarian organizations.

Notably, however, Popper advocated repression of opponents with totalitarian tendencies in only the most extreme circumstances where reason and argument were likely to be futile. He referred to individuals and organizations that were engaged in incitement to persecution and intolerance, and were inclined to respond to reason and argument with acts of violence.

---

[6]Strictly speaking, Riesman presents this contribution to the discussion as one article followed by another, closely related, article in two parts.

After the war, views such as Loewenstein's, Riesman's and Popper's became influential on the world stage and largely prevailed except in the United States, where the tendency went in the opposite direction. In post-war Germany, the politically dominant view was that democracies needed to defend themselves with what would otherwise be considered illiberal laws. These aimed to stifle the worst action and speech from movements committed to overthrowing democracy and liberal toleration themselves. Subsequently, West Germany's Basic Law, approved in 1949 – that is, the country's new, post-war constitution – included a provision enabling the Federal Constitutional Court to ban political parties that it viewed as dangers to 'the free democratic basic order'.

In the United States, a similar thought to Popper's was expressed by Justice Robert Jackson, one of the dissenting judges in *Terminiello v. Chicago* when it reached the US Supreme Court (decided 16 May 1949). It involved a Catholic priest, Arthur Terminiello, who had been suspended by his bishop at the time of the key events. He'd delivered a racist and inflammatory speech with fascist overtones to a crowd of over 800 people, while a larger crowd angrily protested outside, not entirely restrained by the city police. Terminiello was subsequently fined under an ordinance prohibiting breach of the peace, which was interpreted by the state courts of Illinois to include a prohibition against behaviour that (among other things) 'stirs the public to anger, invites dispute, brings about a condition of unrest, or creates a disturbance' (337 US 1, 3 (1949)).

This left the court to consider whether the ordinance, as interpreted by the state courts, was constitutional.[7] Writing for the majority of the judges, Justice William O. Douglas found that it was not. He emphasized that a system of free speech designedly protects speech that provokes unrest, dissatisfaction and anger. Accordingly, governments within the United States could not ban the expression of ideas unless it created a danger that went beyond mere inconvenience to the public.

In dissent, Justice Jackson referred to the global context of struggles between violent ideologies. He feared that a strong reading of the First Amendment would weaken the ability of governments in the United States to hold in check the street-level violence of fascists, revolutionary communists and other such ideologues. He did not seek to suppress

---

[7]Under the American legal system the state courts are the final interpreters of state laws. Accordingly, the US Supreme Court was not in a position to 'save' the statute by reading it more narrowly than the state courts beneath it in the judicial hierarchy.

any particular viewpoint, even a fascist one – here, he departed subtly from Popper's thinking. But he feared that local police forces would lose control of the streets and leave a vacuum for mob rule. He warned that a technical and doctrinaire approach to liberty could 'convert the constitutional Bill of Rights into a suicide pact' (337 US 1, 37 (1949)).

Some Americans at this time looked with favour on enacting new laws prohibiting the vilification of racial and religious groups, and this resulted in efforts to enact group libel laws at state and federal levels, including an attempt within the federal Congress to criminalize group-based defamation sent through the US mail. However, these initiatives ran out of support by the early 1950s and ultimately came to nothing (Walker 1994: 86). Surprisingly – against that general background – an older group libel law, originally enacted in 1917, was upheld as constitutional by the US Supreme Court in *Beauharnais v. Illinois* (decided 28 April 1952).

In this case, the relevant statute had been enacted in response to a race riot in East St. Louis in mid-1917, and it contained broad prohibitions of speech collectively defaming classes of citizens defined by 'race, color, creed, or religion' – exposing individuals to 'contempt, derision, or obloquy' or producing 'breach of the peace or riots' (343 US 350, 351 (1952)). The prosecution of Joseph Beauharnais related to a race riot in the Chicago suburb of Cicero in 1951, emanating from hostilities over housing issues when Black families increasingly moved into what had been all-white neighbourhoods. Beauharnais had not advocated violence or rioting, but as the president of a group called the White Circle League of America he had produced extreme literature vilifying Black Americans and undoubtedly holding them up for contempt, derision and obloquy.

When the case reached the Supreme Court, its judges split five-four in favour of upholding the Illinois statute. The majority held that it was constitutionally valid, since it dealt with a sub-category of defamatory speech, and because defamation was not within 'the freedom of speech' protected by the First Amendment. This case has never been formally overruled by the Supreme Court. Arguably, however, subsequent developments in American law on defamation and hate speech have reduced its value as precedent to almost zero.

From the start, the *Beauharnais* outcome was greeted with caution even by civil rights leaders. The case might have opened a door for more statutes aimed at restricting offensive speech in the United States, but this never happened. On the contrary, the Illinois state legislature eventually – in 1961 – repealed its 1917 law.

By this point, too, David Riesman had written a further article in *Commentary* magazine in which he distanced himself from his earlier views (see especially Riesman 1951: 14), and expressed serious misgivings even about activism and lobbying – as opposed to legal prohibitions – against unsympathetic literary and cinematic portrayals of his fellow Jews along with members of numerous other racial, professional, other groups. For Riesman, this kind of activism and lobbying stifled art and culture, with long-term negative implications for American society.[8]

Post-war anti-communism

In the final years of the Second World War, the Soviet Union played a crucial role in the struggle against Nazi Germany, and in consequence anti-communist feeling within the Allied powers subsided for a time. Tensions with the Soviets grew even before the war ended, but the United States and the UK had no stomach for a new war and made no attempt to save the nations of Eastern Europe from occupation by the triumphant Red Army. Nonetheless, hostility soon ramped up between the rival superpowers and the respective groups of states in their orbits.

Events in the later 1940s and the 1950s intensified Cold War paranoia and fear (Black 2015: 53–5). One geopolitically momentous event was when the Soviets tested their own atomic bomb in August 1949. This destroyed America's post-war strategy of concentrating on the economic reconstruction of Europe and avoiding any significant build-up of its military power (J. Gaddis 2005: 34–6).

The invention of the thermonuclear (or hydrogen) bomb in the early 1950s, and along with it the development of intercontinental strategic bombers and intercontinental ballistic missiles, then changed the meaning of nuclear war (e.g. Black 2015: 83–93, 98–9). The new thermonuclear devices were vastly more powerful than the bombs that destroyed Hiroshima and Nagasaki, and there was now a prospect that they could be hurled between continents in massive numbers. A

---

[8]For my discussions of the various Loewenstein and Riesman articles and their relationship to American legal developments, and for prompting me to track the articles down and consider their ideas, I owe a general debt to Walker (1994: 46–51, 79–99).

full-scale war fought with such weapons could potentially destroy human civilization, if not human life itself, across the entire planet. 'By the 1960s', therefore, 'the US and USSR could hold each other hostage', leading to the logic of mutually assured destruction (Centeno and Enriquez 2016: 113).

Another series of events unfolded from the conclusion of the long-running civil war in China, which ended with victory to the communist forces led by Mao Zedong. In December 1949, the beaten Kuomintang nationalists fled the Chinese mainland, establishing their headquarters on the island of Formosa (now known as Taiwan). In the following year, war broke out in Korea. This led quickly to the nightmare of direct armed combat between the United States and China (whose forces included a large number of Soviet fighter pilots) until the situation on the Korean Peninsula finally reached a stalemate (see, for example, J. Gaddis 2005: 58–60; Black 2015: 63–71).

By 1947, the US government had begun a massive witch hunt against known and suspected communists, and their associates or sympathizers, and as events unfolded, the fears driving this intensified. Thus, we see the beginnings of McCarthyism. For several years, until his downfall in 1954, Senator Joseph McCarthy was free to say whatever he wanted about others, however lurid, vicious, unfounded and even outright false it might have been, without being called effectively to account. McCarthy and other anti-communist witch hunters of the time were responsible for numerous ruined careers and lives.

In the late 1940s, the US government prosecuted eleven members of the Communist Party USA, including Eugene Dennis, its general secretary, for breaches of what was known as the Smith Act (i.e. the Alien Registration Act of 1940). This legislation, which remains in force in amended form, criminalized advocating the violent overthrow of the US government. However, defendants in the case had done nothing unusual for individuals professing revolutionary communist ideas. The crime alleged against them did not involve a specific plan for revolution, but merely the abstract advocacy of revolution, such as might be found in *The Communist Manifesto* by Marx and Engels.

They were found guilty, and their appeal failed even when it reached the level of the Supreme Court. In *Dennis v. United States* (decided 4 June 1951), the judges in the majority upheld the relevant provisions of the Smith Act and affirmed that the activities of the defendants were a sufficient danger to the constitutional order to support their conviction.

Subsequently, however, the authority of *Dennis v. United States* was undermined by *Yates v. United States* (decided 25 November 1957). Here, fourteen Communist Party members had been convicted of crimes under the Smith Act. This time, however, the Supreme Court drew a fine distinction between the advocacy of present-day action towards violent revolution and advocacy of violent revolution as an abstract doctrine to be acted upon at some indefinite future time. If this was the distinction, it is difficult to see how the individuals caught up in *Dennis v. United States* were correctly convicted, but at any rate that case's authority was placed in further doubt by *Brandenburg v. Ohio* in 1969 (for more, see Chapter 7). Although *Dennis v. United States* was not formally overruled, it can now safely be regarded as having no precedential value.

McCarthyism was reflected in American colleges and universities, where '[i]t produced one of the most severe episodes of repression in the universities that the United States experienced in [the twentieth] century' (Hamilton [1995]2017: 19). Many academics who were persecuted by federal and state governments, zealous and sensationalist news media, and/or nervous university administrators were, in fact, not communists at all, or even associated with communist organizations, but became targets in a general environment of accusation and inquisition. The number of academics who were actually dismissed from employment for their political opinions during the McCarthy era was relatively low, perhaps of the order of 70 to 100.[9] Nonetheless, there was a climate of fear. It was not experienced by everyone, of course, but by anyone with potentially controversial views in the 'wrong' direction.

Paranoia about Soviet communism was not confined to the United States, but occupied the thinking of many governments across the geopolitical West. In Australia, for example, the federal legislature passed the Communist Party Dissolution Act 1950, which, as its name suggests, was an attempt to ban and destroy the country's local communist party. This failed when the High Court held in *Australian Communist Party v. Commonwealth* (decided 9 March 1951) that the statute was beyond the federal legislature's powers as enumerated in the Australian Constitution.

---

[9]See Hamilton ([1995]2017: 25–6) for a concise discussion.

The birth of international human rights

At the end of the Second World War, the international community had much to reflect upon: the Holocaust; the terrifying character of fascist states; and the horrors of strategic bombing, including the arrival of nuclear weapons as a factor in wars of societies. The responses – adequate or not – included developments in international humanitarian law (i.e. the law of armed conflict) and international criminal law. These aspects could provide the subject matter for a separate book. In many ways, too, the cataclysmic war weakened the grip of colonial powers on their far-flung territories, contributing to the success of anti-colonial movements, most prominently in Africa and Asia.

Related developments were the foundation of the United Nations and the emergence of a wide-ranging human rights movement that continues to the present day. The story behind the Universal Declaration of Human Rights (the UDHR), and how it came to be, is engaging and inspiring when told by a sympathetic expert such as the conservative legal scholar Mary Ann Glendon. In her 2001 book *A World Made New*, Glendon reveals the immense patience, commitment and intellectual talent that the project demanded. Seemingly endless challenges confronted those most closely involved in drafting, advocating and sponsoring the document, then somehow steering it through difficulties and objections.

The UDHR is largely the work of a group of skilled diplomats who rose to the occasion in the immediate post-war years. Among others, these included the Canadian law professor John P. Humphrey; the Lebanese philosopher and statesman Charles Malik; the French jurist René Cassin; the Chinese philosopher, playwright and scholarly polymath Peng Chun Chang; the Indian feminist and author Hansa Mehta; and perhaps the most important of all, drawing everyone's talents together, the redoubtable Eleanor Roosevelt.

After undergoing many drafts, beginning with a raw first version by Humphrey and then a couple of efforts by Cassin to produce a more integrated document, the UDHR obtained input from the forums of the newly emerging United Nations. Its final version, approved by the UN General Assembly in 1948, was a relatively brief, balanced and widely acceptable pronouncement of standards for human treatment of human beings – especially, though not solely, of standards for conduct by governments towards their own citizens and residents.

The UDHR includes clear affirmations of individual freedoms, but as Glendon emphasizes, the immediate influences on its drafting came from the more 'dignitarian' traditions of continental Europe and Latin America. That is, the UDHR – and hence the many international law documents that followed it and drew upon its language – tends to envisage rights bearers as situated within families and communities. This gives the UDHR a different flavour from, say, the US Constitution or classics of liberal thought such as Mill's *On Liberty* (Glendon 2001: 227).

This emphasis enabled acceptance of the UDHR, and other instruments that followed, by most of the world's nations. But it also contributed to a jurisprudential order where the values of more classic forms of liberalism are treated as somewhat suspect and are balanced against other considerations. The UDHR has a role as something of a modern-day conscience for humanity, while providing a foundation from which to develop international human rights law. But unlike *On Liberty*, for example, it has roots in theological traditions as much as in the Enlightenment project or Benjamin Constant's liberty of the moderns. It does not aggressively assert the value provided to society by non-conformists or eccentrics, who will need to look elsewhere for supportive ideas and language.

In Europe, an effort was soon made to produce a regional document laying down a code of rights and freedoms with more teeth than the UDHR, which was, in itself, only a series of ideals and exhortations. The result was the European Convention on Human Rights (ECHR), or more formally the Convention for the Protection of Fundamental Rights and Freedoms, which came into force in 1953. Other regional or national bills of rights have since followed, including the Canadian Charter of Rights and Freedoms in 1982.

A series of major international conventions became available for signature in the 1960s, expanding on the contents of the UDHR and giving it binding force in international law. These included the International Convention on the Elimination of All Forms of Racial Discrimination, which was adopted by the United Nations General Assembly and opened for signature by individual states in late 1965. It was soon followed by the International Covenant on Civil and Political Rights (ICCPR) and the International Covenant on Economic, Social and Cultural Rights, both adopted by the UN General Assembly in 1966. Years later, in 1979, the Convention on Elimination of All Forms of Discrimination against Women was adopted by the UN General Assembly and became available for signature.

Glendon observes that Articles 3–20 of the UDHR 'refer primarily to what must not be done to people' (Glendon 2001: 187), and in that sense they represent a charter of liberal freedoms. However, much of what is granted by these Articles is then potentially taken away by Article 29, which permits signatory states to limit rights where needed for 'the just requirements of morality, public order and the general welfare in a democratic society'. Since almost any law will be based on some claim related to morality, public order or general welfare, the effect of this is to render the UDHR meaningless unless those concepts are given a narrow interpretation, which will need to derive from a source outside the pages of the UDHR itself.[10]

As a back-stop, Article 30 declares that nothing in the document 'may be interpreted as implying for any State, group or person any right to engage in any activity or to perform any act aimed at the destruction of any of the rights and freedoms set forth herein'. This language is mirrored in Article 17 of the ECHR, and the intention is to withdraw human rights protections from – at the least – the activities of totalitarian movements. Controversies have since arisen over the meaning and effect of such provisions in international instruments and in local laws that draw upon them.

The problem of limits and derogations in international human rights instruments is more pronounced in the ICCPR. This is precisely the international instrument that sets out a detailed charter of individual liberties, but it is riddled with wording that permits, or even requires, limits on those same liberties. Article 20 of the ICCPR, for example, requires that signatory states *deny* certain rights to their citizens and residents. Reflecting the background of the Second World War, the Holocaust and the post-war dismantling of colonialism, signatory states are required by Article 20 to prohibit 'propaganda for war' and 'advocacy of national, racial or religious hatred that constitutes incitement to discrimination, hostility or violence'.

Just how far such provisions restrict liberal freedoms is arguable. In particular, hatred is an extreme emotion that involves or manifests

---

[10]This is, of course, the same problem that I identified in France's 1789 Declaration of the Rights of Man and the Citizen.

intense and destructive antipathy towards another individual or a group.[11] It appears, then, that the word *hatred* sets a high threshold for action by the state, but there is always a danger that concepts can be interpreted expansively once they find their way into legal instruments.

To some extent, this problem is solved in practice. International jurists have tended to interpret human rights broadly and to interpret limits on rights narrowly. The limits on freedom of expression (and other rights) contained in the ICCPR in particular have been given a narrow reading in the respected Siracusa Principles on the Limitation and Derogation Provisions in the International Covenant on Civil and Political Rights, published by the American Association for the International Commission of Jurists in 1985. These principles were developed at a conference of distinguished experts on international law held in Italy in 1984. Where relevant, the interpretations offered in the Siracusa Principles are likely to be given earnest consideration by international bodies and municipal courts. But even the Siracusa Principles grant each state considerable leeway – what is known as a margin of appreciation – to prohibit expression where necessary to protect what the principles call the fundamental values of the community.

Likewise, the jurisprudence of the European Court of Human Rights, hearing cases arising under the ECHR, has often permitted illiberal outcomes in accordance with the doctrine of a margin of appreciation. This body is often known as the Strasbourg Court because of its physical location in the city of Strasbourg. It has accumulated an enormous body of case law, attempting to maintain the relevance of the ECHR as social conditions change, while also showing caution on issues where consensus seems elusive across European societies.

Aftermath

We live in the aftermath of total wars, genocides, the invention and deployment of weapons of mass destruction, the ascent of totalitarian ideologies, the founding and operation of totalitarian states, and the

---

[11]This strict approach to the nature of hatred and the legal meaning of *hatred* or *hate* is consistent with the developed case law in Canada. See *Canada (Human Rights Commission) v. Taylor* (decided 13 December 1990) and *Saskatchewan (Human Rights Commission) v. Whatcott* (decided 27 February 2013).

creative destruction of empires. I've offered only a partial sketch of responses to these huge, almost incomprehensible events. It's fair to observe that events like these, and the imperative to respond, can make the struggle for Benjamin Constant's 'liberty of the moderns' – for individual freedom to live and speak as we wish – seem old-fashioned and insignificant.

If huge geopolitical problems, such as the self-assertion and apparent allure of worldwide fascist movements, demand large-scale solutions, and if those solutions require a bit less individual liberty, so be it – or so the thought might go. We see this thought in writings such as Karl Loewenstein's as early as the 1930s, and in some of the detail of today's human rights law. But human rights law also honours the importance of the individual, and in any event the yearning for freedom has not receded. This sets up a tension that continues in the twenty-first century.

7 LIBERALISM DIVIDED

The Long Sixties

The period from the late 1950s to the early 1970s is often known as the Long Sixties. This decade-and-a-half was a time of rapid social change in Western liberal democracies.

The sequence of events played out against a geopolitical backdrop of Cold War between the Soviet Union (and its allies and client states) and the liberal democracies of the West, with a concomitant fear of unrestrained warfare using thermonuclear weapons. Post-war colonial independence movements arose or continued, among them the protracted but ultimately successful rebellion against France in Algeria from 1954 to 1963. Some Western nations, most notably the United States, became bogged down in a strategically pointless war in Vietnam. Throughout this conflict, American military forces won every open battle, but the United States and its allies ultimately lost the war of societies.

There was much social change that fitted with a broadly liberal agenda for reform. This included developments in racial equality and sex equality, rights to contraception and abortion, and relaxation of literary and cinematic censorship. The outcome was by no means the emergence of a fully liberal society in any Western nation, and each step along the way was resisted strongly – sometimes successfully – by conservatives. Liberal and radical activists gained numerous victories, but even by the mid-1960s some were expressing impatience with the pace and scope of change.

This was a peak era in history for recognition of the Millian harm principle – or one or another interpretation of it – as both a foundation for legal prohibitions and a limit to the law's legitimate role. In the UK, the government established the Departmental Committee on Homosexual

Offences and Prostitution, chaired by a distinguished educationalist, Sir John Wolfenden. This body duly reported its findings in September 1957 – the famous Wolfenden Report – recommending reforms to the laws relating to prostitution and especially homosexual conduct. In the latter case, the report recommended decriminalization of private sexual conduct between adult men.[1] While its recommendations were modest by later standards, the Wolfenden Report rejected any idea that it was a legitimate function of the law to enforce traditional morality or impose a particular way of life on citizens.

The report prompted an earnest public debate in the UK, most famously a series of exchanges between two leading jurists of the time: the eminent judge (Lord) Patrick Devlin and the equally eminent professor of jurisprudence H. L. A. Hart.[2] Despite an initial rejection of its recommendations on male homosexuality, the Wolfenden Report did eventually contribute to decriminalization of 'private' (very narrowly defined) homosexual conduct via the Sexual Offences Act 1967. This initially applied only to England and Wales, but was later extended to Scotland and Northern Ireland.

In the United States, the drafters of the Model Penal Code relied heavily on the harm principle. This was a project of the American Law Institute, completed in 1962 by a team led by Herbert Wechsler – a distinguished attorney and legal scholar. It has since influenced the criminal law in many American jurisdictions.

The Long Sixties – particularly the decade of greatest change from about 1964 – can be remembered as a time of energy and joy, and of youthful optimism about the possibilities for change. I often hear the era recalled nostalgically as a more innocent time than today, and perhaps there's some truth in this picture. But it's also a one-sided one.

Movements for social change were often suppressed ruthlessly. The Free Speech Movement that began on the Berkeley campus of the University of California in 1964 had a clear and attractive

---

[1]However, the report attempted to justify an age of consent of twenty-one for this purpose – despite acknowledging strong arguments for an age as low as sixteen, matching the age of consent for heterosexual encounters. Note that lesbian acts did not need to be decriminalized, as they had never been illegal in the UK.

[2]This debate itself prompted a large body of commentary. However, the best place to start is with Devlin (1965) and Hart (1963).

justification, and it was a trigger point for the larger student movement of the 1960s – across the United States and then beyond. It began as a campaign against an anachronistic regulation forbidding political activity on campuses of the University of California, and especially against a decision by university administrators to enforce the regulation strictly – that is, heavy-handedly and excessively. The students responded with tactics of civil disobedience learned, in part, from the Civil Rights Movement, and the initial response was again heavy-handed, even to the point of brutality.

The great Martin Luther King, who'd led the Civil Rights Movement in the United States through many iconic moments and encouraging victories, was assassinated in 1968. To this we can add the assassinations of President John F. Kennedy in 1963 and his brother Robert Kennedy in 1968. For many thoughtful people, it seemed like a dark time in history. The Civil Rights Movement produced important political changes, but it failed to achieve the social transformation that its leaders and participants hoped for. Similarly, the feminist movement of this era helped to undermine the lingering discourses that surrounded women and their social roles, but Western feminists did not achieve a complete social transformation.

The year 1968, in particular, was marked by dramatic youth rebellions that captured imaginations across the world yet failed in their immediate political goals. In France, the 'May 68' insurrection of students and workers (which in fact persisted through much of June) helped inspire movements as far away as Japan and Mexico. However, the political outcome in France itself was a new election and an electoral triumph for the incumbent president, Charles de Gaulle. In the United States in same year, the Republican presidential candidate Richard Nixon won a crushing victory, suggesting widespread support for a return to 'law and order'. In fact, the rehearsal for this was two years earlier when Ronald Reagan easily won the governorship of California on a similar platform.

In sum, we can see obvious differences between the *mores*, fashions and discourses characterizing Western cultures before and after the Long Sixties, but less was achieved than many theorists, activists and young idealists had hoped for, and whatever was achieved repeatedly came under challenge.

The rise and fall of the Civil Rights Movement

In the wake of the Second World War, the Holocaust and the Nazis' theory of racial hierarchy with an Aryan master race, there was a global reaction against racism and religious/ethnic bigotry. Within the United States, heightened race consciousness, matched by yearnings for a social order without racial enmities and the evils of white supremacism, encouraged Black Americans to challenge the discriminatory laws still operative in the southern states.

Black American activists commenced a social, political and legal campaign for equality which provided a model for other social movements that followed close behind. Their first great legal victory was in the US Supreme Court case *Brown v. Board of Education* (decided 17 May 1954), which held that racial segregation in American public schools was unconstitutional. This signalled the eventual end of Jim Crow laws, but school desegregation encountered bitter resistance in the South, and the burgeoning Civil Rights Movement achieved its victories only through constant and passionate struggle.

The Civil Rights Act of 1964, enacted by the federal Congress, ended up, via some political shenanigans, prohibiting sex discrimination as well as racial discrimination. This statute created a precedent, not only for the United States but for many other nations. The UK followed suit in 1965 with its own Race Relations Act, though this had relatively limited scope in not, for example, dealing with discrimination in employment. For that reason, expanded legislation was enacted in the UK in 1968.

The Civil Rights Act went further than withdrawing government persecution of subordinated groups, in that it gave African Americans and American women positive rights to obtain assistance from the courts if they were discriminated against by non-government parties such as employers in the private sector of the economy. Further legislation enhancing the rights of Black Americans followed until 1968, and the result was an impressive package of reforms. It was, however, viewed differently by white and Black citizens: 'While blacks considered the civil rights legislation a good beginning, white America viewed them as a triumph' (Baritz 1989: 248).

The 1960s reforms brought undeniable benefits, but there was soon a perception that they had not done enough. The elimination of formal barriers to racial equality was complete, but it did not translate into practice on the ground. Even now, over half a century later, Black Americans suffer from numerous social disadvantages that include very high incarceration rates.

Samuel Walker has pointed out that the classic era of the Civil Rights Movement – an era of activism for racial equality, an end to racial discrimination, and a colour-blind approach to employment and other decisions – 'came to an end somewhere in the early 1970s' (Walker 1994: 132). The incomplete benefits obtained prompted a policy shift towards ideas of affirmative action aimed at creating a substantively equal society. This change of direction may have been merited in the circumstances, but it alienated many white voters who were themselves experiencing tough economic circumstances by the mid-1970s. At the same time, some American liberals objected in principle to anything other than an approach based on formal equality and colour-blind decision-making. The outcome, therefore, was one issue among many that splintered American liberalism.

Culture war

The term *culture war* is a translation of the German *Kulturkampf*, originally referring to an 1870s struggle between the Roman Catholic Church and the Prussian government. In more recent times, we see many references to a culture war, or to culture wars (plural), in discussions of American politics and – to a lesser extent – Western politics more broadly. The issues have varied, and they would be somewhat independent of each other if considered on their respective merits rather than as components of rival political platforms. Perhaps most prominently, they've included abortion rights and the legal and social position of gay men and lesbians. However, they've extended to gun control (an issue mainly confined to the United States), church–state relations and many other topics.

One early use of the term *culture war* in this context – the earliest that I'm aware of – was by the American social historian Loren Baritz, who chose it as the title to Chapter 5 of his book *The Good Life* (Baritz 1989: 225–88). Baritz employed variations of the phrase in a vivid account of the social issues and events that dominated US politics in the 1960s, with repercussions thereafter. In the 1990s, the phrase was popularized by the sociologist James Davidson Hunter and the arch-conservative political commentator and presidential candidate Pat Buchanan. Let's consider this in a broader context.

As we've seen in previous chapters, there's a complex story to be told about scholars and thinkers, dating to the centuries of early modernity, who challenged the truth claims of Christianity. They developed alternative worldviews, making non-religious understandings of the universe, and humanity's place in it, increasingly available and intellectually attractive. Through the nineteenth century and beyond, Christianity persisted, if mainly in the form of a discursive rather than overtly coercive religiosity.[3] During the twentieth century, however, and especially during the Long Sixties, even this kind of religious culture encountered dramatic challenges. Christian theology and especially Christian morals lost much of their prestige, visibility and public influence.

What remains under debate among scholars is a set of questions about the timing and causes of the decline of Christian religiosity. We might, for example, note the opposed views of the historians Callum G. Brown (2009, 2017) and Clive D. Field (2017). According to Field, the totality of the evidence does not suggest a catastrophic collapse during the early 1960s, as Brown postulates, and nor does it support Brown's ingenious explanation. For Brown, the key development in the UK and elsewhere was defection from the churches by young women who rejected longstanding ideas – closely entwined with Christian doctrine and practice – of chaste domesticity as a feminine ideal. (By this point, large numbers of men may already have had doubts about the whole business of churches and religion.) Elegant though Brown's explanation seems, Field adduces evidence of a long-term decline in religiosity dating back to the nineteenth century and leading up to the 1960s.

I cannot pretend to adjudicate this debate between experts. What is clear, however, is that there were dramatic legal and cultural changes in the UK and many other countries. Numerous areas of law were liberalized during the Long Sixties. These related, for example, to gambling, capital punishment, abortion, homosexuality, family planning, divorce and censorship. Greater legal freedoms were accompanied by relaxation of informal standards of respectability and virtue. To a large extent, the Victorian system of piety and traditional morals receded from the ways people were assessed, addressed and discussed – and from cultural products such as films, novels and magazines. Second-wave feminism

---

[3]See Chapter 5 for this distinction.

(often known in the late 1960s and early 1970s as the Women's Liberation Movement) grew, prospered and took variant forms; a vibrant and varied youth culture emerged, centred especially on rock music and the phenomenon of student rebellion (for discussion, see Brown 2009: 176).

Writing from an American perspective, though much of his thesis is applicable elsewhere, Baritz portrays 1960s political and social conflict as dominated by four issues, and hence four 'cultural wars', which he describes as 'sometimes overlapping and mutually supportive'. He enumerates these as 'the redefinition of conventional morality, civil rights, radicalism, and alienation' (Baritz 1989: 227). According to Baritz, these issues defined a single movement, and they were joined by a common state of mind involving greater flexibility and tolerance, revaluation of the past, suspicion of authority, a refusal to accept middle-class dictates in personal life, and a sincere, if flawed, commitment to equality and democracy (see Baritz 1989: 227–8). As for the flaws, Baritz refers in his discussion to a restriction of greater equality to the movement's insiders, and observes that at this point there was a blindness to the subordination of women even within the movement itself.

Baritz describes a gap between generational attitudes, with parents fearing for the moral and personal safety of their children, while the latter viewed their parents' generation as a threat to their freedom and even their lives in the context of the Vietnam War. Here is one difference between the United States and many other Western nations: not all were involved in the debacle of Vietnam. Furthermore, other Western nations did not have an exact equivalent of the Civil Rights Movement. Nonetheless, the specifically American struggles over Vietnam, military conscription and civil rights were broadcast across the world and were inspirational elsewhere.

For a time, youthful rebellion against the established moral, political and economic order could be asserted through self-presentation via hairstyles – particularly young men with long hair – and clothing choices. This kind of display gradually lost its symbolic force as it became a matter of conformity to fashion rather than a sign of revolutionary ambition, but for much of the Long Sixties it united rebellious youth. Conversely, it succeeded in provoking anger and outrage from conservative politicians and commentators, as well as many everyday parents and local authority figures. The generation gap included sharply differentiated attitudes to sex, with the youthful commitment to sexual freedom facilitated by the increasing availability of the contraceptive pill.

It's a cliché that each generation of children rebels against – and in turn, is condemned by – its parents, but this obscures the sea change that took place during the Long Sixties. Brown argues that there was much continuity, amid change, between the dominant ideology of 1800 and that of 1958, but thereafter we can identify an impressive cultural interruption: 'The result has been that the generation that grew up in the sixties was more dissimilar to the generation of its parents than in any previous century' (Brown 2009: 190).

The UK became a far more secular society than it once was. Christian organizations and their doctrines experienced a diminished social influence and no longer provided a sense of identity or 'self' for most men and women (Brown 2009: 2). The outcome was similar in Australia, New Zealand and much of continental Europe, but it turned out rather differently in the United States and perhaps to some extent in Canada (Brown 2009: 196–7). Especially in the United States, religious conservatives fought back more successfully than in Europe, employing social prescriptions and public rhetoric that now seem extreme and anachronistic from a European (or Antipodean) perspective. Twenty-first-century American politics is in many ways an ongoing 'discursive battle' between a still-vigorous ideology centred on evangelical Christianity and a secular post-Sixties culture (Brown 2009: 197).

The US Supreme Court

In the United States, battles in the growing culture war were often decided by the nation's Supreme Court as questions of constitutional interpretation. A series of cases that began with *Griswold v. Connecticut* (decided 7 June 1965) established a constitutionally protected freedom from unwarranted government interference in people's deeply personal choices about how they live their lives. This case involved a statute from the 1800s banning all forms of contraception, even when used by married couples, and thus made it an accessory crime for a doctor to prescribe any contraceptive device or medication. The Supreme Court set an important precedent by holding this law to be unconstitutional.

In *Eisenstadt v. Baird* (decided 22 March 1972), the right to use contraception was extended beyond cases involving married couples, although the facts here were somewhat peculiar. The case involved the distribution of a vaginal foam product at the end of a lecture by an individual who was not a doctor. Assuming that *Griswold* was correctly decided, we might doubt whether its logic as a precedent should extend so far. In any event, these and other cases that posited a 'privacy' right provided the basis for *Roe v. Wade* (decided 22 January 1973), which struck down a Texas anti-abortion law[4] and for almost fifty years provided a zone of liberty for women seeking abortions prior to the viability of the foetus. For a time, numerous laws were invalidated if they imposed onerous conditions for access to abortion services.

Two decades after *Roe v. Wade*, however, its central concept only barely survived challenge. In *Planned Parenthood v. Casey* (decided 9 June 1992), a more conservative iteration of the Supreme Court under Chief Justice William Rehnquist upheld significant restrictions on abortion. Moreover, a slightly earlier case, *Bowers v. Hardwick* (decided 30 June 1986), hinted at movement in a more conservative direction when the court refused to invalidate an anti-sodomy statute.

As it turned out, *Bowers v. Hardwick* was eventually overruled by *Lawrence v. Texas* (decided 26 June 2003), which indeed did strike down a comparable statute. Exactly twelve years later, the Supreme Court held in *Obergefell v. Hodges* (decided 26 June 2015) that state laws could not restrict the right to marry to opposite-sex couples. Putting this more positively, the court held that the states must provide for same-sex marriage. Since then, however, *Roe v. Wade* has not fared so well, and it was overruled in *Dobbs v. Jackson Women's Health Organization* (decided 24 June 2022). As a result, the various American states are now free, as far as federal constitutional law is concerned, to enact their own laws regulating or even prohibiting abortions.

This outcome has an obvious and important impact on many American women who can no longer lawfully terminate their pregnancies. More than that, it casts doubt on the reasoning in all cases that relied upon an implied constitutional right to privacy. Despite reassurances in the opinion of the court, delivered by Justice Samuel Alito, there is no guarantee that any decisions based on privacy in the relevant sense are secure.

These cases, especially *Roe v. Wade*, were probably always vulnerable to challenges at a later time, in that they rely on constitutional rights that are

---

[4] A companion case, *Doe v. Bolton*, related to a Georgia statute that was drafted rather differently.

said to be implicit or inferred (and are hence a matter of interpretation). It would have been a more straightforward outcome if privacy rights were explicitly set out in the US Constitution *or* if protection of deeply personal choices were a widely shared value that could be insisted upon in electoral politics. The latter, however, seems unachievable in a nation that remains deeply divided over the legitimate role of the law and over concepts of sexual wrongdoing.

By way of comparison, the ECHR differs from the US Constitution in that it provides explicitly for a right to respect for private and family life. This appears in Article 8. However, the Article is open to interpretation and does not necessarily equate to the constitutional privacy right that has been recognized in the United States. Furthermore, Article 8 contains extensive limitations relating to, among other issues, government action for 'the protection of health or morals'. In practice, the European Court of Human Rights reads limitations and derogations in the ECHR narrowly while attempting to give generous effect to the rights themselves. However, it has balanced this approach with its doctrine of a margin of appreciation, allowing nations that are signatory to the ECHR a measure of flexibility in how they interpret and implement its provisions.

As a result, Article 8, together with other ECHR Articles such as Article 14 on prohibition of discrimination, has provided the basis for a rich and developing body of jurisprudence on the rights of gay men and lesbians. This builds on the foundational case of *Dudgeon v. United Kingdom* (decided 22 October 1981), in which the Strasbourg Court examined an anti-gay law that was still applicable in Northern Ireland despite the reforms enacted in England and Wales in 1967. The court held that Northern Ireland's law forbidding male homosexual acts, even in private between consenting adults over the age of twenty-one, was in breach of the ECHR, although it rejected a submission that the age of consent should be seventeen to bring it in line with the general age of consent in Northern Ireland at the time.

Cases such as this illustrate circumstances in which rights and freedoms can be protected more clearly by a modern human rights instrument than by an older document such as the US Constitution with its appended Bill of Rights. But this does not entail that modern instruments, with their numerous built-in limitations and derogations, will always be more effective. Most notably, the European Court of Human Rights has not been willing to infer a general abortion right from the words of the ECHR.[5] Furthermore, neither approach can guarantee a tolerant society in which speech and action are free from the tyranny of social opinion and informal pressures to conform.

Free speech in the United States

Since the First Amendment to the US Constitution explicitly forbids the federal Congress from making any law that abridges 'the freedom of speech', American free speech jurisprudence stands on relatively strong ground. However, the First Amendment does not apply by its own terms to laws enacted by state governments, or to exercises of executive or judicial, rather than legislative, power. These extensions rely upon judicial reasoning and interpretation, and, as we saw in Chapter 6, the courts refer to the Fourteenth Amendment rather than to the First Amendment in isolation.

Nonetheless, the extensions are settled law. The remaining question is exactly what does and does not fall within 'the freedom of speech' since it is clear enough that the expression was not intended to apply to all expressive acts whatsoever. It does not obviously apply to cases such as the following: communications through essentially non-verbal media such as sculpture, painting and photography (these are not literally 'speech'); narratives that might evoke emotion but do not explicitly contribute to public discussion of ideas; financial contributions to help propagate political, religious and other opinions; and cases of verbal abuse, invective, defamation and revelations of secrets.

On the narrowest readings, 'the freedom of speech' might be interpreted as no more than a freedom of straightforwardly political speech or a freedom to make scholarly contributions to public discussion, as described by Kant in his essay on the nature of enlightenment (see Chapter 4). In practice, however, the US Supreme Court moved during the Long Sixties and thereafter to recognize a uniquely broad zone of protected expression. Here, *Brandenburg v. Ohio* (decided 9 June 1969) was a pivotal case.

---

[5]See especially *A, B and C v. Ireland* (decided 16 December 2010). In this case, the court did find that decisions relating to abortions fell within the meaning of Article 8, but it upheld Ireland's anti-abortion law as a permissible protection of its society's established morals.

The court held that state legislatures could not prohibit 'advocacy of the use of force or of law violation except where such advocacy is directed to inciting or producing imminent lawless action and is likely to incite or produce such action' (395 US 444, 447 (1969)). This is reminiscent of John Stuart Mill's corn dealer example (see my discussion in Chapter 5). In the case at hand, the beneficiary was a Ku Klux Klan leader. However, the outcome potentially assisted many political theorists or activists who, at least in the abstract, advocated resort to violence.

In *New York Times v. Sullivan* (decided 9 March 1964), the *New York Times* successfully defended itself from a libel suit brought by L. B. Sullivan, the police commissioner in Montgomery, Alabama. In the lower courts, Sullivan succeeded in obtaining damages in respect of a full-page advertisement by civil rights supporters trenchantly criticizing the Montgomery police (though not mentioning Sullivan by name). Although the advertisement made inaccurate and damaging claims about police actions, the Supreme Court allowed an area of leniency for good-faith, but inaccurate, allegations about the conduct of public officials in performance of their duties. In such cases, the court introduced a new requirement that the speaker must have shown 'actual malice', which was defined to mean either knowledge that an imputation was false or reckless disregard of its truth or falsity.

American defamation law has developed further since 1964, but the immediate effect was to make it easier for civil rights activists to advocate their case for social reform without falling afoul of lawsuits.

In a series of cases in the second half of the 1960s and the early 1970s, the Supreme Court consolidated its approach to political speech. *Bond v. Floyd* (decided 5 December 1966) unanimously overturned Julian Bond's exclusion from taking up his seat in the state of Georgia's House of Representatives, which he'd been denied for expressing pacifist views including opposition to America's involvement in the Vietnam War.

Cohen v. California (decided 7 June 1971) overturned the conviction of an anti-war protestor, Paul Robert Cohen, who had walked within the corridor of a courthouse wearing a jacket embellished with the words 'Fuck the Draft'. Cohen had subsequently been convicted under a Californian law relating to disturbing the peace. However, the Supreme Court held that he could not be convicted for merely offensive language, and in the leading opinion, Justice John Marshall Harlan famously acknowledged the particular four-letter word under debate as distasteful, while adding: '[I]t is nevertheless often true that one man's vulgarity is another's lyric' (403 US 15, 25 (1971)).

In *New York Times Co. v. United States* (decided 30 June 1971; often known as the *Pentagon Papers Case*) the majority of judges were unwilling to impose prior restraints on publication by the *New York Times* and the *Washington Post* for the purpose of protecting government secrets. The case involved a complex factual situation, but the gist of it was an attempt by the federal government to restrain publication of articles based on a classified, government-commissioned history of American activities in Indochina. This was at a time when US forces had been involved for six years in open, but unofficial, war in Vietnam.

In the field of obscenity law, the *Hicklin* test was overturned definitively at US Supreme Court level in 1957. Early in that year, *Butler v. Michigan* (decided 25 February 1957) struck down an obscenity statute that criminalized the distribution of material which might tend to incite minors to violent or (supposedly) depraved or immoral acts. However, the more important case was *Roth v. United States* (decided 24 June 1957) in which the Supreme Court upheld the conviction of a bookseller, Samuel Roth, but in doing so rejected the *Hicklin* test. The court found that 'material which deals with sex in a manner appealing to prurient interest' was not constitutionally protected, but that the First Amendment protected artistic and literary works legitimately dealing with human sexuality:

Sex, a great and mysterious motive force in human life, has indisputably been a subject of absorbing interest to mankind through the ages; it is one of the vital problems of human interest and public concern.
(354 US 476, 487 (1957))

The next breakthrough was the 1959 case *Kingsley International Pictures Corp. v. Regents of the University of New York* (decided 29 June 1959). This overturned a ban on a French film of D. H. Lawrence's *Lady Chatterley's Lover*. The film's prohibition was not based on alleged obscenity but on its supposed message of encouraging adultery, or at least portraying it as desirable behaviour for some people in some circumstances. Once again, the prohibition failed, and the majority of the court made clear that it was not constitutional in the United States to prohibit a work for its advocacy of an unconventional or supposedly immoral idea.

From this point, there was a tendency towards liberalization of American obscenity law. The nine judges serving at any time on the Supreme Court were unable to reach a consensus on the appropriate legal principles to handle these cases, and most were unwilling to declare unequivocally that controlling the sexual content of publications was none of the law's business. Some outcomes seem anomalous, or at least difficult to reconcile with each other. However, the overall trend was clearly towards less censorship and more toleration.

In the mid-1960s case *Memoirs v. Massachusetts* (decided 21 March 1966) a Supreme Court majority permitted the sale of John Cleland's eighteenth-century erotic novel *Memoirs of a Woman of Pleasure* (better known as *Fanny Hill*). Unfortunately, this case presented no majority opinion on the applicable law. For a plurality of three judges, the central point was that the book could not be shown, taken as a whole, to be utterly without social value. Three other judges agreed with the outcome for reasons of their own, while another three dissented.

When the 1967 Swedish film *I Am Curious (Yellow)* (directed by Vilgot Sjöman) was imported into the United States, it ran into censorship problems for its frank erotic content. It eventually opened in theatres in early 1969, but was the subject of extensive litigation in multiple state jurisdictions and at several levels of the American legal system, including decisions on procedure from the Supreme Court. Despite the film's mixed reception in American courtrooms, its release, commercial success and considerable support from commentators and film critics created a watershed moment for toleration of nudity and explicit sex in mainstream cinema.

Debate over erotic books, magazines, films and other materials became a central feature of the 1960s culture warfare, with clear lines between American liberals who generally supported increased freedoms and their conservative opponents who came to see the suppression of 'smut' as a righteous crusade.

After Nixon won the presidential election in 1968, opportunities arose to make his own Supreme Court appointments. These included a new Chief Justice, Warren E. Burger, in 1969. The result was a more conservative line-up of judges, some of whom were openly hostile to pornographic works and their associated advertising material. Thereafter the test that literature and art must have no social value to qualify as 'obscene' was replaced in *Miller v. California* (decided 21 June 1973).

On the *Miller* test, prurient or patently offensive material of a sexual nature did not have to be *utterly* without redeeming social value before it could be found to be legally obscene, and thus a legitimate target for prohibition. However, it was not a legitimate target if, taken as a whole, it possessed 'serious literary, artistic, political, or scientific value' (413 US 15, 24 (1973)).

The *Miller* test was a step backwards from the viewpoint of civil libertarians – and certainly from the viewpoint of pornographers – but it remained considerably more difficult for would-be censors to meet than the old *Hicklin* test had been. It confirmed the protection of literary, artistic or philosophical works dealing seriously with the theme of human sexuality. Despite Nixon's efforts and the socially conservative mould of the Burger court, there was no prospect, in the state and federal jurisdictions of the United States, of prohibiting erotic material with any plausible claim to thematic seriousness.

The complications and difficulties relating to the constitutional law of obscenity did not end with the *Miller* case (for more discussion of the details than I can deal with here, see generally Hixson 1996). It is noteworthy, however, that throughout this entire phase from *Roth* to *Miller*, and in the latter's immediate aftermath, there was no doubt which was the 'liberal' and which the 'conservative' side of the issue.

Illiberal liberals

In his study of academic freedom in the United States, Neil Hamilton usefully reminds us that the student rebelliousness of the 1960s was not all free speech, free love and freedom from participating in war. Many student radicals sought to disrupt and dismantle existing social institutions, which were regarded as fundamentally oppressive, and these institutions included universities. Thus, Hamilton observes: 'Inherent in this ideology was permission and encouragement of extreme measures to coerce and intimidate others' (Hamilton [1995]2017: 32).

Leaders of the student movement increasingly embraced one form or another of Marxist ideology, and they adopted tactics of disruption as a prelude to what they imagined as a transformation of society. By the mid-1960s, and into the following decade, vandalism, violent imagery and sometimes outright violent acts had become more common tactics of protest. The increasingly ideological and radicalized character of the movement can be attributed in part to its perceived lack of success in influencing public policy, and hence a growing sense of desperation.

Few books, if any, had more influence on the youthful rebels and activists than David Riesman's *The Lonely Crowd: A Study of the Changing American Character*, first published in 1950. To simplify slightly, this advocated the development of autonomous personalities, conforming uncritically neither to the internalized voices of their parents and other elders encountered in childhood nor to the external pressures of society, including peer groups, fashionable role models and mass media influences. In the book's final chapter, Riesman expresses 'the hope of finding ways in which a more autonomous type of social character might develop' (Riesman [1950–1969]2001: 304).

Riesman himself worked with young colleagues from the New Left in the early 1960s, protesting, in particular, against the development and stockpiling of nuclear weapons. And yet, by the late 1960s he had become disillusioned with the direct-action tactics of the political movement that – at least in its American version – he had largely inspired (see Geary 2013: 620). Riesman viewed the most dramatic protest tactics of the young radicals of this time as all too reminiscent of those once employed in Europe during the emergence of fascist parties and ideologies.

Riesman's 'second preface' to the 1969 abridged edition of *The Lonely Crowd* is restrained in its criticism of younger people, but it is cautiously reflective about the book's influence and in places the author seems almost repentant. Riesman observes that a minority within a minority of young people had, as of the late 1960s, 'thrown itself into politics, finding in the antiwar, civil rights, and antiuniversity movements a new secular religion and often a new family' and he contrasted their approach with his own 'more benign and nonviolent view' of what is possible via incremental change (Riesman [1950–1969]2001: xxix–xxx).

This sort of observation is, perhaps, a recurrent one, made by successive generations of middle-aged intellectuals observing the energy and excesses of young activists. For the minority of a minority that Riesman refers to, however, a set of political priorities and theories probably did act as a kind of successor belief system to Christianity (or even to a more conventional Marxism). It came complete with a Durkheimian effervescence arising from the experience of communal participation. Unfortunately, it could sometimes be an intolerant belief system like other political religions before it.

One iconic episode that played out a few years later involved a controversy over the publication of Edward O. Wilson's book *Sociobiology: The New Synthesis* (Wilson [1975]2000). This huge volume synthesized much of what was known about social animals and the working of animal societies, but its final chapter inflamed left-wing ideologues by treating our own species, *Homo sapiens*, as one more social animal among others, thus suggesting that an evolved human nature could be identified beneath the diversity of human cultures. It seems that the underlying fear was that this approach could lead to claims of race- and sex-related differences in cognition, emotional tendencies and behaviour. These could then be used to rationalize racist or sexist beliefs and to justify social inequalities.

In November 1975, the *New York Review of Books* published a letter with sixteen signatories, including the distinguished biological scientists Stephen Jay Gould and Richard Lewontin. Notably, the letter attacked Wilson on ideological rather than scientific grounds, since it claimed that theories such as Wilson's persist in one form or another because they provide a rationale for the status of dominant groups identifiable by class, race and sex. Much the same critique was then published in a lengthier document in the journal *BioScience*. This was authored by Lewontin and others on behalf of a radical left-wing study group (Sociobiology Study Group of Science for the People 1976). In both cases, the authors attempted to smear Wilson's views with guilt by association, alleging a similarity to, and continuity with, earlier theories allegedly endorsing biological determinism.

In responses published in the *New York Review of Books* and in more detail in *BioScience* (Wilson 1976), Wilson objected vigorously to the criticism he'd received, pointed to various distortions of his actual position and reproached what he saw as a form of self-righteous academic vigilantism. In her book on the entire episode, Ullica Segerstråle makes reference to the 'social psychology of witch hunts' operating in such attacks on science (Segerstråle 2000: 15).

Wilson's views were eventually subjected to scientific and philosophical scrutiny – rather than mere ideological rejection – and this led to a richer debate over the evolutionary roots of human nature, the degree to which our nature has become unmoored from its biological origins as a result of cultural developments and the existence (or extent) of any biologically determined psychological differences between the sexes.

Science is improved by criticism, and we would do well to encourage scrutiny of scientific hypotheses for their fundamental coherence as well as their empirical viability: for example, are they supported by the existing evidence and how well do they withstand attempts at empirical falsification? But this does not excuse the highly personal and inflammatory attacks that Wilson endured from Gould, Lewontin and others. It certainly does not excuse a notorious incident in 1978 when chanting demonstrators absurdly accused Wilson of genocide and one woman poured a jug of iced water over him.[6]

Marcuse on repressive tolerance

By the mid-1960s, there was already public debate over the use of disruption and violence by some protestors, and one result was an influential essay by a member of what is known as the Frankfurt School.

The Frankfurt School was a group of scholars associated with the Institute for Social Research, founded in the German city of Frankfurt am Main in 1923. Among its most influential members at one time or another were Max Horkheimer, Theodor W. Adorno, Ernst Bloch, Walter Benjamin, Erich Fromm, Herbert Marcuse and (later) Jürgen Habermas. The Institute evolved its orientation – most dramatically in 1930 when Horkheimer became its director – and in the late 1930s it adopted the deliberately obscure term *critical theory* as a label for its method(s) of analysis. During the 1930s, its scholars were forced out of Germany (initially to Geneva and then to the United States) by the rise of the Nazi Party. After the end of the Second World War, however, some returned to Europe.

The work of the Frankfurt School responds to the fact that the revolution of the industrial proletariat predicted by Marxist theory did not take place. As we've seen, Marx predicted an impoverishment and immiseration of the workers that would force a revolution against the existing political order. But in the most advanced capitalist economies – Britain and Germany when Marx was writing – events did not proceed as the theory envisaged.

At the beginning of their best-known book, *Dialectic of Enlightenment* (originally published in 1947), Horkheimer and Adorno quote extensively from Francis Bacon, who wrote early in the seventeenth century at the

---

[6]For a more detailed discussion of the debate occasioned by Wilson's book, see Blackford (2019a: 453–9). For considerably more still, see generally Segerstråle (2000).

beginning of the Scientific Revolution. Bacon extolled the potential of science and technology to contribute to human welfare, but Horkheimer and Adorno interpreted his programme as an effort to control nature and other human beings. According to *Dialectic of Enlightenment*, the outcome has been catastrophic: 'the fully enlightened earth radiates disaster triumphant' (Horkheimer and Adorno [1947]1988: 3). This approach establishes the book's authors as twentieth-century successors to Rousseau, writing in an anti-Enlightenment tradition where progress in science, technology and philosophical thought is viewed as destructive of personal goods and social relations – and as culminating in a powerful minority's domination over other human beings as well as non-human nature.[7]

During the 1960s, another leading figure of the Frankfurt School became a high-profile public intellectual in the United States. This was Herbert Marcuse, who is perhaps best known for his essay 'Repressive Tolerance' (first published in 1965, with a postscript added a few years later). Though capitalist societies had not, as of the 1960s, produced the environment of poverty and misery that Marx viewed as capitalism's logical outcome, Marcuse – like other Frankfurt School authors – understood them as societies of exploitation and domination. He thus saw a need to replace the capitalist system with something better, but he realized that this was difficult in a situation of overall affluence with increasing living standards for the majority (Marcuse 1969: 107–8).

In response, Marcuse argued for toleration of radically left-wing ideas accompanied by intolerance for the ideas, policies or conduct that (in his view) supported the regressive elements of society and impeded necessary political action (Marcuse 1969: 102). He complained that toleration was being extended to evil ideas, policies, conduct and situations. He did not imagine that his approach would, or could, be pursued through state power. However, he called for – or at least justified or excused – violent political action from radical groups, which he depicted as using violence to try to break a chain of violence (Marcuse 1969: 131).

Marcuse proposed to open up the possibilities for radical groups to take whatever steps might be needed to oppose what he considered regressive and repressive viewpoints. This would involve no longer

---

[7]It scarcely needs saying that this is not a conservative or establishment critique of the Enlightenment that defends the power of enjoyed by monarchs, the Church and the landed aristocracy within Europe's *ancien régime*.

tolerating the speech and assembly of groups and movements associated with a wide variety of political platforms – not only Nazis, fascists, white supremacists and other groups on the extreme Right, but also most social conservatives and political libertarians. For example, toleration of speech and assembly would be withdrawn from groups that opposed 'the extension of public services, social security, medical care, etc.' (Marcuse 1969: 114).

An obvious point in Marcuse's support is that almost anything can be justified in response to an ongoing catastrophe of sufficient urgency and extent. Thus, Marcuse could justify or excuse acts of intolerance and violence, precisely by his claim that he lived, in the 1960s, in a morally catastrophic political and cultural environment – 'an emergency situation' requiring 'an extreme suspension of the right of free speech and free assembly' (Marcuse 1969: 123).

Marcuse acknowledged that radical left-wing opinions were tolerated in current affairs programming and the like, and even that they were allocated similar air time to right-wing views. But he insisted that they were swamped by indoctrination into mainstream assumptions via entertainment and advertising. As he saw it, then, reason was helpless to sway a majority who were deeply socialized to accept the status quo.

This is strong stuff, but – again – Marcuse had a point. Neither liberal tolerance, such as advocated by Mill, nor democratic elections can ensure that whatever is viewed as the correct vision of society will prevail. On the contrary, radical critiques of existing political arrangements and social discourses will always face an uphill battle even when they are not actively suppressed. If we view our situation – as Marcuse perceived his – as a state of emergency, partly because our ideas and policies are not making headway, this might lead us to withdraw all toleration from our opponents, and perhaps even to adopt or countenance political violence.

Fiss on free speech and equality

In the mid-1990s, the distinguished legal scholar Owen M. Fiss published two books – *Liberalism Divided* and *The Irony of Free Speech* – in which he looked back on post-war developments in the United States relating to freedom of speech and First Amendment jurisprudence. In what follows, I will focus on *Liberalism Divided*, a thematically unified collection of his articles and essays from the 1980s and 1990s, though Fiss develops similar themes in both volumes.

In *Liberalism Divided*, he especially homes in on a division over free speech issues that emerged within the tradition of American liberalism in the late 1970s and early 1980s. How far this represents a division over liberalism itself is another matter, since the positions that Fiss defends or views with sympathy had moved on from anything that we would find in the work of, say, Benjamin Constant, Wilhelm von Humboldt or John Stuart Mill. It is more accurate to refer to divisions *within the political Left*, broadly understood, with Fiss particularly focused on developments in the United States.

Since the 1990s, Fiss has been a major figure in debates over the role of governments in permitting, prohibiting or curating speech. For example, Adrienne Stone, a leading constitutional scholar with a special interest in free speech issues, recognizes him as an exemplary exponent of a particular tendency. That is a 'desire to mitigate traditional attitudes of mistrust [toward the government] and rehabilitate a role for the state in the protection of free speech values' (Stone 2007: 75).

Throughout *Liberalism Divided*, Fiss portrays American liberals at war with each other over free speech issues. He describes how American liberals had opposed the post-war efforts to suppress communist ideas, then remained united in the 1960s in defending the protests and demonstrations associated with the Civil Rights Movement. Thereafter, however, the appearance of unity was shattered by new agendas and by tensions between the values of equality (if this is given a strong interpretation) and individual liberty.

On its face, the First Amendment protects 'the freedom of speech' by limiting the power of Congress, and as American constitutional law has developed, all branches and levels of government in America. It provides that the government must 'make no law' that abridges the freedom. Historically, eighteenth-century Americans may have been reassured that the recently established federal Congress could not use its power in an overweening way to impinge on their individual liberties. Fiss, however, sees the *purpose* of the First Amendment as expanding the range of political and social viewpoints that are up for serious public discussion. He views governments and their agencies as having a broad power to curate speech, so long as they act in accordance with this ulterior purpose.

Accordingly, he sketches two rival views of free speech. One sees its purpose as protecting individual interests in self-expression, and identifies the state as 'the threat' (Fiss 1996a: 5; Fiss's emphasis). The alternative view, and the one that he supports, assigns to the First Amendment a markedly different purpose of ensuring full debate on political issues, with all points of view being heard. The deeper idea, therefore, is not to protect individual freedom to dissent from popular ideas or depart from approved ways of life. Rather, it is to preserve the collective right of the people to determine political directions.

As Fiss describes these two approaches, they sound a bit like Benjamin Constant's liberty of the moderns and liberty of the ancients – or like the respective views of Isaiah Berlin and Jean-Jacques Rousseau. But neither approach identified by Fiss quite matches Constant's view – which attempts to embrace both kinds of liberty – or the traditional Millian position. In *On Liberty*, the liberty of thought and discussion is a liberty from the tyranny of prevailing opinion *and* from state censorship. It cannot be said, then, that Mill views the government as *the* threat. Moreover, the approach described in *On Liberty* is to avoid suppression of opinions on a wide variety of topics of general importance, not only those closely related to legislation and government policy. For example, Mill's liberty of thought and discussion included free discussion of philosophical, moral, theological and scientific opinions.

On Liberty has much to say about the importance of individual self-expression, but it also elaborates the collective interest in open discussion of opinions and ideas. That interest arises at the level of human societies but also at the level of humanity itself. It follows that Mill's liberal account of free speech – or more accurately, liberty of thought and discussion – is considerably more subtle than the first view that Fiss describes.

To labour a point that I hope has become clear, Fiss does not in any way seek to protect liberal values such as spontaneity and original thinking. On the contrary, when reading *Liberalism Divided* and *The Irony of Free Speech* as a whole we must inevitably notice how disdainful he is of the whole idea of individual autonomy or freedom.

Fiss would impugn many government actions that have the effect, as he sees it, of cramping public discussion, even if they do so through an indirect and unintended process. But he is not primarily focused on whether certain viewpoints are being officially censored, and indeed he supports silencing viewpoints wherever he believes this will enrich public debate about political topics. Fiss ascribes to the courts a power to determine whether particular actions by the state really do enrich debate, or whether they are counterproductive. As he seems to understand, this would involve the courts in conducting wide-ranging investigations and making politically contentious decisions.

We can also see in *Liberalism Divided* and *The Irony of Free Speech* an emphasis on equality as a constitutional value on a par with liberty. Fiss traces the central place of equality to the Civil War, the guarantee of equal protection of the laws in the Fourteenth Amendment, the outcome of *Brown v. Board of Education* and what he regards as a subsequent transformation of the constitutional order and its underlying philosophy. For Fiss, equality has become a defining goal within American liberal thought, and this has implications for freedom of speech, since 'the pursuit of egalitarian objectives often requires strong exercises of state power, including curbs on speech or expressive activity' (Fiss 1996a: 4). Thus, the political value of equality supports a broad power for governments to act as needed to advance the position of Black Americans and other subordinated groups.

Throughout his analysis, Fiss concentrates our attention on what he identifies as the *purposes* of the First Amendment and other core rights-granting provisions of the US Constitution. Although it is largely implicit, he is clearly not very concerned about whether governments and courts conform their actions to the wording of the constitutional text.

'Liberalism' divided

Fiss suggests, somewhat persuasively, that there was little in the way of division within American liberalism over free speech issues during the 1960s and early 1970s. For example there was little internal disagreement over landmark Supreme Court cases such as *New York Times v. Sullivan*, *Brandenburg v. Ohio* and the *Pentagon Papers Case*. For Fiss, American liberals' support for these outcomes demonstrated that there was little of countervailing value at stake: American liberals of this era were not overly troubled about the reputations of public officials, the dangers posed by a small and isolated Klan rally or the sensitivity of a government report based largely on materials already in the public domain.

Fiss identifies a division within American liberalism that arose in the second half of the 1970s and then into the 1980s, with a new set of issues relating to pornography and hate speech, political activists' access to privately owned spaces, government facilities, and the mass media, and problems associated with state subsidy of the arts. In a succession of later situations, some American liberals wanted stronger, more positive, rights for speech whose content they approved of, combined with restrictions on speech whose content they viewed as harmful.

Fiss echoes Marcuse's complaint from the 1960s that critics of the established order are, though tolerated, given inadequate access to the mass media to challenge mainstream assumptions (see, for example, Fiss 1996a: 50). Thus, fundamental critiques of the existing economic structure, the viability of capitalism and the justice of capitalist markets are kept off the political agenda without being actively censored and suppressed. Writing at a time before the rise of social media, Fiss acknowledges the existence of avenues for dissident voices in op-ed columns, letters to editors, public access cable channels and so on, but he argues that these pale beside the air time on radio and television available to the rich and privileged. Accordingly, he argues for legislative and judicial policies that will facilitate the spread of unpopular views, though he mainly seems to have in mind radical critiques of consumerism and capitalism.

Accordingly, *Liberalism Divided* criticizes several Supreme Court cases, including *City Council v. Taxpayers for Vincent* (decided 15 May 1984), in which the court upheld a city ordinance that prohibited posting material (including political campaign posters) on utility poles and other items of public property. Similarly, in *United States v. Kokinda* (decided 27 June 1990) the United States Postal Service was allowed to prevent solicitation on its property by a political advocacy organization.

In neither of these cases was the government or one of its agencies attempting to suppress an unpopular or disliked viewpoint. Nor was the government creating a space that was open to speech while being selective about which viewpoints were permitted. In short, no law was being made – and nor was any other government action being taken – to suppress a disliked viewpoint or opinion. Nonetheless, the practical effect was more harmful to some groups than others, namely groups that were desperate for forums where their ideas could be presented to the public.

Here, Fiss has a point about the tilt of the political playing field. However, he overreaches when he asks, rhetorically, 'What, then, is left of free speech?' if privately owned shopping malls, government premises and infrastructure and so on are not opened up to provide access for marginalized political opinions (Fiss 1996a: 64). There is, however, a straightforward answer to this question. Pretty much *everything* is left of free speech in its most obvious and traditional sense. Notwithstanding Fiss's reproach, America's governments (and their various agencies) are severely limited in their ability to punish US citizens and residents for their expressed views on controversial topics. Unpopular, unconventional or heretical views are permitted without punishments for their proponents such as existed in earlier eras. Contrast the experiences of the Albigensians (slaughtered in their hundreds of thousands), Jan Hus, Michael Servetus and Giordano Bruno (burned at the stake), Galileo (subjected to lifetime house arrest) or Richard Carlile (who spent much of his adult life in prison).

The First Amendment even permits radicals to question America's fundamental economic and political institutions. What it cannot guarantee is that those radicals will receive equal time, and be taken as seriously by the public, as other speakers who more or less accept their society's fundamental institutions and conduct their debates accordingly. Whether or not radical ideas can make headway will depend on many circumstances, but one difference from earlier times is that radical ideas were once viewed with much greater fear and suppressed far more savagely in case they became popular.

In principle, Fiss accepts the constitutional rule against coerced speech, dating back to *West Virginia State Board of Education v. Barnette* in the 1940s (see my discussion in Chapter 6). He suggests that the rule is misapplied in cases such as *Pacific Gas & Electric Company v. Public Utilities Commission* (decided 25 February 1986), where the Supreme Court struck down an order that a public utility company provide customers with a message by a public advocacy group. This message was an attempted rebuttal of the company's own message in its newsletter. The principle here, and in other cases that Fiss objects to, is that freedom of speech includes a right *not* to convey messages that you disagree with (and might even detest).

Fiss compares coerced speech with the taxation system, which inevitably requires taxpayers to contribute to activities that they oppose or dislike, whether it be wars, particular books bought by public libraries or other things requiring public expenditure. But this is not the same. As taxpayers, we must accept – perhaps grudgingly – that some government revenue to which we've contributed is deployed to finance actions and speech that we object to. This does not entail that we must accept a further step by the government in requiring us to engage in that speech ourselves.

What seems clear is that many radicals by the late 1970s, and then through the 1980s and beyond, had lost trust in liberal values and principles as sufficient for their particular social goals. As we've seen, this was not an entirely new development, since impatience with the pace of change was being expressed even in the 1960s, and with it went disruptive and sometimes even violent tactics. But by the late 1970s and the 1980s, this sentiment extended well beyond David Riesman's minority within a minority, and had become mainstream within what Fiss construes as 'liberalism' – that is, the broader political Left.

I will take up this development more broadly – with less focus on the specific American context – in Chapter 8. Before turning to that, I'll conclude with some remarks about late-1970s feminism, Fiss's reaction to it and the general political mood that emerged in the 1980s.

Feminist disappointment

By the late 1970s there was a sense of disappointment with the achievements of Anglophone second-wave feminism. This movement began in the early 1960s as an effort to emancipate Western women from legal structures, discourses and social expectations that excluded them from positions of power – and indeed, from many everyday jobs and activities – and consigned them to highly restricted life options. Even in the movement's more dramatic styles of presentation in the later 1960s and the early 1970s, its essence had not greatly changed. According to Fiss, 'The early 1970s was an age of unisex' (Fiss 1996a: 69). The struggle against anti-abortion laws was a crucial part of feminist efforts to give women something more like the practical freedoms enjoyed by men.

In itself, all of this was compatible with, and indeed followed from, liberal thought. From its beginnings in the nineteenth century, liberalism sought to do away with dominant and subordinated social classes and to pursue individual liberty for all. Equality for women fitted easily with that goal for change.

As we've seen, American liberals embraced efforts during the Long Sixties to develop a narrow definition of obscenity in the legal sense. As Fiss observes, they 'viewed the sexual politics of the late 1960s as an important source of personal and political freedom' (Fiss 1996a: 2). By contrast, American conservatives supported state censorship aimed at preserving traditional sexual *mores*. In general, the second-wave feminist movement accepted the liberal approach until the mid-1970s.

But beginning around 1975, a new feminist agenda gradually became dominant in the United States and elsewhere – at least in other Anglophone democracies – and it has retained considerable influence ever since. It was especially targeted at what was viewed as the sexual objectification of women. In practical terms, this meant identifying predatory manifestations of male sexuality and, in particular, attempting to eliminate rape, sexual harassment, prostitution and pornography. This does not mean that all feminists embraced all elements of the new agenda. On some issues – especially the regulation of pornography, but more generally the preferred attitude to heterosexual desire – the movement split.

As Fiss observes in what is otherwise a sympathetic account, the 'growing concern with objectification, as both a form and cause of inequality, made even the most ordinary heterosexual relationship suspect' (Fiss 1996a: 70). Feminists with a focus on the new agenda campaigned against pornography in particular, not to preserve traditional ideas of sexual sin but as part of their goal to end the subordination of women as a group.

Fiss's discussion of feminist anti-pornography campaigns concentrates on an ordinance drafted by the feminist legal scholar Catharine A. MacKinnon and the author and activist Andrea Dworkin. The ordinance was introduced by the city of Indianapolis in 1984, but was subsequently struck down as unconstitutional by a US district court (decided 19 November 1984). The court's decision was upheld when the case was heard by the Seventh Circuit Court of Appeals in *American Booksellers Association v. Hudnut* (decided 27 August 1985). Eventually, the US Supreme Court affirmed the outcome without a supporting opinion in *Hudnut v. American Booksellers Association* (decided 24 February 1986).

The ordinance's core element was an elaborate definition of pornography. As cited in the original district court case, the ordinance defined pornography as 'the graphic sexually explicit subordination of women, whether in pictures or in words, that also includes one or more of the following' – followed by a long series of impugned kinds of depictions, arranged in six paragraphs.[8] These ranged from depictions of violent sexual conduct, including of women taking pleasure in being raped, to relatively mild depictions of women 'as sexual objects for domination, conquest, violation, exploitation, possession, or use, or through postures or positions of servility or submission'.

The ordinance provided a complex scheme of prohibitions, remedies, permitted defences and disallowed defences. It is noteworthy that a general ban on 'trafficking' (i.e. producing, selling, exhibiting or distributing) pornography as defined did not apply to all forms covered by the statutory definition. Specifically, it did not apply to depictions of women meeting the definition only because of relatively mild elements. However, other prohibitions and remedies applied to all of the itemized forms of pornography. Some of these provisions were clearly acceptable from a mainstream liberal viewpoint: for example, some were prohibitions on using coercion or fraud to induce participation in creating pornography.

The content and structure of the ordinance made it irrelevant whether the particular portrayal of women had any redeeming literary, artistic, political or scientific value. However, the ordinance specified that the trafficking ban did not apply to isolated passages or parts from a literary or other work. Taken overall, the ordinance contained much wording that can fairly be viewed as rhetorical, obscure, ambiguous, confusing or otherwise open to criticism. Yet it was also a product of much thought, and was doubtless a sincere effort to punish abuses related to the production of pornography and to suppress only the most demeaning hardcore porn.

Although it did not rely on the wording of the *Miller* test, the ordinance was likely to capture little material that added anything to public discussion of ideas and opinions. For liberals, however, there is always a further question as to whether speech or action is so harmful – and harmful in such a way – that it cannot be tolerated. In a book written some years after the failure of the Indianapolis ordinance, MacKinnon uses the familiar language of 'emergency' to justify anti-pornography laws (MacKinnon 1996: 41). But whether the existence, sale, exhibition or distribution of even the most distasteful kinds of pornography ever amounted to an emergency is highly doubtful.

To establish such a claim, rationally compelling evidence would need to be brought of a causal relationship between the availability of demeaning

---

[8]All quotations in this paragraph are from 598 F. Supp. 1316 (S.D. Ind. 1984), 1320.

hardcore porn and a social situation of rampant sexual violence. Despite MacKinnon's anecdotes and speculations, nothing like this has ever been accomplished.

Still, the important point here is not the merits of the anti-pornography critique, or the Indianapolis ordinance in particular. If it comes to that, MacKinnon and others like her had a legitimate concern. Whether or not they were overreacting, they were reacting to something real. There was a possibility that old-style sexist discourses surrounding women – the discursive enforcement of an ideal of chaste domesticity – might be replaced by something just as oppressive in its way. Politically engaged women of the Long Sixties had demanded sexual, as well as social and economic, liberation, but the emerging fear by the late 1970s was that women might now be defined and valued by men *solely* for their sexual appeal and availability, or even worse, as suitable targets for humiliation. As women entered mainstream labour markets in larger numbers, experiences of sexual harassment in the workplace seemed to confirm such fears.

For current purposes, the important point is that debates over these issues revealed conflict within the political Left. In the United States, an important segment within 'liberalism' – the new breed of radical feminists especially associated with MacKinnon – sought to narrow, rather than enlarge, the First Amendment's protection of free speech.

The disillusioned Left

We have never lived in perfectly liberal societies, and my references throughout this book to becoming post-liberal do not suggest that there was a golden age when liberal democracies were fully liberal. But for a time, we seemed to be on the way. During the 1960s and 1970s, a mode of left-wing politics based on toleration, individualism and traditional liberal ideas made progress in obtaining social change and legal reform. The Millian harm principle had prestige and influence; censorship and social *mores* relaxed.

These successes for the Left – and their ongoing consolidation – were significant, but they were not the total transformation of society that many activists had hoped for, and many forms of oppression remained, including continued racism, poverty and inner urban decay. Traditional liberal politics gave ground to new approaches based on group identities rather than an emphasis on individual desires, pleasures and liberties.

As early as the 1960s, American colleges and universities began to introduce schemes aimed at increasing the proportion of African American students in their programmes. This meant more than a policy of non-exclusion or equal opportunity in the strict sense of not discriminating against people from historically subordinated groups. In some cases, colleges and universities rationalized the approach as one of seeking a more diverse student body for its educational benefit to all. This 'diversity' rationale was specifically approved by Justice Lewis F. Powell, Jr. of the US Supreme Court in *Regents of the University of California v. Bakke* (decided 28 June 1978), then by a majority of Supreme Court judges in *Grutter v. Bollinger* (decided 23 June 2003).

The outcome of these cases was that some systems of student admissions would be unlawful in the United States if they plainly discriminated in one way or the other on racial grounds. However, some weight could be given to racial background in order to further the goal of creating a demographically diverse student body. Thanks largely to Justice Powell's opinion in *Bakke*, the word *diversity* came to denote an important public value in the United States and beyond, perhaps even, as the scholar John M. Ellis has suggested, 'the key value in academic life' (Ellis 2020: 62).

Lying behind this educational goal, however, though not always stated openly, was a larger remedial goal: integrating a uniquely subordinated, and to some extent (understandably) alienated, group into the social mainstream. While this seems commendable, affirmative action initiatives in this sense remain controversial in the United States and elsewhere even today. As I complete the manuscript of this book, affirmative action initiatives are under renewed legal challenge in the American court system and may well be condemned as unconstitutional by the current Supreme Court by the time you read these words.

In 1979, Margaret Thatcher became the UK's prime minister, while Ronald Reagan was elected as US president in November 1980. By this time, right-wing politicians in the United States were using the word *liberal* (whether as an adjective or a noun) as a term of a derision. This was a far cry from the efforts – hopeless, but not entirely pointless – of Herbert Hoover in the 1930s to position himself as the true liberal in opposition to Franklin D. Roosevelt.

Black American activists were alienated by Reagan's election on a right-wing policy platform, and by increasing racism – or at least the appearance of it – in grassroots American society. During and immediately after the 1980 presidential campaign, the United States saw an uptick in violent crimes against African Americans (Pinkney 1984: 171–2). On college and university campuses, there was a sense of resurgent racism, including what Samuel Walker calls 'a disturbing pattern of attacks – verbal and physical – on minority-group students' (Walker 1994: 6).

In all, the political Left was disillusioned by the late 1970s. Radicals of the time had grown more pessimistic about their ability to produce rapid, overdue change through political movements based on liberal values. There was a sense that the legal and political victories obtained to date had been incomplete and insufficient, that they'd achieved little in improving the situation of people belonging to subordinated groups. Indeed, there was a perception of hard-won gains actually being reversed. What we call the Long Sixties was thus an era of momentous change, but one that ended with radicals feeling disappointed, disillusioned and open to new approaches.

Postscript: At a late stage of production of this book, the US Supreme Court handed down its decision in *Students for Fair Admissions, Inc. v. President and Fellows of Harvard University* (decided 29 June 2023). The practical consequences remain to be fully tested. However, the undoubted gist of the decision is to tighten the statutory and constitutional restrictions on race-conscious admission practices in American universities.

8 THE MAKING OF A POST-LIBERAL CULTURE

The birth of identity politics

The disillusionment of the political Left at the end of the Long Sixties motivated a further – and now intellectually deeper, more theoretically complex – struggle. By the 1980s, activists increasingly rejected ideas such as racial integration, colour blindness and treating individuals on their particular merits. These ideas had come to seem naïve and ineffectual. In the United States, racist attitudes and racial disadvantage persisted despite victories won by the Civil Rights Movement, and this prompted new kinds of theorizing, notably an approach to legal scholarship called Critical Race Theory (for discussion, see Pluckrose and Lindsay 2020: 111–14).

One revealing text is Derrick Bell's 1987 book – reprinted in 1989 with a new appendix – *And We Are Not Saved*. Bell was a Black American law professor, based at Harvard, and a foundational figure in Critical Race Theory. Like many others, he lamented that legal victories such as *Brown v. Board of Education* in 1954 had not led to racial equality. He formulated hard questions for American society, including people of his own racial background: 'How have we failed – and why? What does this failure mean – for black people and for whites? Where do we go from here? Should we redirect the quest for racial justice?' (Bell 1989: 3).

Bell explored these issues in a book that is both a masterpiece of legal analysis and a literary *tour de force*, using fables and dialogues to illuminate the social plight of Black Americans, the responses of the courts and the possibilities for further legal and social struggle. *And We Are Not Saved* expresses his cynicism about the motives of the law courts, even in cases such as *Brown v. Board of Education*, and about the prospects for genuine good will from white Americans towards their Black counterparts. Accordingly, Bell and other critical race theorists explored more assertive, or even militant, solutions to racial inequality. Some of them published intellectually forceful articles supporting restrictions on racist speech (for discussion, see Walker 1994: 134).

The politics of identity as we now experience it is a product of the late 1970s and especially the 1980s. In fact, a frequency search using the Google Books Ngram Viewer shows almost no use of the term *identity politics* until the mid to late 1980s and then it takes off steeply throughout the 1990s.[1] Online tools such as the Ngram Viewer have limitations, but Ngram searches give at least a reasonable approximation of when a neologism (or a formerly rare expression) takes off and enters into widespread usage.

The OED defines *identity politics*, in the relevant sense, as 'adherence by a group of people of a particular religion, race, social background, etc., to political beliefs or goals specific to the group concerned, as opposed to conforming to traditional broad-based party politics'. The OED records three examples of the term from the 1970s. The first refers to difficulties encountered by the 1960s student movement in establishing a viable role for itself as both a movement protesting against the oppression of students and a vanguard organization to inspire and assist more clearly subordinated or oppressed groups (see Gitlin 1973: 27).[2] Arguably, this is not a clear example of what *identity politics* now means.

The OED's second example, however, is more on point. It is from a manifesto drafted in 1977 by members of the Combahee River Collective, most accessibly available in a 1979 anthology of socialist feminist thought. This document represented the position of a group of Black feminists involved in activism against what they saw as multiple, intersecting and simultaneous oppressions experienced by Black women. Their manifesto

---

[1] All frequency searches with the Google Books Ngram Viewer checked and confirmed 17 December 2022.
[2] Edmund Fawcett states that the first use of the term *identity politics* in its current sense recorded in the OED is from 1989 (Fawcett 2018: 435). But the OED's examples from the late 1970s are close to the current sense. They show the practice and idea of identity politics – originally with a positive valence – first emerging at the end of the Long Sixties as left-wing ideology and praxis.

uses the term *identity politics* to convey their struggle against their own oppression rather than joining movements with the aim of liberating others (Combahee River Collective 1979: 365).

The final 1970s example in the OED is from a 1979 article by the sociologist Renee R. Anspach. Anspach's analysis of identity politics introduces the idea in the context of political activism among physically disabled people and former mental patients. Anspach portrays this kind of activism as a recent development: first manifesting in the mid-1970s and (as of 1979) still taking shape. While the rise of a disability rights movement was significant in itself, Anspach's article is most helpful for current purposes for its author's sense of a new *kind* of politics, albeit one with inspirational precursors such as the Civil Rights Movement and second-wave feminism.

As Anspach observes, identity politics *circa* 1979 was directed at changes in institutions and public policy. However, it was distinctive insofar as each new movement fashioned and promoted a collective identity, and in doing so urged a positive image of the self on its own participants and on society at large (Anspach 1979: 766). Each movement had its own history, and hence its own background conditions that prompted its emergence at a particular time. Perhaps some movements had better founded grievances than others. But at any rate, they fed off each other's public prominence, took heart from each other's successes, and provided successive new movements with the vocabulary and metaphors to support political action (see Anspach 1979: 771).

Implicit in Anspach's analysis is a commonality among these identity movements that is revealed by frequent references to a group's liberation, pride, power or rights (e.g. women's liberation, gay pride, Black power, civil rights). Expressions such as these assert a group identity and ambition, while challenging what is viewed as a disempowering and unjust society.

The mutual support that developed among early identity movements expressed itself in numerous ways, but Anspach provides an illuminating example. At one point, he quotes from the polemical literature of a particular disability rights organization. It states that the organization's goal is 'to transform the classist, racist, and sexist society, with its oppressive power relations, that caused our pain and incarceration' (Anspach 1979: 772). Here we see, in a relatively early form, the assertion of solidarity between activists working on behalf of diverse groups. One change since the late 1970s is that we are now less likely to see hallmarks of classic Marxism such as references to a 'classist' society. That aside, an expanding set of categories came to be analogized with women and racial minorities, and they looked for support from each other.

The usual suspects: The Frankfurt School and postmodernism

Throughout the 1980s and beyond, there was a sense of more diffuse forms of oppression and power than found in clearly discriminatory laws such as those in the United States during the Jim Crow era. New approaches to political activism were supported by new theoretical approaches. In particular, activists looked to critiques of liberal thought and the Enlightenment tradition, based on the Frankfurt School of critical theory and the work of iconic theorists from France such as Michel Foucault, Jean-François Lyotard, Jacques Derrida and Jean Baudrillard. The latter were, at best, a loose group whose ideas are often lumped together, accurately or not, under the label *postmodernism*.

As we've seen, scholars from the Frankfurt School acknowledged the failure (at least to date) of Marxist predictions that the industrial proletariat would be reduced to grinding poverty and forced to overthrow the capitalist order. Nonetheless, the Frankfurt School viewed twentieth-century capitalism as a system of domination, even if it presented a relatively soft and kind veneer: that is, the majority of workers were granted sufficient comforts to acquiesce in the system's overall functioning. From this viewpoint, the Scientific Revolution and the Enlightenment had failed in their goal of improving the human condition, and instead had produced new tools for a privileged minority to dominate the majority as well as nature itself.

In *Zealotry and Academic Freedom*, Neil Hamilton argues that a mix of ideas that arose in the 1980s became the ideology of the academic and cultural Left, and that it hardened into a new form of zealotry. This mix included ideas adapted from European postmodernism and ideas that supported 'the movement for diversity based on race, gender [i.e. sex], or other status' (Hamilton [1995]2017: 56). As Hamilton understands postmodernism, it amounts to the claim that we live in societies whose governing social, political and economic arrangements cannot be given any objective justification, or even improved through processes of rational inquiry that lead to better policy. Rather, our societies should be viewed as systems of power in which some people end up subjugating the rest.[3]

This crudely represents the complex analyses of history, language, power and much else that appears in the work of so-called postmodernists, but it's a fair summary of how these authors have been interpreted by political activists in the English-speaking world. It's a worldview that could, in principle, be paralysing, since no new set of structures could be conclusively justified as an improvement on the status quo. But in practice, it can give support to an activist process. The aim is, first, to identify the mechanisms of subjugation and, second, to empower subjugated groups. That initially involves raising their awareness of the social reality and hence their level of resentment. This can motivate resistance, if only by revealing the hidden dynamics of power, undermining the prestige attached to certain discourses and institutions, and encouraging small acts of nonconformity or rebellion.

But such an approach can also encourage efforts to *obtain and employ* power. It can lead to an attitude that the sphere of public discussion is a site for struggle: the aim is cultural and political victory rather than a search for truth or understanding. This leaves no room for the Kantian or Millian idea of public discussion as a progressive enterprise. On a vulgar postmodernist approach, participants in the public sphere might guard their own freedom to take part in cultural conversations. Once they have the upper hand, however, they have little reason to refrain from suppressing rival ideas to whatever extent is achievable. Thus, some postmodernists – or their imitators – tended in the 1980s and beyond to convert political controversies into matters of, as Charles Taylor has expressed it, 'power and counterpower' and 'taking sides in solidarity' (Taylor 1994: 70).

To illustrate with just one example of how this could work, I'll turn to an article by the legal scholar Martin F. Katz, published in the *University of Western Ontario Law Review* in 1985. Katz's thesis is that the meanings of statutes and other legal materials are indeterminate, and can be chosen for their social impact. To illustrate the point, he refers to debates

---

[3]How, if at all, does postmodernism in this sense relate to 'postmodernist' art, architecture, narrative fiction and so on – a set of styles, often playful or parodic, that partly assimilate and partly react against high Modernist forms and techniques? That's a good question, but it would take us well outside the scope of this study.

over abortion, where the 'pro-life' side is likely to claim that 'abortion is wrong because it involves the murder of an unborn baby' (Katz 1985: 64). The 'pro-choice' side, of course, will likely make claims about the autonomy of the pregnant woman (though *pace* Katz, it might also offer arguments about the moral status of embryos and foetuses).

For Katz, it is possible to cut through all this by asking what subjugations are instigated by the respective positions.[4] 'After the deconstruction', he puts it – once we're enlightened by the works of Derrida and Foucault – we can recognize that the law is merely 'an elaborate system for the exercise of political power' (Katz 1985: 66). We can reinterpret its norms freely irrespective of what initially seem to be clear words in statutes and reported cases.

It then becomes a matter of deciding between policies. One policy subjugates women by imposing on them 'the full weight of the social burden of the sex act' and denying them 'the choice of what their role in society will be' – thus assigning them 'the time-honoured role of wife and mother' (Katz 1985: 64). Conversely, the pro-choice policy excludes men from the decision of whether or when to have children 'except to the extent that the women enjoying full self-determination choose to consult them' (Katz 1985: 65).

Katz's rhetoric reveals his preference for the pro-choice position, even though he does not explicitly spell this out. I share that political position for different reasons, but Katz's analysis completely sets aside arguments as to whether abortion can be regarded as the murder of an unborn baby. It will not satisfy anyone who sincerely believes that abortion is murder to be told that the entire moral and metaphysical debate involving the status of the unborn can be replaced by a simple choice to take a side in solidarity with either women or men. Once postmodernist theory is invoked in this way, public discussion is reduced to an effort to identify which groups are most affected by various kinds of subjugation or oppression, and the further tendency is for those groups to be regarded, in effect, as sacred. In the extreme, illiberal methods such as 'monitoring and controlling permissible speech' are used to accommodate the real

---

[4]For this idea of 'instigating subjugations', Katz cites an article by Michael J. Shapiro (Shapiro 1984). Shapiro's article, in turn, draws on material in Michel Foucault's collection of interviews and other shorter works *Power/Knowledge* (see especially Foucault 1980: 92–108) among numerous other citations of Foucault and other continental European thinkers.

or imagined sensitivities of subjugated demographic groups (Hamilton [1995]2017: 61).

This does not mean that the usual suspects – the Frankfurt School and postmodernism – *caused* identity politics as it began in the 1970s and developed in the 1980s and thereafter. That can be better accounted for by experiences in the Long Sixties and afterwards, including various sources of disappointment and disillusion on the political Left but also anxieties on the Right. It is most unlikely, for example, that the multicultural policies of Margaret Thatcher's right-wing UK government in the 1980s had anything to do with influences from Marcuse or Foucault, or with any earnest theorizing about social domination and subordination, instigating subjugations, and the like.

These schools of thought did, however, provide tools for social and political analysis that were seen by many theorists and activists as more promising than traditional styles of liberal thought based on ideas of toleration, liberty, meliorism, pluralism and harm.

Developments in Anglo-American philosophy

At the start of the 1970s, academic political philosophy in the mainstream Anglo-American tradition was something of a moribund field. However, it was soon revitalized when the Harvard philosophers John Rawls and Robert Nozick published important books (Rawls 1971; Nozick 1974) drawing upon concepts of a social contract going back to Hobbes, Locke and earlier.

Rawls defended a strongly egalitarian variation of liberal theory, fitting smoothly with the American style of New Deal liberalism, though supported by innovative and striking arguments. Nozick developed a version of political libertarianism that proposed only a minimal role for state action and somewhat resembled the radical liberalism of Wilhelm von Humboldt or Herbert Spencer in the nineteenth century – not necessarily employing their arguments, but with similarly individualist conclusions. At this stage, the debate was largely about rival conceptions of justice in the distribution of material rewards and wealth, and what kind of political institutions would produce defensible outcomes. Rawls's thinking became highly influential not only within academic philosophy but in the wider world of public policy. Nozick's response, meanwhile, was viewed as a challenging critique if not a viable alternative.

During the 1980s and 1990s, political philosophy developed in a new direction that it has largely followed since. Anglo-American (including Australian, Canadian, etc.) political philosophers showed increased interest in the situations of religious, ethnic, cultural and racial groups – as well as in feminist theory. Titles and topics increasingly involved issues of *identity, inclusion, diversity, difference* and *recognition* in special senses that those terms acquired. Debates about immigration, multiculturalism and the issues surrounding equal opportunity became more commonplace.

Thus, Canadian philosopher Will Kymlicka's *Liberalism, Community, and Culture* (originally published in 1989) and *Multicultural Citizenship* (1995) were important contributions to political philosophy at the time. Kymlicka sought to defend liberal theory (of a sort) while also defending the ambitions of cultural groups within larger societies to *survive* – not necessarily unchanged, but nonetheless without being dissolved into the surrounding culture. This entailed a liberal argument for at least some rights to be held by collectives such as the Aboriginal peoples of Canada or the Francophone culture of Quebec.

The issue of recognition became prominent in political philosophy as well as in practical politics. Here the debate was over demands for acknowledgement made on behalf of minority cultures, religions or (usually traditional) ways of life. The demands, that is, extended beyond toleration, indifference or even guarantees of survival, to include positive ascriptions of worth.[5] An important collection on this general topic, edited by Amy Gutmann, was entitled *Multiculturalism: Examining the Politics of Recognition* (Gutmann 1994). This included thoughtful essays by Charles Taylor and other major philosophers.[6]

Like Kymlicka's work, Taylor's wide-ranging essay considers the ambitions of minority cultural groups to survive within larger societies. This desire for distinct cultures to survive without losing their identity is not easily accommodated by liberal theory, where the emphasis is

---

[5]One important contribution to this debate from outside the Anglosphere was Axel Honneth's *The Struggle for Recognition* (1995), originally published in German 1992.
[6]An earlier version of this book with a slightly different title was published in 1992. The 1994 volume includes additional contributions by Jürgen Habermas and K. Anthony Appiah.

on individual liberty and it's accepted that the cumulative choices of individuals might lead over time to the dissolution of present-day collectivities and their replacement by something else. Nonetheless, Taylor suggests that liberalism can grant this desire up to a point. That is, liberals of a less doctrinaire sort can find value in the integrity of cultures and the ways of life that they enable (Taylor 1994: 60–1).

Be that as it may, the problems become more difficult when cultural representatives demand more – that is, when they demand recognition, and hence an attitude of something like esteem, or that Westerners 'acknowledge their *worth*' (Taylor 1994: 64; Taylor's emphasis). This demand has inevitable difficulties, some of which Taylor explores in his own terms. Broadly: By what standards can we make judgements about the value of cultures? Are there objective – that is, culture-transcending – standards that can be used, and if there are, why assume that all cultures will measure up well (let alone equally well) when they are applied? Conversely, if modern Westerners are expected to apply *their own standards* for making such judgements, there is even less guarantee that this will produce positive ascriptions of worth. If there are really no standards to apply, and it's just a matter of taking sides, this may not grant what is actually demanded, and it might, once understood by those on the receiving end, be viewed not only as second best but even as condescending and insulting.

This leaves Taylor with no more than what he views as a reasonable and good-willed presumption or working hypothesis: 'the claim … that all human cultures that have animated whole societies over some considerable stretch of time have something important to say to all human beings' (Taylor 1994: 66). Expressed at such an abstract level, this does sound reasonable (doesn't it?), and perhaps difficult to deny without prejudice or ill will. I am happy to embrace Taylor's presupposition about human cultures other than my own, but even so, this does not preclude finding much in them that seems objectionable.

A difficulty with *recognition* in the sense at hand is that individuals might have sincere and plausible objections to particular cultures, religions or ways of life, or at least to ideas or practices associated with them. In that case, any attempt to push beyond mutual forbearance can lead to censorship of at least some people's serious and principled beliefs, and the ways in which these are expressed. That is: if we push beyond toleration, some things will not even be tolerated. Applied to them, the virtue of tolerance becomes a vice.

Conversely, it's possible to maintain an objection while also exercising toleration and even entertaining the possibility that there is an element of truth or value to be found in whatever is being tolerated. The relevant degree of toleration might depend on numerous aspects of a situation. Depending on the circumstances, we might tolerate cultures, religions or ways of life that we object to, even to the extent of not publicly criticizing them in any harsh way. Alternatively, we might criticize them harshly but go no further into territory such as punishment and censorship. Either way, an approach that involves significant toleration might fall short of a positive ascription of worth. In many cases, a demand for recognition might be excessive or unrealistic.

Consider, for example, religious beliefs that seem implausible to most people in Western societies, such as belief in the existence of the Olympian gods or in a literal Satan – a vastly powerful and evil being who works mischief in the world. For all I know, some of my readers might hold these particular beliefs, but even they are likely to view some religious beliefs as simply absurd. There is no guarantee that such beliefs will avoid being marginalized in a particular society where they are widely regarded as not even rational candidates for truth. The same applies to moral beliefs that are widely viewed as ridiculous and obviously untenable. These might retain some adherents, but there is no guarantee that they won't be marginalized and viewed with suspicion by the great majority in a particular society. A real-world example in current Western societies might be the belief in a moral imperative to perform female genital mutilations.

In the late 1990s, the feminist philosopher Susan Moller Okin initiated an important debate about tensions between feminist hopes and policies of multiculturalism (see Okin et al. 1999). Okin acknowledged that Western liberal democracies were far from perfect in attaining an ideal of sex equality, but she argued that they were further advanced in that direction than more traditional cultures. This prompted a question of how such an uncomfortable truth, if such it was, ought to affect policy deliberation. How far, that is, should Western governments tolerate or encourage cultures where women (and indeed others, such as children) are subjected to illiberal constraints?

Iris Marion Young, who was influenced by continental as well as Anglo-American philosophy, made important contributions to the emerging debates with books entitled *Justice and the Politics of Difference* (1990) and *Inclusion and Democracy* (2000). Young saw herself as developing a post-liberal political philosophy addressing inequality and oppression at the level of groups, rather than focusing on individual rights and liberties or on specific harms suffered by individuals.

John Rawls himself published an important book, *Political Liberalism*, in 1993. Here, he defended a tolerant and pluralistic society, based on no single comprehensive worldview or theory of the good, and characterized by familiar liberal rights. The hope expressed throughout was that such arrangements could be endorsed by the society's constituent individuals and communities from within their own comprehensive understandings, and not necessarily for the same reasons. Rawls devoted attention to the issue of how to interact with people and communities whose comprehensive understandings of the world did not permit them to endorse such pluralism and mutual toleration.

I have sketched this body of philosophical literature only briefly and incompletely. We could find many other examples of the transformation of political philosophy in the 1980s and 1990s, and I've passed over important developments such as the critique of liberal assumptions from 'communitarian' perspectives, such as the Harvard-based philosopher Michael Sandel's critique of Rawls in *Liberalism and the Limits of Justice* (1982). Work such as this inspired responses from a new generation of liberal theorists such as Kymlicka.

The new developments in political philosophy did not necessarily mean endorsement of multiculturalism or any particular position related to identity politics. They did, however, involve dramatically increased attention from English-speaking political philosophers to cultures, demographic identities and group interests.

Hate speech and the campus speech codes

As Samuel Walker has explained, groups representing African and Jewish Americans during the 1950s and 1960s did not seek restrictions on hate speech, however defined. Instead, their priority was constitutional protection of their own speech and activism. They employed tactics that included hyperbolic, provocative, intensely emotional and often inaccurate rhetoric to rally their supporters and attack opponents – an approach that might well have failed in a legal regime that was less protective of free speech. During the Long Sixties, restrictions on free speech attracted no powerful advocates on the Left. On the contrary, the American Council for Civil Liberties (ACLU) advocated forcefully and effectively for the freedoms in the First Amendment. In the United States, therefore, hate speech laws failed to materialize because they were stranded 'without an advocate' (Walker 1994: 11).

However, 1980s university and college campuses were very different environments from American society as a whole. Here, the ACLU was not strongly represented. Instead, well-organized student bodies that supported restrictions on the speech and conduct of students faced poorly organized opposition (Walker 1994: 16). The motive and opportunity were aligned for efforts to stamp out campus-based expressions of racism.

This was the background to the college speech codes adopted in the 1980s by many educational institutions in the United States. These codes drew on theories and priorities that were inconsistent with previous post-war American thinking about freedom of speech (though not necessarily with developments at the time in feminist theory or in international human rights law). Once legally challenged, however, the speech codes were quickly defeated. US district courts struck down codes developed by the University of Michigan (ruled as constitutionally invalid in 1989) and the University of Wisconsin (ruled as invalid in 1991).

The University of Wisconsin's speech code was relatively narrow in its drafting. Although it referred to a raft of protected characteristics – race, sex, religion, colour, creed, disability, sexual orientation, national origin, ancestry and age – it prohibited only comments or other expression that amounted to attacks on individuals. Interpreted and applied sensibly, this might fall within the long-established 'fighting words' doctrine. Furthermore, the Wisconsin code specifically exempted opinions on general topics that might be expressed in classroom discussions.

Taken as a whole, the 1980s speech codes have a bad reputation among free speech advocates. However, their content and implementation varied, and in some cases they were arguably consistent with traditional liberal thinking such as in chapter II of Mill's *On Liberty*. But in any event, their fate was sealed by the US Supreme Court when it scrutinized the St. Paul Bias Motivated Crime Ordinance, enacted by the City of St. Paul in 1990. This contained a prohibition on placing symbols that could reasonably be known to arouse 'anger, alarm or resentment in others on the basis of race, color, creed, religion or gender' (505 US 377, 380 (1992)). It made specific reference to burning crosses and Nazi swastikas.

In June 1990, a group of teenagers burned a crudely made cross in the front yard of an African American family. One of the teenagers, known in the court records as 'R.A.V.', was found guilty of violating the ordinance, which led to a series of challenges to its constitutionality, culminating in a hearing before the Supreme Court. In *R.A.V. v. St. Paul* (decided 22 June 1992), all nine judges held the provision to be constitutionally invalid, but they were divided in their reasoning.

Five judges held that even if the ordinance referred only to symbols that amounted to fighting words, it was nonetheless invalid. Although fighting words formed one of the categories of unprotected speech, this group of judges held that laws relating to such unprotected categories could sometimes violate the First Amendment. By analogy, a law banning artistically meritless hardcore pornography – which would fall into the 'obscenity' exception to freedom of speech – would be constitutionally invalid if it were directed at only those pornographic movies in which certain political symbols were displayed. Thus, the St. Paul ordinance failed the constitutional test because it banned only those fighting words expressing racist or similarly bigoted viewpoints.

The other four judges would have reached the same result, but they were critical of the majority's reasoning. They would have invalidated the ordinance on the ground that it was overly broad in including expressive conduct that caused mere hurt feelings, offence or resentment, and did not fall into the narrow category of fighting words. But on either the majority or the minority theory, the case permitted governments and their agencies only limited scope to prohibit racist or otherwise bigoted expression. This restricted the discretion of publicly funded universities to regulate speech on their campuses.

A decade later, however, the Supreme Court upheld a law that prohibited burning a cross in public with intent to intimidate. In *Virginia v. Black* (decided 7 April 2003), most members of the court analysed cross burning in accordance with constitutional doctrine relating to 'true threats' (rather than 'fighting words'). The court held that a state might discriminate between levels of intimidation, and might therefore prohibit only the *most intimidating* symbolic acts, as opposed to prohibiting acts of intimidation that expressed *only certain viewpoints*. To uphold the Virginia statute as constitutional on this basis, it was sufficient that burning a cross in the manner of the Ku Klux Klan had a long and well-known history as a means of announcing impending violence and inducing terror.

Virginia v. Black involved two separate incidents that took place in 1998. In one incident, the cross was burned at a Ku Klux Klan rally on private property with the permission of the owner, who was present throughout. The leader of the rally (Black) was subsequently charged under the statute and found guilty. In the other incident, two individuals (Elliott and O'Mara) attempted to burn a cross in the yard of a Black American man, and they were also found guilty of crimes under the statute. When appeal proceedings reached the Supreme Court, Black's conviction was overturned because the cross had not been burned as an act of intimidation. For technical reasons that need not detain us, the legal proceedings involving Elliott and O'Mara were remanded to the Virginia courts for further proceedings to determine their guilt.

In all, the combined effect of *R.A.V.* and *Virginia v. Black* was to allow prohibitions on threatening speech, while considerably restricting the scope for prohibitions on speech that is merely hurtful, offensive or provocative. That hardly resolved the numerous issues involving discrimination and oppression of Black Americans, but it did set one allowable boundary to racist expression in the United States.

British developments and the problem of blasphemy

Immigrants from former colonies in Africa, Asia and the Caribbean began arriving in the UK in large numbers in the 1950s and early 1960s, leading to racial and cultural tensions when they were met – too often – with incomprehension and bigotry. In these circumstances, imperatives of racial harmony and civil peace became overriding, often of more significance than liberal freedoms in the minds of those shaping policy directions and developing the law. On occasion, this produced surprising results.

In 1976, the British magazine *Gay News* published a homoerotic poem (with an accompanying illustration) about the crucifixion of Jesus of Nazareth. The poem was by an established poet, James Kirkup, and entitled 'The Love That Dares to Speak Its Name'. In response, the morals campaigner Mary Whitehouse initiated a private prosecution under the common law of blasphemous libel. Her targets were the magazine's editor (Denis Lemon) and its publishing company. In the initial trial, both were found guilty, and Lemon was given a suspended prison sense as well as a fine, but the case then worked its way through the judicial system until it reached the highest appellate court. At the time, prior to reforms in 2009 that created the Supreme Court of the UK, this was the House of Lords.[7]

In *Whitehouse v. Lemon* (decided 21 February 1979), the court upheld the convictions. In the circumstances of the 1970s, this was an astonishing result, seemingly against the grain of developments throughout the twentieth century if not before. There had been no recorded prosecution for the crime of blasphemous libel since 1926, and no one had been sent to prison for it since John Gott in 1921. The crime was considered obsolescent by the 1970s, but it had never been removed by statutory reforms (this eventually happened as recently as 2008).

The main legal issue was whether or not the offence required proof of an intention (which might include reckless indifference) to attack the Christian religion and so arouse emotions of shock and resentment in believers. Alternatively, was it sufficient that Lemon had intentionally published the impugned material and that it *actually was blasphemous in that sense*?

The majority of the Law Lords hearing the case upheld the convictions, mostly based on examination of past precedents and whether previous courts had required more in the way of *mens rea* (guilty mind – or the mental element of a crime) than an intention to publish. However, the concurring judgement of Lord Scarman introduced a further twist in the understanding of blasphemy law. He construed its purpose as protecting the beliefs and feelings of Christians – which, in itself, was not especially controversial since the late nineteenth century – and he proposed that it be extended to protect adherents of the full variety of religions:

My Lords, I do not subscribe to the view that the common law offence of blasphemous libel serves no useful purpose in the modern law. On the contrary, I think that there is a case for legislation extending it to protect the religious beliefs and feelings of non-Christians. The offence

---

[7] The technicalities of the old system, prior to 2009, need not detain us. The important point to grasp, to avoid any confusion, is that such a case was, in fact, heard by an 'appellate committee', rather than by the actual House of Parliament.

belongs to a group of criminal offences designed to safeguard the internal tranquillity of the kingdom. In an increasingly plural society such as that of modern Britain it is necessary not only to respect the differing religious beliefs, feelings and practices of all but also to protect them from scurrility, vilification, ridicule and contempt.

([1979] AC 617, 658)

Accordingly, Lord Scanlan saw the law of blasphemous libel as a tool for deterring highly offensive attacks on Christianity. On this approach, there was a case for extending blasphemy law – presumably via statutory reform – to protect other religions. If that had happened, religion in general would have been placed beyond reach of severe or highly aggressive expressions of disrespect.

In addition, Lord Scanlan interpreted Article 9 of the ECHR, which grants a right to freedom of religion, as imposing a positive obligation on 'all of us' to avoid 'insulting or outraging the religious feeling of others' ([1979] AC 617, 665). This approach to the Article is worth dwelling on for a moment. It is somewhat alarming, as it converts what is most naturally understood as a negative right against the state – in this case, a right not to be subjected to religious persecution – into a limitation on free speech.

The European Court of Human Rights has since wrestled with these issues in cases involving blasphemy laws or laws relating to disparagement of religion.[8] It has developed an extensive body of jurisprudence dating back at least to the mid-1990s: see *Otto-Preminger-Institut v. Austria* (decided 20 September 1994) and *Wingrove v. United Kingdom* (decided 25 November 1996).[9] The court has maintained that the expression *the rights of others*, where it appears in the ECHR, includes their right against fellow citizens – as opposed to the state – not to have their feelings hurt by offensive attacks on their religious or moral convictions. According to the court's jurisprudence, this right not to have feelings hurt can impose a positive obligation on the state to restrict the freedom of expression granted in Article 10 of the ECHR.

---

[8]In 1982, a challenge to the outcome of *Whitehouse v. Lemon* was blocked by the European Commission of Human Rights, a body that acted at that time as a gatekeeper for whether cases would be heard by the Strasbourg Court.

[9]I discuss these two cases, among others, in Blackford (2012: 180–5).

However, no such right against other citizens, or positive obligation on the state, is mentioned explicitly in the ECHR itself. Recall that this document was introduced shortly after the Second World War as a protection for individuals – including their ability to express themselves – against overweening exercises of state power. It is not a code of civility between citizen and citizen.

In one recent case, *E.S. v. Austria* (decided 2 October 2018), the court upheld an Austrian law against disparagement of religion. This case involved a right-wing politician who had accused the prophet Muhammad of paedophilia for his supposed (according to the historical sources) sexual intercourse with his child bride Ayesha when she was nine years old. Even more recently, in *Rabcewska v. Poland* (decided 15 September 2022), the court provided a detailed analysis of its past jurisprudence on blasphemy/religious disparagement laws. This case involved a pop singer known as Doda, who'd given an interview in which she made mocking and disparaging comments about the authors of the biblical texts, suggesting that they wrote under the influence of alcohol and marijuana. She was subsequently fined under Polish law, leading to her complaint that her right to freedom of expression under Article 10 of the ECHR had been infringed.

Doda's complaint against the Polish authorities was upheld, but this does not mean that the court overruled its earlier approach in the line of cases culminating in *E.S. v. Austria*. It maintained its view that there are positive obligations on the state to deter extreme religious insult and maintain religious peace. On the factual situation before it, however, the court held that the authorities in Poland had failed to conduct a proper exercise of balancing the singer's freedom of expression against the justifications for constraining it.

An initial, perhaps cynical, guess might be that the court is simply more solicitous towards Islam than to Roman Catholicism. On the other hand, it might have been equally or similarly unwilling to protect accusations of deeply stigmatized conduct, such as paedophilia, if they were aimed, not at Muhammad, but at Jesus or some other universally revered figure in the Christian tradition. By contrast, the court might have viewed Doda's light-hearted remarks for the amusement of her fans as comparatively innocuous and undeserving of punishment. All that said, the cynics might have a point: this case can be interpreted as one example among many of a trend for political and judicial authorities to protect Islam in particular from what is seen as harsh and inflammatory criticism.[10]

Lord Scanlan's observations on multiculturalism in 1979 were not vital to the outcome of *Whitehouse v. Lemon*, since they were made by only one of five judges hearing the final appeal. However, they exemplified a way of thinking that was emerging by the late 1970s, and they were a precursor of what was to come. The outcome confirmed that the law of blasphemous libel was very much alive in the UK – it had only been sleeping – and that the courts were not inclined to liberalize it. Previous blasphemy cases under the English common law had involved deliberately provocative or abusive expression directed at Christian doctrines, symbols or sacred figures. By contrast, it appears that nothing like this was intended by James Kirkup in writing his poem or Denis Lemon in publishing it. The Law Lords accepted that the poem was likely intended as a gesture of inclusion for gay men within the fellowship of Christianity rather than as a malicious attack on Christianity or Christians.

This result was reached against a backdrop of racial and ethnic tension, and a felt need to maintain harmony. But any connection between that problem and the obsolescent law of blasphemous libel is implausible. Kirkup's poem in *Gay News*, however outrageous it might have seemed to 1970s morals campaigners, had no connection with Britain's fascist and white supremacist groups, which had congealed in the late 1960s into the National Front.

The Rushdie Affair in context[11]

The National Front was a violent movement that grew rapidly in membership and power. By the early 1970s, it was able to gain large numbers of voters in some parts of England when it ran candidates in

---

[10]For discussion, see Cliteur (2021a: 79–82). The impulse to protect Islam from any unpleasant criticism doubtless extends well beyond political and judicial authorities to influence much thinking and activity within the news media, the academy and the 'knowledge class' more generally in a sense that will be a focus of discussion in Chapter 9. For a recent example of how this can play out in the academy see generally Greer (2023).

[11]The analysis in this section draws upon that offered throughout Malik (2010) and on my discussion of some of these issues (especially the Rushdie Affair) in Blackford (2019b).

local and general elections. Economic recession in the 1970s and into the 1980s made it easier to target immigrant families as scapegoats. The National Front was frequently involved in street violence at this time, often in conflict with anti-fascist groups that sought to confront it. Although its influence declined in the 1980s and 1990s, and its role as a movement of the far Right was taken over by new political parties, it remains a cautionary symbol of British society's ugliest side.

During the movement's heyday, radicalized white bigots stabbed, bombed and killed. They made life hell for innocent people who attempted no more than to make a decent life for themselves and their families. The police were unhelpful when not outright hostile – especially in their dealings with young dark-skinned men. All of this aroused resentment and anger, and the 1980s are now remembered in the UK as a decade of inner-urban riots, mainly involving young men from African and West Indian backgrounds. Most dramatic was the Brixton riot of April 1981, which inspired further rioting across much of England and Wales.

One official response to the waves of immigration since the 1950s, and more particularly to the riots of the early 1980s, was the politics of multiculturalism. With different emphases, and perhaps different motives, this approach was pursued aggressively by the Conservative government of Margaret Thatcher, but also by local councils that often had left-wing leanings. The Greater London Council, in particular, sought to identify and support community leaders, and to encourage relatively insulated – but hopefully peaceful – racial and cultural enclaves.

This enabled the affected individuals to associate in communities that did not conform to a traditional – and no doubt somewhat falsified – picture of English or British culture. Taken beyond a certain point, however, multicultural policies raised a challenge to more cosmopolitan ideals from the Enlightenment and the heritage of liberalism. Multiculturalism tended to assign immigrants and their British-born children to newly formed communities within, and partly separated from, the UK's larger population. These racial, ethnic and cultural communities were not intended to be *internally* liberal, pluralistic and tolerant of non-conforming individuals. From the viewpoint of governments at all levels, it was simplest to expect a degree of homogeneity within communities and to work with leaders who could assert local authority.

Thatcher's policies achieved some success insofar as racial violence declined during the last two decades of the twentieth century. At the same time, they involved a degree of balkanization of British society. Moreover, they tended to push Asian communities further towards *religious* identities, as governments and their bureaucracies looked for plausible community leaders and often found them in the form of religious leaders and their immediate supporters.

Any such development disenfranchises religious sceptics – or simply non-religious individuals – within the newly structured and government-funded community groups. And of course, such developments reflected an unattractive form of racial and ethnic essentialism taking shape within policymaking circles. It's as if politicians and bureaucrats of the 1980s were unable to think of people from non-European cultures as individuals with their own diverse viewpoints, understandings and value orientations.

During this period, Salman Rushdie's novel *The Satanic Verses* caused uproar internationally and specifically in the UK where Rushdie made his home. Rushdie was born in India but had been educated in the UK and took out British citizenship in 1964.[12] As of 1988, when *The Satanic Verses* was published, he was already one of the most admired novelists in the world, especially for his 1981 book *Midnight's Children*. He came from a Muslim family but was not himself the adherent of any religion.

The Satanic Verses contains material that is open to interpretation as satirizing, critiquing or even mocking Islam and its origins, and this made it notorious in February 1989, when Ruhollah Khomeini, a Shi'ite Grand Ayatollah and the Supreme Leader of Iran, issued a ruling on Islamic law – a *fatwa* – against Rushdie. The *fatwa* called for Rushdie's death for allegedly blaspheming Islam, the Koran and the prophet Muhammad. This long-range death sentence extended to all who were involved in the book's publication and aware of its contents.

An episode such as this highlights a potential weakness in John Stuart Mill's classic commentary on the liberty of thought and discussion. Recall that Mill makes an exception when someone addresses an angry mob outside the house of a corn dealer, proclaiming that corn dealers are starvers of the poor. Such examples involve the physical proximity of the incitement to a potential victim of physical violence or other serious unlawful conduct. In such cases, there is little opportunity for the law to intervene between the incitement and the action. In today's circumstances, with incomparably more advanced communication

---

[12]More recently – since 2000 – Rushdie has lived in the United States. He took up American citizenship in 2016.

technologies than existed in 1859, effective incitements to assassinations and other lawless acts can originate from speakers who are as physically remote from their victims as Ayatollah Khomeini was from Rushdie.

Subsequently, a would-be assassin died in an attempt on Rushdie's life in August 1989. Rushdie's Italian translator, Ettore Capriolo, was wounded in a knife attack in July 1991. In the same month, Hitoshi Igarashi, the Japanese translator of *The Satanic Verses*, was stabbed to death. In 1993, its Norwegian publisher, William Nygaard, was shot outside his home and spent a lengthy time in hospital with his wounds. In 1994, the distinguished Egyptian author Naguib Mahfouz was almost killed in yet another knife attack. Mahfouz was the author of another controversial book, *Children of Gabalawi* (first published in Arabic in 1959 and translated into English in 1981), but it seems that his more immediate crime was expressing support for Rushdie during his plight. Years later, in August 2022, Rushdie himself was attacked by a knife-wielding assailant and was gravely wounded to the extent of losing an eye and the use of one hand.

Over the years, many others have been threatened, hurt, kidnapped or killed. Perhaps most notable of all was the massacre carried out by a mob of radical Salafists in Sivas, Turkey, in July 1993. Enraged by the presence at a cultural festival of Aziz Nesin, the translator of parts of *The Satanic Verses* into Turkish, the mob set fire to a hotel, killing thirty-five people. Two of the rioting Salafists were also killed in this deplorable incident, bringing the total count to thirty-seven.

In *Joseph Anton* (2012), his memoir of the years immediately after the *fatwa*, Rushdie laments the number of people on the Left who denounced him at the height of the Rushdie Affair, many of them writing columns for major British newspapers such as the *Guardian*. Some of these pieces called on him to be humbled by what had happened, or to learn from it and atone for the offence he'd caused. Meanwhile, as he describes in *Joseph Anton*, he was leading a difficult, cramped, furtive life, constantly beset by housing and other crises.

The Satanic Verses was banned in many countries, including Pakistan, Bangladesh and Indonesia, and indeed, most of the Islamic world, but also in nominally secular states such as India. In the West, many politicians went out of their way to distance themselves from Rushdie, with some Labour Party figures in the UK outright condemning his novel and associating themselves with the angry campaign against it. Major political leaders such as Margaret Thatcher, the US President George H. W. Bush and leading members of their respective cabinets offered only weak responses to the *fatwa*. The British Foreign Secretary, Geoffrey Howe, distanced himself and the government from Rushdie and *The Satanic Verses* to an extent that bordered uncomfortably on denunciation, though the British government did subsequently condemn and oppose the *fatwa* (for discussion see Ruthven 118; Cliteur 2019: 188–9).

As Kenan Malik observes in *From Fatwa to Jihad*, 'Western politicians seemed incapable of taking an unequivocal stand in defence of free speech and against the threat to Salman Rushdie's life' (2010: 34). This included left-wing academics and commentators who turned against Rushdie for his alleged insensitivity to religious and cultural feelings. Some of Rushdie's fellow authors spoke up to support him, but others responded with hostility to him and solicitude to pious Muslims who were somehow insulted or hurt by a lengthy novel that (in most cases) they had not even read (for discussion, see Cliteur 2019: 178–88). The Archbishop of Canterbury, Robert Runcie, gave support to the idea – advanced by Lord Scarman a decade before – that the law of blasphemy should be extended to include hurt to the feelings of religious adherents other than Christians (Cliteur 2019: 192).

In the decade between Lord Scanlan's dicta in *Whitehouse v. Lemon* and the 1989 Rushdie Affair, a sentiment had quietly developed in Britain and beyond that ideas themselves can be candidates for recognition and respect, and that this applies particularly to traditional religious and cultural ideas closely interwoven with people's understanding of their identity. It is not surprising that pious Muslims treat Islam's narrative about its own origins and founding figures as sacred, imposing a strong interdiction on any questioning or satire. More surprising is the acquiescence in this by many Western outsiders. This places ex-Muslims who are critical of their former religion – perhaps having experienced it as oppressive – in an invidious position. Secular intellectuals from Muslim backgrounds, such as Rushdie, are under pressure to self-censor any expression that might hurt Muslims' religious feelings.

In an article published in 1989, Charles Taylor took a somewhat nuanced, but nonetheless questionable approach to the Rushdie Affair. Taylor emphasized his own opposition to laws against blasphemy, but he expressed sympathy for the view that religion merits special protection, such as via blasphemy laws, since it 'is the locus' of a believer's 'stand on the deepest and most fundamental issues – death, evil, the meaning of life' (Taylor 1989: 118). From another viewpoint, however, with a different system of values, this is exactly why we should subject religion to sceptical scrutiny and *not* grant it any special protection.

Religions tend to make very large claims, including claims about how human beings ought to live in relation to a real or imaginary transcendent reality. They strive to inculcate metaphysical and moral beliefs, along with particular attitudes to the world (sometimes including a negative attitude to the empirical world itself, and to many everyday pleasures). They impose significant demands on their adherents and sometimes on others, either by expecting non-adherents to accommodate adherents' unusual or inconvenient behaviour or in the more extreme form of expecting non-adherents to conform to a specifically religious morality.

Religions have, moreover, a long record of enforcing their demands through acts of coercion or violence. Some have been unwilling to tolerate either non-belief or rival religions, or have granted only the limited toleration of consigning non-believers and the adherents of rival religions to a second-class social standing. In many cases and circumstances, then, it is reasonable to respond to religions with expressions of defiance, as did Richard Carlile, Charles Southwell and others in the nineteenth century, even though they paid a heavy price. Many people with non-religious or anti-religious philosophies view religious beliefs – from their perspective – as ill-founded, false, socially harmful and damaging to the welfare of individuals in the everyday, empirical world. Such people might well be motivated to engage in satire, ridicule and denunciation in the tradition of Voltaire.

Political Islam as a challenge to liberalism

As we've seen (Chapter 2) the Islamic empires of the Middle Ages contained a hierarchy of religions in which other religions were subordinated to Islam. Judaism and Christianity were tolerated, and to some extent favoured, for their monotheism and because of a belief that 'People of the Book' (basically Christians and Jews) had received genuine revelations from God. Unlike Christianity, Islam never developed a doctrine in which the Jews were understood as a destructive, Satanic force. Nor did Islamic populations develop Christians' anxieties over the Jews' success as traders, merchants and financiers. With notable exceptions such as the Almohad Caliphate, Islamic rulers treated Jews and Christians relatively well.

For centuries, even as the Islamic empires repeatedly fought the kingdoms of the West, this social arrangement was relatively stable. However, the balance of factors began to change in early modernity as the West forged ahead economically, technologically and militarily. From the turn of the nineteenth century, marked dramatically by Napoleon's invasion of Egypt in 1798, Islam's relationship to the West altered forever. Muslims in the Middle East were increasingly exposed to Western ideas, not least varieties of anti-Judaism and antisemitism, but especially the rising nationalism that directed much of Europe's energy at the time.

In the second half of the nineteenth century, Muslims decisively lost their dominance in the region to the ascendant European powers, and this culminated in the destruction of the Ottoman Empire during and immediately after the First World War. From the 1890s, anxieties arose in the Islamic world over the emergence of a visionary Zionist movement in Central and Eastern Europe, with large numbers of Jews soon embarking to Palestine and seeking to establish a Jewish nation state. This eventually led to the founding of the State of Israel in 1948 and to ongoing conflict in the region.

It is foolhardy to generalize about such a large topic, but it's fair to say that some Muslim societies experienced challenges in reconciling to these developments and, more generally, in adapting to the distributions of geopolitical power that characterize the modern world. In addition, Western conceptions of freedom of religion demand a form of toleration that extends far beyond that granted historically by the Islamic *dhimma* system. The modern Western approach and the traditional Islamic one are fundamentally incompatible.

One response in the Middle East, though by no means the only one, was an attitude of protecting Islamic ideas, customs and culture, or even retreating to a harsher, more reactionary version of them. Ideas and movements were stirring in the region throughout the twentieth century, including the founding of the Society of the Muslim Brothers (more commonly abbreviated as the Muslim Brotherhood) in Egypt in 1928 – followed by a spectacular growth in its numbers and influence. Later, the influential Islamic scholar Sayyid Qutb, who was executed in 1966 for plotting to assassinate the Egyptian president Gamal Abdel Nasser, denounced the considerable separation of religious and secular authority in the liberal democracies of the mid-twentieth century. He advocated control by Islamic law of every aspect of public and private life.

From a perspective such as Qutb's, the Islamic world is under cultural and philosophical attack, as well as military threat, from Israel and the West. Such perspectives can develop in more than one direction. They range from efforts to enforce Islamic law within Muslim communities in the West (and perhaps to incorporate some Islamic values and concepts into the general law), to efforts to build entire nation states around the requirements of Islamic law, to acts of violence aimed at Western civilians in hope of obtaining political concessions and shaking the self-confidence of the West.

The Organisation of the Islamic Conference (OIC) was founded in 1969 to represent the shared interests of Islam-majority countries and to engage in mutual assistance and cooperation. It has since (in 2011) changed its name to the Organisation for Islamic Cooperation, while keeping the same abbreviation (for more detail on the organization and its status, see van Schaik 2016: 178–9). Since its founding, the OIC has consistently opposed liberal understandings of human rights and free speech, adopting its own Cairo Declaration on Human Rights in Islam in 1990, according to which human rights are to be read narrowly so as to conform to Islamic law. At the time of the Rushdie Affair, the OIC condemned Rushdie for what it viewed as blasphemy. Thereafter, for many years, beginning in 1999, it strived to obtain international commitment to condemnation – or even outright prohibition – of what it referred to as defamation of religion (Blitt 2011; van Schaik 2016).

This campaign led to numerous resolutions from bodies associated with the UN, most notably the UN General Assembly and UN Human Rights Council, condemning defamation of religion. Although the campaign was eventually dropped in this form, the resolutions showed the interest of many nations in opposing disparagement or mockery of religion, and particularly of Islam (McAdam 2018: 95). Over time, support among nations represented at the UN gradually declined, though resolutions continued to be passed. The turning point was a resolution in rather different form adopted by the Human Rights Council in 2011. However, as legal scholar Robert C. Blitt elaborated in a journal article published in the same year, this action by no means repudiated the previous resolutions or the concept of defamation of religion (see generally Blitt 2011).

Accordingly, the OIC and its member nations can plausibly argue that these earlier resolutions were never superseded or replaced, that they express the will of the international community and that prohibition of defamation of religion has thereby become an international norm. As Blitt demonstrates, Western nations opposed to the concept of defamation of religion appear to have been outmanoeuvred. Thus, the OIC maintains its opposition to what it regards as defamation of Islam, in particular, and it remains a leading anti-liberal force in contemporary geopolitics.

The Iranian Revolution of 1978–9 was an especially important geopolitical development, bringing to power an Islamic government in a large and potentially wealthy nation. The spiritual leader Ayatollah Khomeini established himself as the country's supreme ruler, leading to conflict with the West as well as rivalry with other resource-rich Muslim states such as Iraq and Saudi Arabia. Within the Middle East, the key event for the next decade was the Iran–Iraq War from 1980 to 1988, which left half a million deaths. By comparison, the number killed or wounded as a result of the Ayatollah's *fatwa* against Rushdie in 1989 was orders of magnitude smaller, but attempts to assassinate a British citizen merely for publishing a novel struck directly at the professed values of the West and tested its commitment to liberal ideas of free expression.

Reflecting on the situation in France during the 1980s and 1990s, but with wider implications for Western liberal democracies, the political writer Paul Berman portrays a shift over time in the activism of politically aware young Muslims. In Berman's portrayal, they went from participation in broadly left-wing and liberal causes that included opposition to anti-Muslim bigotry to participation in Islamist causes. They went from campaigning against nightclubs that excluded Muslims to campaigning 'to prevent young Muslims from going to nightclubs' (Berman 2011: 173).

For Berman, the rise of Islamism, or political Islam, as an assertive force in the West during the 1980s and 1990s posed a question for the political Left. This challenge was especially salient in Europe, but also relevant to North America and other European colonial offshoots: to support the Islamists or not? Islamist leaders and organizations rejected much liberal and left-wing thought, but they purported to represent a subordinated group: that is, Muslims living in the nations of the West, but also Palestinians in the Middle East caught up in the ongoing struggle between their people and the State of Israel. For many left-wing intellectuals and activists, therefore, Islamists could seem, in their fashion, a progressive group, or at least one whose aims merited sympathy and respect.

Stages of identity politics

The course of world events during the Second World War and the following decades brought about a new consciousness of groups that suffered from one or another form of oppression. These groups were often defined on the basis of racial, ethnic or cultural characteristics, and they increasingly sought acknowledgement of their worth as groups, rather than mere toleration, individual rights or civic respect for their members. This provided the setting for what is now understood and experienced as identity politics.

Even as identity politics rose to prominence during the 1980s and 1990s, Soviet-style communism crashed across Eastern Europe in a sequence that included the formal dissolution of the Soviet Union itself in December 1991. By this point, communist ideology was largely discredited in the West, even within the forums of the political Left, but left-wing activists had already moved on to other sources of theory and to concerns that had little to do with the material interests of workers as a social class.

Fawcett (2018: 435–7) traces three stages of identity politics over the past several decades. First was a campaign against discrimination and for equal rights; second (already beginning to emerge in the 1960s and 1970s) were selective efforts at affirmative action or positive discrimination, with an aim of establishing more equal access to opportunities in education and the workforce. The third stage went further and antagonized many liberals who would have accepted the first and possibly the second, thus creating a new division within the liberal-left quarter: this was a demand to 'recognize, respect, and celebrate previously stigmatized groups as such' (Fawcett 2018: 435).

This third stage is exemplified by the term *inclusion*, which shifted beyond its previous meaning: that is, a reversal of the exclusions of the past so that everyone is now free to participate in the workforce, education and all other areas of social life. Inclusion in this sense can be seen as a counter to – among other things – racism, cultural xenophobia and religious persecutions. But in many settings, the idea of inclusion became something more demanding. On a strong interpretation, it involved altering environments, and creating new systems and institutions, so that everyone could feel recognized (also in a new sense) and no one need experience discomfort. This idea has a certain rhetorical appeal and emotional attraction, but it can soon entail efforts to forbid provocative speech and conduct. That way post-liberalism lies.

9 THE NEW NORMAL

Rise of a mega-movement

The course of events during the Second World War and the following decades brought about a new consciousness of groups that suffered from one or another form of oppression. This was reflected in international efforts to prevent a resurgence of racial ideologies such as Nazism, and in the efforts of Western nations to address their own legacies of racism. At the same time, post-war social, economic and technological developments provided the conditions for success of a confident and effective feminist movement.

By the second half of the 1970s, as we've seen, numerous movements moved away from past efforts based on liberal themes such as toleration, liberty, meliorism, social pluralism and the harm principle. Instead, they flaunted collective identities as they challenged the existing legal, institutional and discursive systems of power. These movements looked to each other for support, borrowed each other's rhetoric and coalesced into an overarching mega-movement.

We saw the beginnings of this in Chapter 8, when studying a 1979 article by the sociologist Renee R. Anspach. To take a more recent example, in her foreword to a multi-authored Runnymede Trust report published in 2017, Baroness Sayeeda Warsi complains about what she calls a 'covert form of Islamophobia couched in intellectual arguments' (Warsi 2017: v). For a quarter of a century, since the late 1990s, the Runnymede Trust has popularized the term *Islamophobia* to label a kind of bigotry against Muslims and/or Islam itself. Warsi continues:

> Discrimination has always been subject to ideological and intellectual justification. Whether this is directed against women, black people, Jewish people or LGBT communities, history shows that it's always

possible to rationalize racism and couch bigotry in 'acceptable' arguments; this form of hatred is the most dangerous.

(Warsi 2017: v)

Note how this passage conflates the situations of several historically subordinated groups ('women, black people, Jewish people or LGBT communities', and by implication Muslims living in Western societies) as if their situations are straightforwardly and obviously analogous. It's also worth stopping for a moment to notice how Warsi's rhetoric poisons the well of public discussion. She rejects any serious criticism of Islam or Islamic culture as based on hatred and bigotry. Intellectual arguments are dismissed without a hearing, since their motivation can be known in advance. Warsi might benefit from John Stuart Mill's advice to avoid branding our opponents as simply bad and immoral people, and to acknowledge whatever can be said in favour of positions that we disagree with (Mill [1859]1974: 117–18).

There are doubtless many intellectually weak arguments against Islam, its historical record and the cultural practices with which it has been associated in some places and at some times. Very often, these arguments might be advanced by individuals who are motivated by irrational hatred or fear. However, there are also powerful criticisms that can be made of Islam, not least the fact that its major truth claims are likely to be false (there's at least a good chance that the monotheistic deity Allah does not exist, that the prophet Muhammad did not really have contact with an archangel or any other supernatural being, that the words of the Koran are not the product of a divine intelligence and so on).

Similar criticisms can be made of Christianity and other religions. But we can go on to discuss the historical records of these religions and others, including their treatment of women, gay men, Jews and many other categories of people that Warsi runs together as if their rights stand or fall with each other and with those of Muslims. We should acknowledge that Islam was a relatively tolerant religion in the Middle Ages, while being clear that its historical mode of toleration, the *dhimma* system, would not be a workable or acceptable model for contemporary liberal democracies.

As an even more recent example of such conflation of political causes, the Black American 'antiracist' author Ibram X. Kendi wrote in 2019: 'We cannot be antiracist if we are homophobic or transphobic' (Kendi 2019: 197). But why? It is, for example, quite possible to be antiracist in any conceivable sense while also believing that men commit a sin against God when they engage in sex with other men, or that the existence of trans women is somehow inimical to the interests of women more generally and is therefore objectionable. Whatever the merits of the individual arguments relating to Black, gay and trans rights, they are not all tied together by the same logic or based on the same empirical facts. Nonetheless, it has been politically and rhetorically expedient to advocate on behalf of these groups and others as a kind of package deal.

In early 2022, the Australian journalist Guy Rundle published a long essay entitled 'Necessity Has No Law', in which he referred to the rise of 'a massive social and cultural movement' over 'the past six to eight years' – that is, beginning in about 2014 or 2016 (Rundle 2022: 22). Irrespective of the details of the chronology,[1] Rundle is correct to perceive the rise of something new that, as he points out, has adopted no single name, although the term *social justice* is often used by its participants, while its detractors are likely to refer to its outlook as *wokeness*, to label its active participants as *social justice warriors* and/or to identify its activist practice as *cancel culture* (Rundle 2022: 22). Of late, as I finalize these words in March 2023, it has become fashionable in some circles to employ the capitalized term of derision *Wokeism* and the adjective *Woke*.

Rundle lists various events and phenomena that have marked the rise of what we might as well term *the Social Justice Movement*, including its insistence on censorship and behavioural controls 'in the interests of a widely defined notion of justice' (Rundle 2022: 22). We should, however, keep in mind that the foundations were laid for this during the 1980s and 1990s, and even with the beginnings of identity politics in the 1970s. The Social Justice Movement that Rundle describes is in some ways an intensification rather than an entirely novel phenomenon. By 1990, say, the Anglophone liberal democracies were already post-liberal in the sense used throughout this book. Nonetheless, there was further change in the new millennium, and it's worth pondering what this involved and how it came about.

---

[1] I first encountered this movement a few years before the dates that Rundle mentions, i.e. in 2010 and 2011. By this time, it was well established in many online forums, if not yet mainstream.

The Social Justice Movement

For Rundle, the Social Justice Movement is best understood as a political expression of the values of the knowledge class (Rundle 2022: 23): that is, a social class of people involved in scientific and scholarly inquiry, the creation of technology and cultural products (including art and literature in their various forms), and the production of public policy and law. On Rundle's account, this class in its contemporary form arose after the Second World War. It gradually became larger, somewhat definite or identifiable, and increasingly powerful. Its members are cosmopolitan in outlook, detached from their local communities' traditions and assumptions, and trained to think in highly abstract and flexible ways. In recent decades, they've evolved shared assumptions and values that have now become their version of common sense – of what seems obvious and undeniable.

If we follow Rundle's account, therefore, the Social Justice Movement has behind it an entire social class – perhaps 30 per cent of the population – that exercises significant power in today's industrialized societies and implicitly supports the movement's goals. The Social Justice Movement focuses on revealing (and consequently opposing) hidden and overlapping layers of oppression endured by marginalized demographic groups. (This fits well with the vulgar postmodernism that fed into the theory and practice of identity politics in the 1980s.)

Not surprisingly, once we're familiar with the history of left-wing disenchantment with liberalism, the Social Justice Movement includes elements that are not only post-liberal but unashamedly anti-liberal. Elements of the movement explicitly reject liberal ideas of unrestricted public discussion – instead, they seek a partial closure of the public sphere to shut out what they perceive as harmful or hurtful speech. As Rundle observes, this attempt to constrain discussion may, depending on the circumstances, be carried out through action by the state or by other powerful bodies. I'd only add that it might not be a 'body' at all that attempts to close discussion or punish the advocates of politically unacceptable ideas. This can result from nothing more than informally organized or semi-organized tribal opinion and feeling.

Rundle views the rise of the Social Justice Movement with its distinctive priorities as something of a repeat of events in the late 1970s – though again, it strikes me as more a continuation and intensification of the history of identity politics and its associated tactics.

He and I agree, however, that the later 1970s, and then the 1980s, saw a new concern on the political Left with issues to do with the representation and portrayal of demographic groups. Such issues were now treated as urgent in their own right, rather than as components of a wider struggle over economic power or individual liberty.

Rundle perceives a kind of interregnum in identity politics from the mid-1990s to about 2010, with a return to the politics of anti-capitalism and material demands, albeit in rather minimal form. I confess that I recall no significant interregnum in identity politics. For example, the supposed period of interregnum was marked by strong and organized campaigns to counter Islamophobia, especially after the 9/11 terrorist attacks in 2001. Rundle, however, is approaching the question from a background in Marxist theory, and perhaps he's correct to identify a period of renewed, if sporadic, activism over material inequalities. This could reasonably describe some of the anti-capitalist and anti-globalization activism that began in the late 1980s and continued through the 1990s and beyond, as well as anger over the global economic crisis of 2007–8, and finally the rapid rise and fall of the Occupy Movement in 2011 and 2012.

Be that as it may, Rundle's sense of social shift around 2010 matches my own. Beginning about then, if we follow the general contour of his argument, there has been further transformation. This was partly driven from below through the interactions of young, and even very young, people using social media and smart phones. In 2010, outlets for self-expression and interaction such as 4chan, YouTube, Reddit, Facebook, Twitter Tumblr – and others that followed – were relatively new but becoming ubiquitous. For example, 2006 was the year that Twitter first appeared and Facebook was opened to the public. Added to earlier forms of social media such as bulletin boards and blogs, such giant IT platforms brewed a ferment of ideas, profoundly altered the character of public discussion, and helped strange thoughts to bloom with little in the way of corrective criticism. Thus, the language of activism changed further, and as Rundle duly observes, some kinds of activism intensified. Let's dig a bit deeper.

This happened at a time when employers were already engaged for their own reasons in ever-increasing surveillance and control of their employees' private lives as well the minutiae of their activities in the workplace. While some comforts and safety measures were injected into workplaces during the later decades of the twentieth century, and some forms of harshness were ameliorated, employees came under more scrutiny than ever from line managers and corporate executives. This was partly aimed at increasing productivity and was partly engineered to comply with legislation that assumed or required close workplace control, but it was largely to protect employers' brands or corporate images. Since then, the trend has continued. Many employees now work under task-performance rather than time-service contracts of employment: this means that they are employed to complete certain tasks or play a certain role within the employer's operations, rather than merely turning up to provide allocated hours of service in a factory or an office. Hand-in-hand with this, employers increasingly demand conformity to extensive and sophisticated codes of conduct.

Together with the use of social media to distribute information about perceived transgressions, all of these developments made employees more vulnerable to campaigns aimed at getting them disciplined or fired. This provided activists with a tactic for punishing individuals who engage in politically unacceptable speech. The fear of bad publicity encourages employers to engage all the more in dystopian practices of surveillance and intolerance. They are often unwilling to support employees whose speech and expression cause trouble.

As an example of knowledge-class thinking, Rundle observes that the question of whether trans women are fully women will be viewed differently within or outside the knowledge class. From outside, there will be a spectrum of approaches and answers, some more sympathetic than others. But for most members of the knowledge class this is a question that 'should not even be asked' – asking it 'is an offensive, indeed violent, act' (Rundle 2022: 35). This phrasing conveys, without specifically drawing attention to, an enlarged meaning of *violence*.

Linguistic transformations

As identity politics developed from the mid-1970s through the 1980s and beyond, it produced a transformation in the language of the political Left. Terms such as *toleration, free speech, individuality, spontaneity, original thinking, personal autonomy, sexual liberation* and *artistic freedom* fell largely into disuse, if not a form of disrepute. Even some of the language of equality – such as *equal opportunity* and *equal rights* – eventually suffered in this way, though the word *equity* is still doing well, often as part of a contemporary mantra: *diversity, equity, inclusion*.

Stocks have risen for *diversity, inclusion, difference, identity, recognition* and *community*. In more politically radical circles, we can find ample references to *subjugation(s)* and *domination*.

Nor is this merely a linguistic change. The new language does not mean completely new political goals, but it reflects significantly changed emphases, principles and values. One effect is a loss of the language of dissent. Here, an important vocabulary has been jettisoned: we have lost the words that we could once call upon to justify diversity of thoughts, desires, viewpoints and policy preferences, as opposed to a diversity of demographic groups. Words such as *individuality* and *spontaneity* played a crucial role in the traditional language of liberalism such as we'd find in Mill's *On Liberty*, and were used to defend personal eccentricities or experiments in living. By contrast, these are not important within the Social Justice Movement, which understands human beings as belonging to intersecting or overlapping identity groups rather than as unique individuals.

In a related development, the author Alice Dreger has identified a desexualization of gay rights advocacy and a linguistic change from talk of trans*sex*uals to trans*gender*. Presumably this shows an effort to downplay the perennially contentious issue of sex (for discussion see Dreger 2015: 63; Blackford 2019b: 136–7). The newer vocabulary and rhetoric tend to situate gay men, lesbians, bisexual people and transgender people as arbitrarily subjugated groups, rather than emphasizing the freedom of individuals to experience and act upon unconventional or statistically unusual desires. To some extent, this might relate to the AIDS crisis of the early 1980s, which altered many priorities among gay men in particular, as well as arousing fears of contagion within the more general – straight – population. The new vocabulary and rhetoric support a strategy of accommodation to the permanent sensibilities of straight society, with an aim of deflecting any thoughts of pathology or abnormality.

In Chapter 8, I mentioned that the Google Books Ngram Viewer has limitations as a research tool. In particular, it cannot be used reliably to track changing meanings for ordinary English words. For example, the word *inclusion* gained in frequency during the second half of the nineteenth century, and perhaps there's an interesting story behind this. But its up and downs since the middle of the twentieth century do not show any remarkable changes, despite the recent emergence of a specific meaning, or set of meanings, related to identity politics. By way of comparison, the word *diversity* climbed steeply during the 1980s and

1990s, before falling off slightly and then somewhat stabilizing in the new century. We might guess that this reflects its particular meaning of demographic diversity within the language of identity politics, but we can't draw robust conclusions: the Ngram Viewer does not tell us what proportion of the word's present-day use reflects that specific meaning, as opposed to its more general meaning as an approximate synonym of *variety*.

Another interesting example is *gay*, which climbed steeply from the mid-1970s, and especially from the early 1980s, after a gradual decline since its halcyon days as a popular word from around 1750 to around 1850. It has now achieved something like its former heights, but this almost certainly reflects a change in its most common meaning. That is, during the 1970s and thereafter it lost its general meaning as a rather old-fashioned equivalent to *bright, light-hearted, carefree, joyful* and similar words. Instead, a slang meaning in which it referred to homosexuality started to become common and received much encouragement.

The Ngram Viewer comes into its own with neologisms. It shows, for example, almost no record of the expression *LGBT* before 1992 or 1993, at which point there was a sudden rise in its use. As confirmation, the OED's online draft additions provide a first citation for the term in 1992. Ngram searches show that variations such as *LGBTQ* and *LGBTQI* are even more recent, coming into use only in the new century – with steep increases in their popularity beginning around 2010. The term *transphobia* was almost unknown until the early 1990s. When graphed by the Ngram Viewer, it rises fairly slowly at first. It shoots upwards from about 2005, then rises even more steeply – once again from about 2010.

The term *Islamophobia* was almost unknown in English until 1993, but rose steeply from 1998 after being popularized by an important report published by the Runnymede Trust in the preceding year. It then rose even more steeply from 2010. The term *microaggression* (or *microaggressions*), referring to small or subtle acts of prejudice against members of a subordinated demographic group, came almost out of nowhere around the start of the new century, although the OED does have a citation of *micro-aggression* as far back as 1970. It rose steeply but inconsistently until about 2010 – and then rose more steeply still.

Ferreting out these small facts hardly amounts to rigorous scientific investigation, but it broadly indicates new concerns and emphases that entered identity politics over the past few decades and especially since about 2010. Here we see the rise of a new ideological formation with its own jargon. In addition to a relative phasing out of 'liberal' words such as *individuality*, at least in political and philosophical discussion, and the accretion of new significance to words such as *diversity, inclusion* and *recognition*, we can see new terms becoming popular as and when new centres of attention arise for left-wing activism. For example, the expression *fat shaming* was almost unknown until 2010, then climbed very steeply in popularity. The expression *slut shaming* arrived a couple of years earlier, but also had its sudden rise from about 2010, as did *trigger warning* whose frequency graph goes almost vertical in that particular year.

Concept creep

In his 2016 paper 'Concept Creep: Psychology's Expanding Concepts of Harm and Pathology', University of Melbourne professor of psychology Nicholas Haslam identified an ongoing trend over the previous decades – beginning, perhaps, around the 1980s and thus roughly coinciding with the rise of identity politics. In Haslam's paper, the expression *concept creep* refers to an expansion of meaning for terms that refer to 'undesirable, harmful, or pathological aspects of human experience and behavior' (Haslam 2016: 2). Haslam's research specifically examined concept creep as it appeared in the disciplines of behavioural and social science, but the creeping of harm-related concepts has either spread beyond those fields or occurred more widely in a parallel development.

In his original 2016 paper, Haslam focused on an expansion of meaning for the terms *abuse, bullying, trauma, mental disorder, addiction* and *prejudice*. He observed that the meaning of these words had extended since, say, the 1970s both horizontally (to new kinds of speech and conduct) and vertically (to less dramatic or severe levels of apparent nastiness or psychological impact).

This expansion of harm-related concepts has an attractive side, in that it derives from a humane motivation: it shows concern for the welfare and happiness of others. Indeed, some specific expansions can probably be justified. For example, we now recognize a broader spread of phenomena as mental illness or disorder, bullying or child abuse. The latter includes certain kinds of conduct that were once viewed as normal, or even benign, aspects of children's upbringing. Various kinds of physical and other punishment, harshly judgemental language and sheer neglect might have seemed unremarkable just a few decades ago, but are now viewed as unacceptable ways of treating children. In that respect, society has become slightly kinder. But there can also be negative implications as the meanings of many concepts – not limited to Haslam's original six – expand both horizontally and vertically.

Haslam and his collaborators continue to research the phenomenon of concept creep and to publish their findings. But even without formal data, we can observe a similar expansion with *violence, hate* (or *hatred*), *distress, vulnerability, bigotry,* and feeling or being *unsafe,* as well as with *harm* and *hurt* themselves. The list could grow very long, but for our current purposes, concepts of violence and harm are especially troubling. In liberal theorizing, these set a high threshold before speech or other kinds of behaviour become candidates for prohibitions and restrictions, or even for serious disapproval. As their meanings expand, however, they capture much behaviour that commonly provokes nothing more than disagreement, annoyance, transient and low-impact offence, or frustration of certain desires. In short, we can see harm-related concepts expand – what Haslam calls *harm inflation*.

As this continues, there is a risk of pathologizing the experience of everyday challenges and stigmatizing more and more sorts of everyday speech and behaviour. Even in the domain of child rearing, where increased solicitude for the welfare of growing, dependent people has been more than reasonable, there is room for concern. As harm inflation continues in this area, there is a risk of teaching children to think of themselves as permanent victims, and as justified in not tolerating even the slightest divergence from their own opinions, values and standards. Once certain speech or conduct can credibly be labelled as violent or harmful, this can support an extreme moralistic response. The tendency is then to remove any concept of a middle ground between straightforwardly benign behaviour and behaviour that is considered beyond the pale of toleration.

Completely uncontroversial definitions of concepts such as *violence* and *harm* are not possible. Nonetheless, the issue is worth further consideration because it affects what kinds of speech and action fall either within or beyond the zone of tolerance in liberal democratic societies. One difficulty is that the word *violence* has various extended or metaphorical meanings. For example, we can speak of the violence of a film that merely portrays – and certainly cannot *commit* – violent acts. Likewise, we can speak of one philosopher 'violently attacking' another's ideas, but no actual violence is involved.[2] Sometimes the word *violent* means little more than *forceful*, but this also has extended and metaphorical meanings.

In its primary sense, however, *violence* signifies the damaging infliction of physical force against people, other living creatures or non-living things (usually, but not always, property). Most centrally and significantly, violence is deliberate infliction of physical force with an intention to cause another person physical injury, death or significant pain. So understood, violent behaviour attracts so much fear – and potentially causes such serious and unequivocal harm – that it is viewed as socially intolerable in most contexts[3] and is typically prohibited by the core criminal law. Against that background, to stigmatize actions and speech, or in some cases even concepts, theories and opinions, as violent is tantamount to demanding their legal or social suppression.

By contrast with *violence*, the word *harm* is difficult to define without resorting to synonyms that are no more helpful. Thus, the primary definition in the OED is: 'Evil (physical or otherwise) as done to or suffered by some person or thing; hurt, injury, damage, mischief.' This is sufficiently vague to leave room for trivial physical or mental discomforts to count as harm of a sort. However, the point of the harm principle, as developed in *On Liberty*, was not to open the door to a vast range of actions to suppress opinions and ways of life that might cause discomforts of these kinds. Rather, it was to set a limit to the tyranny of local opinion and feeling (as well as the more obvious tyranny of the formal law) and provide a zone for toleration of eccentricity and unorthodoxy.

This is important because Millian liberalism was about legal and social toleration. By contrast, it has become an unstated assumption of the Social Justice Movement that expressions of opinion can cause harm, that merely hearing opinions can render the hearer unsafe – and indeed that being in physical proximity to the expression of an opinion (such as being present on a college or university campus where it is happening) can produce distress or trauma. These are, in a sense, self-fulfilling claims, since participants in the Social Justice Movement may be trained

---

[2]Of course, there's nothing wrong with metaphorical or extended use of words as long as it's clear that that's all they are.
[3]This is a generalization that admits of exceptions, including the limited and regulated use of violence in certain sports. A separate book could be written about the socially accepted uses of violence.

and encouraged to experience severe emotional reactions to disliked viewpoints.

Thus, a new vocabulary has been superimposed on that of 1980s/1990s identity politics. This new vocabulary of hurt, distress, hatred and violence, of feelings of being unsafe, and other overwrought references to pathology and harm – now applied to mere clashes of opinion on social and political issues – forms an instantly recognizable linguistic register. When employed in the domain of social and political discussion, this language, with its associated posture of childlike vulnerability, provides its users with new tools to censor ideas and punish conduct.

If examples are needed, many can be found in a recent book by Keith E. Whittington, a constitutional scholar based at Princeton University. In defending free speech on American college and university campuses, Whittington adduces numerous examples of students, and sometimes even academic staff, claiming to be in pain, to be (or at least feel) unsafe, or to be victims of violence – merely because of the presence elsewhere on campus of speakers with whom they disagree. The speakers discussed by Whittington are not, by any means, always far-right radicals or aggressive provocateurs. Many are distinguished academics, public intellectuals or mainstream political figures.

One of Whittington's examples is a speech at Wellesley College in 2017, delivered by Laura Kipnis (Whittington 2018: 134–7), a professor of media studies at Northwestern University with research interests that Whittington neatly summarizes as 'the cultural politics of sex' (Whittington 2018: 137). In recent years, Kipnis has been critical of what she sees as the excesses of sexual harassment policies and procedures on American campuses – this stems, in particular, from her view at close proximity of a disciplinary hearing against a particular male professor at Northwestern University. This led to her 2017 book on the subject, *Unwanted Advances*. While Kipnis's views are controversial, she supports them with scholarly argument and they gain some credibility from her years of relevant research.

In *Unwanted Advances*, Kipnis observes that there was a brief period between the sexual revolution of the 1960s and the AIDS crisis of the 1980s when sex might sometimes involve hurt feelings, but was generally treated as life experience, and in this context 'words like pleasure and liberation got tossed around a lot' (Kipnis 2017: 7). But by the time she was writing *Unwanted Advances*, some forty years later, this rhetoric of pleasure and liberation had disappeared, and was replaced by a vocabulary of danger, encroachment, contamination and vulnerability, and by an implicit denial of women's agency. As Kipnis observes, once such a lexicon becomes the prevailing discourse, 'sex is going to feel threatening more of the time, and anything associated with sex, no matter how innocuous … will feel threatening' (Kipnis 2017: 9).

Kipnis is nuanced about this. She does not deny that there are current problems with relations between the sexes, particularly on American campuses. On the contrary, she attempts to identify the problems, based in part on discussions with her own students, many of them writing autobiographical or confessional material for her creative writing classes. She concludes that young men and women on American campuses participate in a genuinely alarming culture of partying while extremely drunk. If she's correct – something on which I'm unqualified to comment – a lot of sex happens at, around and after these parties. Some of it might be enjoyable for all concerned, but too much of it might not be. That is, it's unwanted by the women involved, even though they are not subjected to violence or force, or even to threats of violence or force. Rather, they give reluctant consent under social and emotional pressure while confused about their choices and cognitively impaired from drinking large amounts of alcohol. Some might have no regrets, but others might later feel violated, guilty and/or ashamed.

If Kipnis is correct, however, there's another side to the situation: many colleges and universities in the United States (and probably elsewhere) are scrutinizing the details of seemingly innocuous interactions that show no obvious 'grey' area of exploitation or abuse. This includes prying into romantic relationships after they have broken down and one party or the other holds a grudge.

Situations differ, but Kipnis argues persuasively that at least some of these investigations take place against the expressed preferences of the alleged victims – thanks to third-party complaints – and in any event, that they require impossible judgements based on patently inadequate evidence. As concepts of abuse, and the like, expand, higher education institutions can be pressured to investigate accusations that fall outside their proper jurisdiction and are far beyond their competence. And yet, college and university administrators might fail to recognize and address genuine problems with contemporary campus culture.

Some of Kipnis's analysis relates to particular aspects of American campus life that might not have a precise equivalent in other countries. My point here is not to express agreement with any particular claim that Kipnis sets out in *Unwanted Advances*. It is merely to emphasize that she has something to say that might have considerable value and might be supported to a greater or lesser extent by open-minded and more rigorous research. At a minimum, she has developed a viewpoint that merits consideration and discussion (which does not exclude scrutiny and critique). Yet, when she presented her ideas at Wellesley College they were not treated by opponents as merely incorrect. Their expression on campus – indeed, her very presence as a speaker – was denounced as a threat to the community's safety and welfare.

Examples and their discontents

This phenomenon deserves deeper, more adequately scientific study. Meanwhile, we must rely on individual examples to illustrate the point. In my 2019 book *The Tyranny of Opinion*, I discuss many cases of individuals being targeted for trivial or entirely imaginary transgressions. Each of these cases raises issues that merit reflection. Among numerous others, they include:

- Justine Sacco, whose life was overwhelmed by a Twitter mob in January 2013 after she posted a relatively innocuous, if arguably tasteless, tweet on the way to South Africa from the UK. This particular cybermobbing, initiated by the *Gawker* journalist Sam Biddle, came complete with its own Twitter hashtag: #HasJustineLandedYet. As a result, Sacco lost her job with a media and internet company, and her career was derailed for several years even if it was not ultimately destroyed (for detail and discussion, see Blackford 2019b: 181–2).

- Tim Hunt, an eminent scientist who delivered a well-received and humorous speech at a conference in South Korea in June 2015. The speech was falsely reported as arguing for sex-separated science laboratories to protect men from the distraction of working with attractive women. Like Sacco, Hunt was the victim of a Twitter mob, this time with the hashtag #DistractinglySexy. He was pressured out of his honorary appointment with University College London (see Blackford 2019b: 179–81).

- Erika and Nicholas Christakis who were, respectively, the Associate Master and Master of a residential college at Yale University. Beginning in October 2015, they were subjected to a campaign of daily abuse after Erika distributed a thoughtful, gently worded email questioning the need to police students' Halloween costumes. At one stage, Nicholas was physically surrounded by a large mob of students who were literally screaming at him, as captured on video that became available online. Erika was driven out of her connection with Yale and both were forced out of their positions with the residential college (see Blackford 2019b: 142–9).

- Rebecca Tuvel, who was the author of an article published in early 2017 in the feminist philosophy journal *Hypatia*. This paper argued for the theoretical possibility of racial transitioning by analogy with the experience of transgender people (whom she clearly and expressly supported). This led to a campaign for Tuvel's article to be retracted, including an open letter to *Hypatia*'s editors carrying over 800 signatures (see Blackford 2019b: 153–5).

- Laura Moriarty, who published a Young Adult novel entitled *American Heart* in January 2018. Even before the novel's formal publication, it was widely denounced by online social justice advocates, most of whom would have had no opportunity to read advance copies. *American Heart* depicts a near-future United States in which Muslims are persecuted and sent to detention camps – an obvious reference to anti-Muslim sentiment at the time, much of it whipped up by Donald Trump. Nonetheless, the book was considered unacceptable because the help given by a white American girl to a Muslim women made it a 'white saviour narrative'. It is doubtful that the campaign against *American Heart* ultimately harmed its sales, but it was at least successful in pressuring the influential book-reviews magazine *Kirkus Reviews* to publish a revised and less favourable version of its original review, and to withdraw its starred endorsement of the book (see Blackford 2019b: 158–63).

We could go on indefinitely finding and adding such examples. In August 2017, James Damore, a software engineer employed by Google, was fired for writing an internal memo that offered views about sex-related psychological differences. After the memo was publicly leaked, Damore was shamed on social media platforms, and then promptly fired. In his recent book *Dangerous Ideas*, Eric Berkowitz adduces this episode as an example of private employers in the United States being able to shut down what they view as offensive speech, and in context Berkowitz is clearly expressing disapproval. However, even he misrepresents the memo as stating 'women were inferior to men in jobs such as engineering' (Berkowitz 2021: 245).

In fact, Damore said nothing so crude or obviously sexist. Rather, he suggested that over-representation of men in software engineering at Google might be due to differences in what activities the sexes tend to find attractive and enjoyable. To support this suggestion, he cited a body of mainstream, though often controversial, scientific research that suggests population-level trends in personality differences between the sexes. In other words, he did not refer to intellectual or competency differences, but to a tendency to be interested in different activities, which could lead to an imbalance in men and women pursuing certain careers. There was no suggestion that those women who were, in fact, motivated to pursue careers in software engineering were inferior to their male counterparts. Accordingly, Damore argued that Google should focus on equality of opportunity for individuals, without necessarily expecting statistically similar outcomes for men and women across its workforce.

Some or all of the research that Damore cited might be open to criticism for its methodology and/or for drawing premature conclusions from the available data. For all that has been established by science at this point, the identified personality differences between men and women might be small. They might even be an illusion that will vanish as further studies are conducted. Alternatively, they might result from different ways in which boys and girls are socialized, perhaps even from the moment they are born. In the latter case, the differences in careers favoured by young men and young women might likewise be real, but the solution to this problem, if it is one, lies outside the control of Google or other employers.

The problem with offering examples is that they are easily dismissed as atypical. However, this phenomenon has become so ubiquitous that its existence can no longer be doubted in good faith. Every day we see individuals who have been shamed and punished merely for expressing unorthodox opinions, or for wording their comments in an off-message way from the viewpoint of the Social Justice Movement. These individuals are often bullied into giving obsequious apologies for the 'harm' that their words have caused. Alternatively, any refusal to recant and apologize will be condemned as 'doubling down' and displaying a hateful or callous attitude.

Most notably, the victims are often left-wing, liberal or progressive by one definition or another. James Damore is evidently a political conservative of some kind, but Moriarty, for example, was writing from a broadly left-wing viewpoint and expressing her concern about anti-Muslim bigotry in Trump's America. None of these viewpoints resembles the totalitarian ideologies that worried Loewenstein, Riesman and Popper in the 1930s and 1940s, and inspired the protections baked into international human rights law.

The issue here is not whether these tactics of surveillance, shaming and punishment always upend someone's life and career. Indeed, they often fail. For example, Rebecca Tuvel received support from her academic colleagues at Rhodes College in Memphis, and her career seems to have gone ahead just fine. Nonetheless, there's a *culture* of cancellation within the Social Justice Movement.

More examples enter the news every time we look. Earlier this month, for instance, students at Stanford University shouted down an on-campus speech by Stuart Kyle Duncan, a conservative federal judge, and prevented him from giving his prepared remarks. Worse, the university administration failed at the time to take any effective action to control the disruption. A senior administrator with a diversity, equity and inclusion portfolio did intervene at the microphone to suggest that heckling students give the judge some space to express his views. At the same time, however, she berated him for his 'harmful' views and the damage to 'the fabric of [Stanford's] community' caused by his mere presence on campus.[4]

---

[4]This incident in March 2023 is too recent for me to endorse any one published account as definitive, and indeed events continue to play out at Stanford as I write. However, a Google search incorporating terms such as *Stanford* and *Judge Duncan* will identify numerous and accumulating media sources.

Gender storms

If even more examples are needed, there's a rich lode of them in contemporary debates between transgender activists, on the one hand, and opponents who refer to themselves as gender-critical feminists on the other. The latter are suspicious of the term and concept *gender* or *gender identity*, which is sometimes understood as an inner feeling of maleness or femaleness, or of being a man or a woman.[5] In her popular book *The Transgender Issue*, Shon Faye, a British journalist and transgender activist, interprets a person's gender identity as 'their personal sense of their own gender' (Faye 2021: xiv).

By contrast, second-wave feminists often used the word *gender* to signify the social norms, practices and discourses that shape men and women, respectively, into different kinds of roles, activities and forms of self-presentation. To put this in a fancy way, *gender* in this sense is a system of discursive as well as coercive power operating in human societies. At the least, gender-critical feminists insist upon the reality and importance of biological sex as a characteristic of our species, *Homo sapiens*, irrespective of how we understand gender identity or what significance we assign to it.

Adding to the complications, the word *gender* also gained ground in the second half of the twentieth century as a more euphemistic or polite alternative for *sex* in the sense of the biological categories of male and female. As noted by its entry in the OED, this now seems to be the word's most common usage, and indeed, it has been driving *sex* out of that niche, at least when we're discussing members of our own species. Thus, we now talk about such things as gender reveal parties: parties where prenatal sex discernment technology is used to identify an unborn baby's sex. Conversely, the little word *sex* has more than held its ground overall: since the 1950s and early 1960s, it has largely replaced expressions such as *sexual union* or even *sexual intercourse* to refer to the act of copulation.

Despite these linguistic developments, scientists continue to study, and refer to, the biological category of sex. This can now be understood in terms of male versus female reproductive strategies and smaller (male) versus larger (female) types of gametes. In *Homo sapiens*, sex in this

---

[5]Or in many cases, as a boy or a girl. We will have to pass over complications such as individuals who assert, and live in accordance with, a 'non-binary' gender identity.

sense is coded through genetic mechanisms that have received much study and are well understood in their fundamentals. Prior to the rise of modern science, of course, with its microscopes and other instruments, the distinction between male and female life forms could not have been understood in this way. Indeed, there was a long history of speculation and proto-scientific efforts to understand the unseen processes involved in sexual reproduction.

All of this leaves much room for debate about scientific and everyday (or 'folk') understandings of a distinction between people by sex (that is, as male or female), the logic by which various conceptions of sex and gender/gender identity relate to each other, and what the implications might be for sensible public policy. If, in the extreme, the emerging policy in liberal democracies is that considerations relating to gender identity should straightforwardly supersede those relating to sex, this prompts sincere concerns about trans women's presence in settings such as prisons, public bathrooms, crisis shelters and women's sport.

This is not, as Shon Faye has called it, merely a 'confected debate' (Faye 2021: 233). Concerns such as these must be discussed publicly, even if they can ultimately be assuaged if everybody shows good will. In a relatively short book with a quite different focus, I cannot examine possible compromises or stake out a substantive position of my own. But I take an interest in recent attempts to constrain the debate itself.

In the UK, efforts at legal and social censorship of gender-critical feminist views reached an extreme point during recent litigation over the non-renewal of a consultancy contract between Ms Maya Forstater and an organization called CDG Europe. The decision not to renew Forstater's contract followed her participation in debates on the social media site Twitter, in which she'd expressed strong opinions to the effect that biological sex is distinct from gender identity, that sex is immutable and that, for example, trans women are biologically male. After the non-renewal of her contract on these grounds, she alleged that she'd been discriminated against for her gender-critical views, contrary to the terms of the Equality Act 2010. This statute prohibits (among many other things) discrimination by employers on the basis of philosophical belief.

When Forstater's case was heard by the Central London Employment Tribunal, CDG Europe argued that her gender-critical views did not amount to a philosophical belief, and therefore her claim should be dismissed at the threshold, irrespective of what other facts might be established. At first sight, this seems a bizarre submission, since

Forstater's gender-critical beliefs do, indeed, seem to involve the mix of empirical claims and conceptual reasoning about fundamental existential questions that would normally qualify them without question as philosophical.

However, legal counsel for CDG Europe argued that the relevant statutory provision must be interpreted compatibly with the ECHR. This, in turn, does not protect all otherwise-philosophical beliefs (or their expression) whatsoever, no matter how dangerous to society they might seem to be. In that respect, recall that the ECHR contains, in Article 17, a kind of let-out clause. Article 17 provides that nothing in the convention implies a right to engage in activity that is destructive of the rights and freedoms enumerated in the ECHR itself. This means, for example, that Nazis are unlikely to be able to claim protection of their freedom of belief under Article 9 of the ECHR, their freedom of expression under Article 10, or their freedom of assembly and association under Article 11.

Given the relationship between the Equality Act and the ECHR, therefore, the protections in the Equality Act would probably not be extended to a British employee who is fired for expressing Nazi-like ideas and advocating a totalitarian state. Nor would they protect someone blatantly inciting terrorism or other acts of violence. Accordingly, relevant courts and tribunals in the UK have developed a test to the effect that the Equality Act will not protect beliefs that are not worthy of respect in a democratic society. One issue before the employment tribunal was whether this category is just the same as, or is broader than, the category of beliefs that are not protected by the Article 17 of the ECHR.

My exposition of these intricacies, which I've slightly simplified, may be testing the patience of readers who are not legally trained. The intricacies are, however, necessary as background to the case. The shorthand version is that the employment tribunal was called on to decide whether Forstater's gender-critical views were unworthy of respect in a democratic society and therefore (by a tortuous route) outside of legislative protection. As an even shorter version, did her views lie beyond the pale of social toleration?

In a decision that issued in December 2019, the Central London Employment Tribunal held that Forstater's views were, indeed, unworthy of respect in a democratic society and thus dismissed her case against CDG Europe. But with all respect to the tribunal member who decided the case, this decision was manifestly wrong. Forstater's views were undoubtedly philosophical, and to claim that such views, which were by no means fascist or otherwise totalitarian, were beyond the pale of respect in a democratic society was remarkably illiberal. The 'respect' involved here does not mean esteem or any other kind of high regard, or even a concession of rationality or plausibility, but merely an acknowledgement that a belief falls within the zone of tolerance when expressed in public discussion.

As events turned out, the tribunal's decision was reversed on appeal to the Employment Appeal Tribunal, and no further appeal was launched. In *Maya Forstater v. CDG Europe* (decided 10 June 2021), the appeal tribunal held that the issue at this stage of proceedings was only whether Forstater's views were so fundamentally intolerable as to fall altogether outside the intent of the Equality Act. This was held to be essentially the same question as whether her views fell outside the protection of the ECHR as a result of Article 17. The appeal tribunal found that Forstater's views were *not* beyond the pale of toleration in a democratic society.

This did not, in itself, mean that Forstater had won her case. It gave her no more than a green light to proceed with her case on its substantive merits and demonstrate that she had, in fact, been subjected to unlawful discrimination. In the end, she was successful in further proceedings.

In Maya Forstater's case, freedom of philosophical belief was defended successfully against an illiberal interpretation, but the outcome was less happy in late 2021 when the feminist philosopher Kathleen Stock was hounded from her professorial post at the University of Sussex. As viewed by her attackers – seemingly students from the university itself – Stock's crime was defending a moderate form of gender-critical feminism. She resigned after a campaign of targeted, personal hate that became too much for her to bear. As I mentioned in Chapter 6, *hate* and *hatred* are very strong words that refer to an extreme emotion. But I am not employing the word *hate* in any expanded sense. Caught up in the shared fervour of their campaign against her, Stock's attackers really did appear to view her as an appropriate object of hate.

In her recent book *Material Girls: Why Reality Matters for Feminism* (2021), and in other writings and public appearances, Stock examines the fraught concept of gender. In doing so, she displays obvious care and sympathy when discussing the problems and issues faced by trans women and trans men. There is no doubt that transgender children, adolescents and adults frequently experience problems such as exclusion, violence, homophobic and transphobic taunting, poverty and homelessness (for general discussion, see Faye 2021). It is well to bear these realities in mind when participating in debate over transgender issues. However, no fair reading of *Material Girls* could support the conclusion that Stock is unaware of them or that she is herself motivated by hatred.

This outcome at the University of Sussex can only inspire fear in other academics who hold views similar to Stock's. Anyone working in an academic post in British universities – and perhaps in universities beyond the British Isles – who doubts the coherence, or the empirical foundations, of contemporary transgender theory will need to take note. Such a person would need to be brave to enter the current transgender debate through either academic publishing or discussion in the broader public sphere.

Cannon to left of them

In recent years, some books that deal with identity issues have sold in enormous numbers, and have been treated in some parts of the Social Justice Movement as almost akin to holy scripture. They have thus earned their authors large fortunes and a degree of social influence out of all proportion to the merit of their ideas. Prominent among these works have been Robin DiAngelo's *White Fragility* (first published in the United States in 2018 and in the UK in 2019) and Ibram X. Kendi's *How to Be an Antiracist* (2019).

To say the least, the ideas proffered in these books are contentious and merit scrutiny, analysis and critique. Carried out adequately, this would require a separate study, but I can at least offer some brief comments and suggest where the authors' approaches might reasonably be questioned.

DiAngelo's thesis is that white people are, without exception, racist, and that they demonstrate a kind of psychological fragility when they resist this claim. DiAngelo concedes that many people understand the word *racism* as meaning 'a conscious dislike of people because of race', and she acknowledges that it would be offensive for her to suggest that someone whom she does not know is, in this sense, racist (DiAngelo 2019: 13). Instead, she explains racism as a group's collective pattern of racial prejudice when it is supported by 'the power of legal authority and institutional control' (DiAngelo 2019: 20). Hence, she tells us that in her stipulated sense only white people can be racist:

When I say that only whites can be racist, I mean that in the United States, only whites have the collective social and institutional power and privilege over people of color. People of color do not have this power and privilege over white people.

(DiAngelo 2019: 22)

To be fair, DiAngelo is undoubtedly correct to find a difference in power when viewed at a group level. Viewed at this level, there is a reality in the United States and other nations of racial dominance and subordination in the socioeconomic sphere. In everyday English, however, the term *racism* conveys something quite different from DiAngelo's idea of differential power and privilege at the level of demographic groups. Racism in common understanding is not a complex sociological phenomenon but an emotion of race-based hatred or a belief in inherently superior and inferior 'races'.

Common imagery associated with these emotions and beliefs includes Jewish prisoners being gassed or worked to death in Nazi concentration camps, chattel slavery in the old American South and Ku Klux Klan lynchings. When someone is accused of racism, this evokes emotions of anger and fear connected with such imagery. Thus, any such accusation of racism, aimed at somebody who is *not* racist in the everyday sense, will inevitably cause confusion and resentment. The problem is compounded when DiAngelo also stipulates her own definition of 'white supremacy' (DiAngelo 2019: 28–30).

DiAngelo makes claims that sound dramatic, such as her insistence that all white people, including herself, harbour and express racism, and that they need to have this constantly identified by themselves as well as drawn to the attention of others. Unfortunately – so the story goes – our ability to 'sustain challenges to our racial positions' (DiAngelo 2019: 112), that is, our ability to endure DiAngelo's style of insisting that we are in some sense racist, is fragile. Hence the 'white fragility' of the title. It follows that the book's rhetorical force relies on retaining the highly emotive connotations of words and phrases used in their everyday senses, even while purporting to employ the same words and phrases in a different and more technical sense.

White Fragility is permeated throughout by various formulations of the claim that any disagreement with its author's ideas is akin to Freudian resistance. But this is another example of poisoning the well of public discussion. *Pace* DiAngelo, disagreement with her ideas is more likely to reveal a perfectly understandable impatience with equivocation and propaganda.

It is also worth observing that *White Fragility* offers no political programme to improve the material conditions of Black Americans or any other group. Rather, it proposes what seems an endless, obsessive self-interrogation by well-intentioned white people who might, at any time, cause emotional hurt through a comment that has no malicious intent behind it but cuts across someone's sensitivities. In these situations, *White Fragility* teaches us, the only approach is self-abnegation and deference to whoever claims to have had their feelings hurt.

In *How to Be an Antiracist*, Kendi calls for racial discrimination where it will tend towards what he calls 'racial equity' (Kendi 2019: 18). By this, he means a broad equality of outcomes between racial groups. On this approach, there can be no causal factors that innocently produce unequal outcomes. Likewise, there can be no such thing as simply being *not* racist in the sense of not being motivated by racial hatred or by beliefs and attitudes of racial superiority. For Kendi, 'there is no such thing as a not-racist idea, only racist ideas and antiracist ideas' (Kendi 2019: 20). That is, we are – at any time – either actively (or better, aggressively) supporting policies that will tend to produce equal outcomes or acting in a racist manner.

Furthermore, Kendi states that even approaches that aim to produce equal outcomes are racist if they propose that existing non-white communities or cultures undergo change of any sort. This applies even if the call for change comes from within a racial community and asks only for voluntary initiatives. Such proposals may seek to undo the effects on communities of a history of discrimination and unequal kinds of education and socialization, and they may in no way manifest racial animus or any theory of biologically inferior racial groups. Nonetheless, in Kendi's terminology, they are 'assimilationist' (Kendi 2019: 24), and hence another form of racism.

One effect of all this is that the concept of racism does not merely creep, but boldly accelerates where it has never gone before. It leaps beyond what makes racism so feared and censured in the first place. Like DiAngelo, and as another example of poisoning the well, Kendi can then deflect any scrutiny or criticism with the claim that even moderate critics are expressing racist views. Mere inaction, such as failure to support policies that have merit by Kendi's lights, is dismissed as yet another form of racism.

Kendi ultimately favours a partly segregated – or he would say 'separated' (see Kendi 2019: 173–80) – society. That is, he wants a society with separate spaces for people from different racial backgrounds, and therefore (as he sees it) from different cultures. This would mean, for example, separate White, Asian, 'Latinx', Middle Eastern, Native American and Black neighbourhoods, churches and schools. However, he does not break this down further and suggest – for example – separate schools for children from Indian, Pakistani, or Chinese backgrounds, separate schools for Sunni and Shia Muslims, separate Jewish schools, or separate schools for Italian or Polish Americans.[6] In short, he does not propose separation of actual cultures that have developed historically and continue to exist.

Racially separated spaces would not be entirely insulated from each other: for example, if I understand Kendi correctly, a child of Japanese Americans could attend a Native American school. However, the child would experience an education dominated by Native American teachers, catering to the parents of Native American students, and socializing students into some version of Native American culture. Likewise, any child sent to a Middle Eastern school would consequently be immersed in, and moulded by, some generic version of Middle Eastern culture. There would also be some institutions where no particular race or culture would predominate. These would be bodies with obvious political or social power, such as legislatures and the editorial boards of newspapers. Overall, however, the society would be balkanized.

Kendi's analysis of race and society raises deep questions, proposes radical social restructuring, and provides a challenge to liberal conceptions of racial relationships. Like DiAngelo's *White Fragility*, it merits scrutiny and critique, but once again it resists these in a way that bypasses reasoned discussion.

Cannon to right of them

None of this criticism of left-wing positions exonerates the traditional Right. It has a long history of intolerance for religious heresy, political dissent, literary and artistic challenges to social convention, and

---

[6]In fact, something much finer grained even than this would seem to be required if the idea were taken seriously.

individuals' deeply personal decisions about how they wish to live to their lives. All of the freedoms obtained in the West during the twentieth century, and especially in the Long Sixties, required tireless campaigning from individuals and groups broadly associated with the Left. As we've seen, it was largely left-wing activists' disillusionment with the pace and profundity of change that led to a loss of trust in liberal ideas. In the United States, in particular, we still see vigorous and intolerant culture warring from the Right, much of it associated with evangelical Christian groups.

The political Right runs an Outrage Industry (see generally Berry and Sobieraj 2014; for discussion, also see Blackford 2019b: 109–13) that pumps out blatant propaganda, distorts political deliberation and is at least as callous as the Social Justice Movement when it comes to intimidating and attempting to destroy opponents. In recent times, the Right has spawned nostalgic populist movements with echoes of fascism in some of their goals and tactics. In many European nations it has produced movements with more than echoes of the fascist parties of the past.

Allow me, therefore, to emphasize that the new normal is *not* anything as simple as an illiberal movement – the Social Justice Movement – capturing many important institutions and exercising cultural hegemony. There's an element of this, and Guy Rundle is correct to state that the movement has obtained 'extraordinary social, economic and cultural power' (Rundle 2022: 23). But this power is far from total and it meets strong resistance in electoral politics and day-by-day cultural warfare. The Social Justice Movement has evidently alienated many people who do not share its assumptions, and this makes it vulnerable to backlashes such as the election of Donald Trump as US president in 2016.

More significantly, *no* major political party or movement, at least in the Anglophone liberal democracies, now seems committed to liberal ideas. No such commitment ever existed on the political Right, and in fact this partly defines the nature of right-wing politicians, movements, parties and social institutions. What has changed through the process described in this chapter and the previous two is a defection of the Left from liberal ideas, and its embrace of a new, significantly illiberal ideology – the ideology of the Social Justice Movement. For its more effervescent participants, this is now a political religion. The result is a war of illiberal tribes, viscerally despising one another and hurling radical moral condemnations.

10 THE NEWEST NORMAL – CURRENT CHALLENGES

One among the philosophies

R. A. Knox was a priest in the Church of England when, as a young man, he converted to Roman Catholicism and soon joined its priesthood. In its day, his 1927 book *The Belief of Catholics* was a popular exposition of the Church's doctrines and an important work of Catholic apologetics. It concludes with a vigorous defence of the Church's traditional willingness to ally itself with territorial governments to suppress ideas opposed to its teachings. Knox suggests that this is most likely to happen in a country with a Catholic government, a 'very strong Catholic majority' and intellectual opposition from only a minority group of 'innovators' with (supposedly) no established traditions or vested interests to be protected (Knox 1927: 241).

In these circumstances, Knox insists, it would be legitimate for the government to impose a system of compulsory Catholic education and to punish (e.g. by deportation or imprisonment) 'those who unsettled the minds of its subjects with new doctrines' (Knox 1927: 241). Considerations of prudence might incline a Catholic government not to involve itself in a campaign of indoctrination and persecution (as it would doubtless seem to non-Catholics). But according to Knox, the government would have the right to go ahead if and when it became expedient. That right has historically been claimed and exercised by the Catholic Church and by governments acting under its influence.

Knox emphasizes that the Church does not view itself as advocating merely one philosophical position among others that vie for adherents: 'The Catholic Church will not be one amongst the philosophies' (Knox

1927: 242). Instead, the Church views its doctrines as true and not up for debate. Where it has power to do so, it will ensure that Catholic doctrines are taught and that even parents cannot refuse their children an education in them. Knox denies that Catholic doctrine is reasonably contestable, but he remarks that it can, in practice, be opposed with 'the sophistries of plausible error' so as to seduce 'simple minds' (Knox 1927: 242). Moreover, he claims, permitting such sophistries to spread will lead to dangerous ideas and aberrations that threaten the social order. Accordingly, Catholic patriots and governments are justified, wherever it is practicable and prudent, in suppressing rival beliefs.

This was the Roman Catholic Church's view for many centuries, but it's somewhat startling to see it expressed so clearly and even defiantly – not by a medieval hierarch, but by a mainstream and respected churchman of the twentieth century.

Liberalism's discontent

The Catholic Church's rhetoric began to soften during the 1960s. In 1965, Pope Paul VI promulgated a declaration entitled *Dignitatis humanae* (Of the Dignity of the Human Person) which represented the Church's embrace of a form of religious freedom. The document was developed in sessions of the Second Vatican Council during 1964 and 1965, and to some extent it represents a break with past positions. In his history of religious toleration in the West, Perez Zagorin sees *Dignitatis humanae* as reversing the Church's long history of intolerance and religious persecution (Zagorin 2003: 310), and indeed, it does reject coercion of religious organizations by means of state power. However, it also demands that the government show favour to religion, rather than, say, being neutral between religious and non-religious worldviews.

If it comes to that, it's questionable how far the Church has genuinely softened. Wherever it retains social and political power, it continues to oppose conduct that it regards as sinful, such as homosexual encounters, same-sex marriage and abortion. It claims authority under God in its interpretation of what it calls the divine law. Since its rise to power in late antiquity, the Church has never been a force for practices of toleration or the moral virtue of tolerance. Quite the opposite is true.

This was exemplified by the 'immediate and intense' response (Tribe 1992: 139) from Catholic organizations and leaders in the United

States when abortion access was liberalized by the Supreme Court's 1973 decision in *Roe v. Wade* – an event almost a decade after the release of *Dignitatis humanae*. Catholic bishops spearheaded a national mobilization of anti-abortion sentiment. Their strategy included efforts at several levels: attempting to amend the US Constitution to prohibit abortion; attempting to overturn the court's decision by gradually filling it with anti-abortion judges; lobbying for restrictions on public funding for abortions; and seeking new processes and rules to frustrate access to abortion rights. Eventually, this mix of tactics by the Catholic Church and other organizations of the traditional Right was successful in the sense that *Roe v. Wade* was overruled in 2022 by *Dobbs v. Jackson Women's Health Organization*.

This is one of many examples that could be adduced of the Church continuing, long after Vatican II and *Dignitatis humanae*, to resist social and legal change in the direction of greater toleration. As another example, the Church has consistently resisted gay rights. This has included political lobbying, such as the opposition of several major political and religious organizations (including the Catholic Church) in Northern Ireland to legalizing male homosexuality years after it became legal in England and Wales (see Chapter 7). This is typical of the Church's ongoing *modus operandi*.

The important point, however, is not to single out the Roman Catholic Church, despite its unique power and influence throughout history. It's an especially prominent example, but *many* powerful religious organizations, governments and political parties, cultural and political movements, and the like take a similar attitude. At least for certain purposes, they do not regard themselves as 'one amongst the philosophies' but as purveying clear-cut, incontestable truths. For them, it follows that their respective viewpoints must prevail through any available means of social or legal enforcement. This requires censoring heretical or dissenting opinions, and persecuting others for allegedly immoral ways of life even in the absence of significant or obvious harm to non-consenting others. The higher the imagined stakes, the stronger the incentive.

This creates a standing challenge to liberalism. More substantive, or 'thicker', understandings of the world and human societies claim to teach incontrovertible and important truths, whereas liberals treat even liberalism's framework for social pluralism and open discussion as subject to debate and possible revision. Liberals may disagree among themselves on many issues of substance. While the liberal framework, or some version of it, might provide the rudiments of a fighting faith, liberals can seem ill-equipped to defend their central ideas in contests with more dogmatic opponents.

Justice Oliver Wendell Holmes, Jr. put his finger on the problem in the 1919 US Supreme Court case *Abrams v. United States*. In his dissenting opinion, he states candidly: 'Persecution for the expression of opinion seems to me perfectly logical' (250 US 616, 639 (1919)). Imagine, that is, that you believe yourself correct on some issue where the stakes are high. If you care deeply enough, if your opponents' speech does not seem merely futile – and tolerable at least for that reason – and you have the power to persecute your opponents for promulgating their 'wrong' and 'dangerous' opinions, why *not* persecute them?

There are, of course, also good and logical reasons for toleration, but they depend on the circumstances of the place and the era. For example, many ancient and medieval empires had reasons to tolerate a diversity of religious beliefs and practices. In part, this was simply to enable social peace and stability in conquered territories. Sometimes it was the logical outcome of syncretism. Sometimes, as in ancient Rome, the state needed only a veneer of formal participation in rites aimed at obtaining the gods' favour; beyond this, issues of individual spiritual salvation were not seen as the state's concern. Various cults and sects with their own soteriological doctrines could look after themselves. In later times, many people concluded that religious knowledge – knowledge of a transcendent world and a transcendent dimension to human life – lies beyond the competence or the proper role of the state.

We could go further in restating and elaborating the reasons for an attitude of tolerance and a practice of toleration. Sometimes the idea might be a policy of maintaining peaceful coexistence through mutual forbearance and avoiding persecutions. Contemporary postmodernists are likely to offer a narrative explaining the historical contingency of current norms and institutions – demonstrating how they came into being and arguing that they needn't be preserved if something else seems more desirable. This approach can become an ideological programme that aims at specific changes and brooks no dissent, but in principle liberals might be sympathetic. At least since Mill, liberals see a possibility of social progress through individual freedoms that permit unorthodox ideas and experiments in living. They will also embrace pluralism as the best path to social peace in contemporary societies marked by divergent worldviews and value systems.

These arguments and others provide a counterweight to the simple logic of persecution. They don't, however, entail that liberalism or toleration comes naturally to many of us. In every era, persecution's logic exercises a powerful attraction. That is liberalism's discontent.

Woke versus anti-woke, or the newest normal

Historically, liberalism was a powerful set of ideas. These were tools for social critique and reform. And yet, as of the mid-1970s it had expended much of its transformative potential. It had overturned outworn restrictions on speech and action, and had undermined many dogmas, practices and discourses that had worked to the disadvantage of women and other subordinated groups. But at every step, it met resistance, and a point was reached where liberal ideas could not produce further change at the rate these groups yearned for. In response, 1980s and 1990s identity politics filled a vacuum.

In the twenty-first century, social media platforms enabled a vast expansion of the public sphere. Many more people were able to take part in discussion and debate, even if they were not celebrities, politicians or professional journalists. One result, increasingly visible as the century has progressed, is an entire new hothouse of ideas built upon late-twentieth-century identity politics. This forms the belief system of the contemporary Social Justice Movement. It fixates on group identities, while deprecating individual freedom. Within this ideological system, particular human beings are not viewed as individuals with unique skills, values, perceptions, life experiences and even personal weaknesses, but as members of overlapping or intersecting demographic groups.

The new belief system shares some goals with traditional liberal theory, in that it emphasizes equality and aims to eliminate hierarchies of social rank. However, it replaces the core idea of toleration with solicitude to certain communities and identity groups that it views as subjugated. It imagines people from these groups as if they are sacred, and it has an imperative not to challenge their beliefs or offend them in any way. It operates with strengthened concepts of diversity, recognition, inclusion and related ideas, and with expanded harm-related concepts: among others, concepts of hate, violence, distress, bigotry, racism, harm itself – of course – and what it means to be or feel unsafe. In freely employing harm concepts, but with new and expanded meanings, the Social Justice Movement pays lip service to liberal principles while rendering them almost meaningless.

The Social Justice Movement's system of beliefs about society and politics arises from a place of kindness and good will. However, it can lead to new kinds of zealotry, intolerance, ruthlessness and even the cruelty of an excited mob when individuals are singled out as targets for social and psychological destruction. Because the stakes seem high, the new system of beliefs is treated as undeniable truth, and any opponents or dissenters are regarded as bad-faith actors. The result is an authoritarian ideology with a logic of persecution, a praxis of surveillance and strong interdictions on various kinds of thinking, speech and behaviour.

Some critics of this ideology view it – or one or more of its sub-components – as a twenty-first-century religion. One such critic is John McWhorter, a Black American academic whose primary expertise is in linguistics. In his 2021 book *Woke Racism*, McWhorter insists that present-day antiracist ideology is not merely similar to a religion, but 'actually is a religion' (McWhorter 2021: 23). He does not examine the concept of a religion, but his point is something like the following.

Antiracist ideology of the kind associated with best-selling author Ibram X. Kendi is incoherent (indeed, according to McWhorter, blatantly self-contradictory), insisted upon dogmatically by its adherents, and notable for many features that can be analogized to the doctrines and practices of Christianity. These include concepts resembling those of evil and sin, along with a kind of canonical status granted to certain books and essays. More generally, it's clear that McWhorter views antiracist ideology as playing the religion role in its adherents' lives: giving purpose; identifying what must not be questioned or otherwise profaned; and inspiring collective exaltation, fervour and hope.

McWhorter is not alone in this regard. The French author Pascal Bruckner, for example, makes a similar point in calling today's politicized antiracism 'the civil religion of modern times' (Bruckner 2018: 11). Such comments are persuasive as far as they go. However, it is overly narrow to focus on contemporary antiracist ideology. Similar remarks apply to much other ideology involving demographic identities, subjugated groups and so on and to the overarching belief system of the Social Justice Movement, which subsumes numerous identity movements and regards them as standing or falling together.

Unlike McWhorter, I baulk at calling this political, or civil, religion a *literal* religion. There is no idea of a transcendent reality or a transcendent dimension to human life. For example, there's no goal of obtaining salvation (or at least a good reincarnation) after death, avoiding offence to God (or to one or more of a plurality of gods), obtaining divine favour for the state and the like. Nonetheless, for many people on what passes as the contemporary political Left, a converging set of political priorities and social theories has become a successor belief system. That is, it's become a successor not only to Christianity, but also to older ideas and ideologies such as Marxism. Especially in the world of academia – and more widely among what Guy Rundle calls the knowledge class – the priorities, theories and jargon of the Social Justice Movement have gained a status much like that of religious doctrines and sacred texts.

They have also produced an ugly reaction in the form of an anti-wokeness culture (indeed, a loosely formed Anti-Wokeness Movement), and even – as we'll soon come to – misguided anti-wokeness legislation. We now see politicians and literary/cultural commentators taking on an anti-woke identity and reflexively opposing everything that the Social Justice Movement approves of – not only its illiberal excesses. This leads to excesses of its own, including an anti-woke version of the Social Justice Movement's conspicuous philistinism. That is, both sides of this culture war spend inordinate effort on examining cultural products such as novels, films and television series with an intolerant eye: obsessing about their ideological acceptability or otherwise, rather than, for example, considering their creative intensity or artistic skill.

The newest normal is cultural warfare between rival illiberal tribes with no thought of learning from each other or even putting up with each other. Both sides police ideological purity and view any tolerance towards the enemy as a sign of corruption or weakness. Much like the Roman Catholic Church, neither side can imagine itself as one among the philosophies.

Political anti-wokeness

While that is partly a matter of impression, we can see the problems more clearly when we turn to governmental manifestations of a contemporary Anti-Wokeness Movement. Here, the recent and continuing efforts of the government of Florida are illuminating. In 2022, Florida's legislature passed the Individual Freedom Act, which was originally planned to be called, in a gimmicky style, the 'Stop Wrongs to Our Kids and Employees (W.O.K.E.) Act'.

This legislation affects public educational institutions in Florida, where it forbids training or instruction that advocates any of eight specific political doctrines. Each of these *forbidden claims*, as we might call them, relates to demographic groups defined by race, colour, national origin or sex. The first such claim is to the effect that members of one race, colour, national origin or sex are morally superior to those of another. Read cold, this looks like a prohibition of long-established forms of prejudice or bigotry. In its social and political context, however, the Act is addressed to a different issue. The objective is to prohibit various related claims made by antiracism activists, feminists and others who form the Social Justice Movement. Antiracism activists, feminists and so on are likely to criticize certain groups, such as white people and men, which they regard as privileged and oppressive, and may sometimes denounce as morally corrupt.

As another example, the eighth of the forbidden claims is: 'Such virtues as merit, excellence, hard work, fairness, neutrality, objectivity, and racial colorblindness are racist or sexist, or were created by members of a particular race, color, national origin, or sex to oppress members of another race, color, national origin, or sex.'[1] Here, the intent is to prohibit teaching such ideas as that white (or European) people invented the concept of merit as a tool to oppress Black (or non-European) people.

The Act is confined to doctrines that relate to groups defined by race, colour, national origin or sex. Accordingly, it does not mention other demographic markers such as religion, sexuality and gender identity. But with that caveat, the Florida legislature has evidently made an effort to nail down what it considers the most egregious and dangerous claims found in 'Woke' ideology. Some of the forbidden claims are sufficiently implausible on their face to prompt doubts as to how many people really support them, let alone teach them to students, but this was not the issue when the constitutionality of the Act was challenged in a US district court.

---

[1] The eight forbidden claims are listed in the Act itself and are also set out in the opening pages of the decision in *Novoa v. Diaz*, issued on 17 November 2022 by the United States District Court for the Northern District of Florida.

An injunction was granted in November 2022 against defendants representing Florida's system of public universities, preventing them from taking action to enforce the statute. In a 139-page decision, the court ruled that Florida could not treat the views expressed in class by academics as the state's own speech which it has the right to control.[2] That is, academics are not merely servants of the state, paid to express its message, but enjoy a measure of independence concomitant with the idea of academic freedom. The court acknowledged previous legal dicta that a state government has wide authority to decide what topics will be taught by its own educational institutions, but held that it does not have the same authority to control what viewpoints academics may express on those topics.

The court was unimpressed by a provision in the Act that allowed the eight forbidden claims to be discussed in a classroom setting, but only in an objective way – which was not defined – and thus without receiving endorsement from the teacher. While the detail of the Act somewhat defies interpretation, it seemingly permits criticism or denigration of the eight claims, as well as factual, non-partisan discussion of them in class, but forbids teachers from endorsing them in any way, however minimal or nuanced. This opens a door to oppressive censorship and surveillance. Moreover, the state's theory that academics' remarks in the classroom of a state university are the government's own speech has the potential to destroy academic freedom entirely.

Accordingly, the legislation was ill-conceived and appropriately met with disdain and mockery from the court. So, was its enactment just an Orwellian exercise in which state censorship of disliked opinions was relabelled as freedom?

The Act's title – referring to individual freedom while introducing new provisions for censorship – is definitely Orwellian. At the same time, we can be too quick to pass judgement, especially if we view the arch-conservative governor of Florida, Ron DeSantis, as a political enemy.

---

[2] This decision is currently under appeal and finding its way through the higher courts. As I finish the manuscript of this book in March 2023, the most recent development is an order, dated 16 March and signed by the United States Court of Appeals for the Eleventh Circuit, refusing to stay the lower court's injunction pending the appeal outcome. Meanwhile, the Florida legislature is considering further legislation that would restrict academic freedom, while similar proposals have been introduced in several other American states.

In trying to extract some insight, we might ask whether anything can be said in the legislation's favour.

There is, in fact, a bit more to say. The academics who challenged the Individual Freedom Act offered evidence of their own standing to sue in the district court. This included presenting evidence that they really did – prior to the legislation – teach doctrines that fell within the eight forbidden claims or were at least near enough in meaning and spirit for the Act to pressure them to self-censor. We don't know how typical these individuals are of academics in the Florida university system, and they mostly revealed little about their pedagogical practice. Still, what they stated, and was subsequently reported by the court, was sufficient to suggest that some senior academics in Florida do, indeed, teach highly contentious ideological doctrines associated with the Social Justice Movement. These are not taught as interesting or important viewpoints among others, provided for students to examine, discuss and possibly argue against, but as the truth.

How far these academics countenance dissent in their classrooms or examination papers is unclear, but nothing in the court's decision assuages a lurking concern. That is, some academics in Florida (and elsewhere) may be teaching illiberal and divisive ideological positions in a dogmatic rather than academic way. If so, this opens their institutions to attack from the political Right.

That observation could lead us to murky questions of educational philosophy and good pedagogical practice. Pedagogical approaches may vary, but academics have some latitude to introduce their personal views in the classroom, so long as they're relevant to the subject matter, and to identify which arguments they find most persuasive. But it's another thing if students (or less powerful staff) are given no opportunities to disagree: for example, if repeating the teacher's views is compelled through teaching and marking practices, or if materials needed to locate and develop counterarguments are not provided to balance the teacher's own views. Beyond a certain point, teaching or training on contentious issues can harden into indoctrination.

A better approach than the state of Florida's might come, yet again, from John Stuart Mill. Insofar as universities form part of the infrastructure of the modern public sphere, we might hope that academics would display the virtues appropriate to public discussion. These include '[the] calmness to see and honesty to state what [their] opponents and their opinions really are, exaggerating nothing to their discredit, keeping back nothing which tells, or can be supposed to tell, in their favour' (Mill [1859]1974: 118).

Perhaps most academics in Florida's state universities are already following Mill's advice. Perhaps some are not, but really should be. For its part, Florida's legislature could look for less heavy-handed and censorious approaches to any problems on its public campuses of indoctrination or ideological purity policing. Outright banning of ideas, declaring them beyond the pale of social toleration, is illiberal and unnecessary.[3]

Current challenges

As we've seen over the past several chapters, liberalism has faced challenges from totalitarian ideologies that seek to control all facets of public and private life and flatly reject any vision of individual freedom. On a world scale, these have included varieties of fascism and the various revolutionary communisms that arose in Russia and other nations. More recently, the liberal democracies of the West have been confronted by political Islam, which has taken more than one form but always with the ambition of establishing theocratic states. Within the liberal democracies themselves, progress towards genuinely liberal arrangements has been contested at every stage by traditional conservatives who try to sustain what they see as Christian moral standards.

These are huge societal and geopolitical forces, active in world history. As they operate, they show how illiberal ideologies produce challenges to liberalism at two levels rather than one. At one level, anti-liberal ideologies are *rivals* to liberalism and its values and principles. At another level, they prompt questions about the *limits* of liberal toleration. In particular, how far must liberals tolerate ideologues who aim to destroy liberal freedoms and establish totalitarian governments?

The European Court of Human Rights has struggled with these issues. In some cases arising under the ECHR, the court has considered attempts to ban political parties based on, or associated with, totalitarian ideologies. In response, it has been reluctant to uphold these bans. The court takes into account the crucial role of political parties within

---

[3]But does this apply to *all* ideas? Perhaps not. Even the most Millian of liberals might not countenance classroom advocacy of Nazi ideas about racial hierarchy. Mill notwithstanding, *some* ideas might be beyond the pale. I'll turn to this in the following pages.

a system of representative democracy. For example, in a 1990s case involving Turkish politics the court protected the rights of a self-styled communist party, notwithstanding the dismal human rights records of communist dictatorships in the Soviet Union and elsewhere (see *United Communist Party of Turkey v. Turkey*; decided 30 January 1998).

This reluctance has, perhaps, been defensible. There's a danger to political and personal freedoms from totalitarian regimes, should they come into being, but there's also danger in overreacting. Recall (from Chapter 6) the harsh approach of American governments and courts during the era between world wars. Prominent among these was the case of Eugene Debs, a socialist leader who was jailed, with the approval of the US Supreme Court, over what now seems an innocuous speech. Likewise, the excesses of the McCarthy era continue to stand as a cautionary example.

In one important case, however, the Strasbourg Court upheld the ban on a political party, and it thereby offered what might be workable guidance for other jurisdictions. As background, a Turkish party had been banned by the nation's Constitutional Court in 1998. At that time, it held power within a coalition and was the largest party in the Grand National Assembly. It had every prospect of obtaining power in its own right at the following election, thus freeing itself from the compromises of coalition government and giving it a path to pursue radical social change. In *Refah Partisi (the Welfare Party) v. Turkey* (decided 13 February 2003), the court upheld this particular ban despite the strong protection for political parties given by Article 11 of the ECHR, relating to freedom of assembly and association.

The court confirmed the right of political parties to exist in the face of hostile state action provided they met two conditions: first, they must use democratic methods to bring about the changes they want, which particularly means not engaging in or calling for violence; second, they must not seek changes that are fundamentally incompatible with democracy itself. The court viewed with disfavour various statements that senior figures in the Welfare Party had made to the effect that they would establish a restructured society based on Islamic law. In other statements, senior figures in the party had spoken of introducing a plurality of legal systems based on the respective religions of the citizens concerned.

The idea of a legal system based on Islamic law and the idea of a plurality of legal systems might sound mutually contradictory. In context, however, the likely implication was that senior party figures planned to introduce an Islamic theocracy, with religions other than Islam enjoying some limited power to govern the lives of their adherents. In effect, the Welfare Party planned to re-establish the *dhimma* system of the Ottoman Empire and its historical predecessors. Furthermore, the court commented adversely on references, again in speeches by senior party figures, to a need for violence, hate and possible bloodshed to achieve what was needed.

From the viewpoint of the court, this added up to an imminent threat to Turkey's democratic order. As the court understood, banning political parties is itself anti-democratic and illiberal, but the issue remains unsettled from the 1930s and 1940s as to how far liberal democracies – as Turkey officially aspired to be – can afford to tolerate the intolerant. The outcome of this case offers one plausible view: beyond a point where the source of the threat has gained significant power and the threat itself has become imminent, a time might legitimately arrive to take decisive action. As a bottom line, some political mechanism might be needed to frustrate totalitarians when they're actually close to gaining power.

Even this need not entail suppression of all speech and expression of the leaders and members of a potentially totalitarian party. It needn't include prison sentences and the like as happened to Eugene Debs. One dimension of toleration, recall, is the *degree* to which we tolerate whatever we have objections to. There is room to provide a degree of toleration even for the speech and activities of would-be totalitarians and theocrats.

And yet, we cannot leave the issue there. No solution to our current predicament appears entirely satisfactory. Notwithstanding the *Refah Partisi* case, Turkey drifted in the following years towards an authoritarian Islamist regime under Recep Erdoğan: 'In Turkey we see a leader who has come to power by democratic means and now slowly, but nonetheless clearly, develops into a religiously mandated dictator' (Cliteur 2021b: 129). We might wonder whether this can be avoided indefinitely in societies where untamed religions and their associated moralities still enjoy majority support. In such a society, the values of pluralism, tolerance and dissent may encounter deep resistance.

Accordingly, the Dutch legal scholar Paul Cliteur expresses sympathy for views such as those expressed by Karl Loewenstein, David Riesman and Karl Popper in the 1930s and 1940s – arguing against toleration of intolerant political movements that would doubtless suppress liberal democracy itself if they ever came to power. At the same time, he refers to the dangers of a 'militant democracy' approach based on suppression of these movements; in particular he acknowledges the excesses of McCarthyism (Cliteur 2021b: 139–43). As Cliteur insists, this creates a genuine problem for liberal democratic states. The occasional ability of illiberal ideologues to obtain power through democratic means should not be underestimated, and what seems unthinkable during a period of civil peace and complacency might become all too thinkable in a time of crisis.

Part of the answer may be found in constitutional safeguards, but even these may not be adequate. Whatever the complete solution might be to this predicament, we at least need a willingness to identify, name, discuss, critique and oppose illiberal movements such as the fascist and communist movements of the past and today's variants of political Islam (Cliteur 2021b: 144–6). In the latter case, our political and community leaders have tended to be non-confrontational. They show discomfort with any expression that tends towards mockery or severe criticism of Islam itself, which can feel, to some, too much like religious, ethnic or even racial bigotry. But religions have their dangers as well as attractions, and these ought to be appreciated. Religions make claims that are inherently controversial, and they strongly motivate their adherents. Some religions, specifically including Christianity and Islam, have powerful inbuilt tendencies to control all aspects of public and private life whenever their organizational leaders are given the opportunity and means.

Islam and Islamism in French society

In France, intense debate over Islam and Islamism arrived in September 1989 with a contest of wills between some female school students who insisted on wearing the Islamic head scarf while school authorities initially resisted this and expelled them. This took place against the background of the Rushdie Affair, and it evoked broader fears of political Islam.

Prior to the twenty-first century, the restrictive garments called the *niqab* and *burqa* were almost unknown in France, but they began to appear in small numbers, apparently as an expression of Muslim identity and commitment to certain Islamic interpretations of sexual modesty. The *niqab* leaves only a slit for the wearer's eyes, while the *burqa* covers even the eyes with a mesh screen. This set up a collision of values, insofar as many public officials in France (and doubtless many ordinary French citizens) experienced the *niqab* and *burqa* as personally confrontational and defiant of the values of the French Republic. Since then, France has continued to struggle in its efforts to come to terms with Islam.

Unlike Christianity, and specifically the once-dominant Roman Catholic Church, Islam is a latecomer to French society. It has no history of compromising with France's long-established suspicion of overt religiosity and its demands that religion play an unassuming social and political role. By contrast, French society is deeply shaped by Enlightenment thinking, a tradition of scepticism and sharp satire, the general spirit of the French Revolution, and the anti-clerical currents of the 1870–1940 Third Republic. France's aggressive conception of secularism, *laïcité*, reflects its unique history.

In 2010, France's National Assembly and Senate enacted a ban on publicly wearing garments that conceal the face, and although this was expressed in general terms the true purpose of the legislation was clear to all. The ban was aimed at the *niqab* and *burqa*. The legislature unashamedly intended to suppress religious/cultural/moral practices that had caused controversy and disquiet. Inevitably, the legislation was challenged on the ground that it breached the ECHR – in particular, Article 8 (respect for family and private life) and Article 9 (freedom to manifest religious belief). The case was heard as *S.A.S. v. France* (decided 1 July 2014).

In its reasoning, the Strasbourg Court fairly swiftly dismissed the French government's argument that such a ban was justified for reasons relating to equality of the sexes, respect for human dignity and public safety. It was, however, willing to consider other concepts that the government put forward. In summary, these included the traditional French value of fraternity, the requirement to observe certain minimum requirements for living together in French society and the requirement for a minimum of civility in social interaction. All of these – or the combination of them, since they are much like alternative formulations of the same point – were said to fall within the ECHR's provision for limitations imposed to protect the rights of others.

The court accepted this argument, holding that it was open for a state party to the ECHR to assign weight to such factors and so enact a ban on garments that impeded interaction between individuals. This is, however, a case where we might wonder just what *rights* the legislation protects. For example, there is no positive right in the ECHR that individuals be able to communicate conveniently with other individuals who may or may not desire this. At most, some Articles provide French citizens with *a negative right against the state* that it will not impede interpersonal communications. This concern is reflected in the dissenting opinion of Judges Nußberger and Jäderblom, which is arguably preferable to that of the judges in the majority.[4]

The clash of values between French republicanism and an exaggerated form of Islamic morality escalated further in 2016. In that year, some local councils in France attempted to prohibit the wearing of a garment colloquially known as the burkini (or burqini). This was a swimsuit designed to preserve sexual modesty in covering almost all of the wearer's body, including her hair. It does not, however, conceal the wearer's face. The burkini's opponents saw it as rejection of the common identity and destiny of the French people in favour of a separate Islamic identity that was ostentatiously affirmed in a public space.

Although the French courts upheld the freedom to wear a burkini – essentially on a liberal interpretation of *laïcité* – this conflict of cultures, traditions and moralities is likely to continue. The conflict is also between ideas of religious freedom and social pluralism (on the one hand) and a desire to tame an assertive and ambitious religion whose adherents cannot easily embrace modern France's proudly secular traditions. The situation will not be resolved easily without a widespread consensus about the relationship between identity as a devout and intensely committed Muslim and identity as a citizen of the French Republic.

Contemporary France is one of the most tolerant societies that have ever existed. Its citizens enjoy ample freedoms. It does, however, affirm certain Enlightenment values that can operate in intolerant ways. In disputes over the *niqab, burqa* and burkini, some French politicians and citizens have displayed a logic of persecution. Given their values, they may have good reasons to *object* to these garments, but it does not follow that they lack grounds to *tolerate* them. That said, they are also right to demand toleration of French traditions, culture and freedoms from dissenting minorities in the country.

France has suffered more than most countries in its encounters with Islamist ideology. A long list of deadly attacks by jihadists could

---

[4]The court adopted closely analogous reasoning in *Dakir v. Belgium* (decided 11 July 2017) after a similar ban was enacted by the Belgian government and subsequently challenged under the ECHR. For critical discussion of these and related cases, see generally Doomen (2018).

be compiled over several decades or, in fact, for the past decade alone. They've included the murderous raid on the Paris offices of the satirical magazine *Charlie Hebdo* in 2015; a series of shootings and bombings that killed over 130 people in November of the same year; and a vehicle ramming, using a cargo truck, on Bastille Day in 2016, leaving over eighty people dead.

The *Charlie Hebdo* murders led to an international outpouring of sentiment in support of France, but even on this occasion there was no shortage of supposedly liberal or left-wing commentators who went close to stating that the victims had it coming (for discussion, see Blackford 2015). Within France itself, one reaction from certain Islamic and Left groups was to denounce Islamophobia rather than fanaticism and murder (Bruckner 2018: 59–60).

Since the gruesome murder of Samuel Paty in October 2020, there has been much attention in Europe to the topic of violence in response to exercises of free speech. Paty was a secondary school teacher in the suburbs of Paris who was attacked and beheaded by an Islamic terrorist, apparently in response to a class that he'd delivered on freedom of speech in which he'd shown one or more cartoons (the exact situation is murky) of the prophet Muhammad, and had drawn attention to the attack on the office of *Charlie Hebdo* five years before. Paty's murder happened when accomplices in the *Charlie Hebdo* murders were on trial. It received little coverage in the Anglophone news media, suggesting a lack of interest in events in France and perhaps some unwillingness to criticize terrorist actions associated with Islam.

Concluding remarks

The twentieth century saw massive programmes of organized violence and the rise of totalitarian political systems with accompanying dislocations, mass murders and purges. Since the 1930s and 1940s, such events have prompted a question of the limits of liberalism. How far can, or should, liberals tolerate the worst actors and their speech and expression?

Oftentimes in human history, societies have confronted opinions that seemed too dangerous to permit. Recall the long history of persecutions for heresy, blasphemy or political dissent. In the seventeenth century, John Locke argued for official toleration of most religions and their teachings, but claimed that some beliefs were beyond the pale of toleration: it was legitimate to suppress them with fire and sword, not because they were false but because they were inherently destructive of the social and political order. Many years later, John Stuart Mill argued forcefully against the core examples that Locke provided. For Mill, unlike many thinkers including Locke and Rousseau, there was no need to suppress denials of the existence of God, or of an afterlife with rewards and punishments (Mill [1859]1974: 91–2).

Historically, Mill had the better of this argument. It does not, however, follow that no opinions at all merit suppression or efforts at driving them to the margins. Must we, for example, tolerate Nazi hate propaganda under the guise of free speech or public discussion, or – should the occasion arise – academic freedom? Since the 1850s, when Mill was writing, a certain innocence has been lost: humanity's experience of total war, genocides and other monstrosities of human action suggests that some things are worse than constraints on free opinion, and that some ideas are too destructive, yet perennially alluring, to be tolerated (compare Barendt 2005: 171). Many taboos have faded, but we no longer countenance claims (whether in so many words or conveyed through rhetoric and imagery) that certain demographic groups are vermin, predators, demons or otherwise fit to be killed. We can view this change as progress (Bruckner 2018: 15) without losing our liberal credentials.

Thus, liberal toleration comes up against limit cases, and in that sense Locke had a point even though he had bad examples. But must we ban all expressions whatsoever of support for revolutionary and potentially totalitarian ideologies, whether fascist, communist, Islamist or otherwise? What about support for terrorist groups, such as glorifying their fallen combatants as heroes and martyrs?[5] These are serious questions, but experience with McCarthyism and its abuses suggests caution. Not every case is a limit case.

Wherever exactly they lie, the outer bounds of toleration must be very wide. Put another way, exceptions should be narrow, precise and readily understandable. As concepts expand, any exceptions at all can become a weapon for censorship and purity policing, so that is one reason for an attitude of maximal tolerance of opinion in the public sphere and even, as far as practicable, in the workplace. Otherwise, we function

---

[5]See, for example, *ROJ TV A/S v. Denmark* (decided by the European Court of Human Rights, 24 May 2018).

in environments of fear. We find ourselves in societies where people conceal what they really think. Expertise is distorted, creativity is stifled, objectivity cannot be assumed, what presents as public opinion no longer reflects the state of opinions privately held in the community, and trust in institutions is undermined.

This sounds all too much like our current plight, so is there a future for liberal toleration? We might feel pessimistic when hearing today's political discourse, with its dogmatism, anger and mutual anathemas. Recall from Chapter 1, the fears expressed by Waleed Aly and Scott Stephens for the future of civil society if this continues. As we've seen, our plight is a product of contingency and history, but does it permit a way forward?

And there, I leave my readers with a question that I can't honestly answer. No events since I wrote *The Tyranny of Opinion* fill me with optimism. If anything, there seems even more acceptance of shaming, bullying and intolerance as responses to ideas, cultural products or ways of life that we object to. There is now even deeper social division relating to ideology and culture.

Pragmatically, what seems obvious to activists from the knowledge class is far less so to the other seventy per cent of society, and this is a structural weakness for what now passes as the twenty-first-century Left. Guy Rundle has suggested, sensibly enough, that a contemporary movement which aims at material improvement for the broad majority of people will need to accept an element of intellectual and social pluralism (Rundle 2022: 36–7). But there are few signs that this will actually happen. On the other side of politics, the emerging anti-woke culture, with its own excesses, is not a satisfactory answer to the illiberal excesses of the Social Justice Movement.

To offer one note of hope – and on this much I follow Friedrich Nietzsche and Michel Foucault – genealogical understanding of ideas and institutions does not leave everything as it was. Ideas and institutions might be justified, even when revealed as products of history: after all, I think there are good arguments for the rule of law and (almost?) unrestricted public discussion, even though these ideas have a history that formed them. But ideas and institutions are at least *denaturalized* once subjected to a genealogical approach. That is, the more we know about how certain ideas became popular, certain institutions became entrenched, certain kinds of language came to be fashionable (while other language was crowded out), the more we see that it might have happened otherwise. And then we might wonder whether different ideas, institutions and language would serve us better.

For my part, I place more trust in the older language of liberal tolerance than the current language of identity groups, harm inflation and performative cries of emotional hurt. In politics and public discussion, we now hear little about liberty, individuality, spontaneity, original thinking or, indeed, about tolerance and toleration. This sort of talk might still appeal to citizens and voters, but it's no longer central to politics and public debate. Perhaps it's too late to revive it. But perhaps it's worth the attempt.

REFERENCES

Adcock, Robert (2013), *Liberalism and the Emergence of American Political Science: A Transatlantic Tale*, New York: Oxford University Press.

Aly, Waleed, and Scott Stephens (2022), *Uncivil Wars: How Contempt Is Corroding Democracy*, Melbourne: Black Inc.

Anspach, Renee R. (1979), 'From Stigma to Identity Politics: Political Activism Among the Physically Disabled and Former Mental Patients', *Social Science and Medicine*, 13A (6): 765–73.

Arnold, John H. (2011), *Belief and Unbelief in Medieval Europe*, London: Bloomsbury.

Balint, Peter (2017), *Respecting Toleration: Traditional Liberalism and Contemporary Diversity*, Oxford: Oxford University Press.

Banner, Stuart (1998), 'When Christianity Was Part of the Common Law', *Law and History Review*, 16 (1): 27–62.

Barendt, Eric (2005), *Freedom of Speech*, 2nd edn, Oxford: Oxford University Press.

Baritz, Loren (1989), *The Good Life: The Meaning of Success for the American Middle Class*, New York: Alfred A. Knopf.

Barnett, S. J. (2003), *The Enlightenment and Religion: The Myths of Modernity*, Manchester and New York: Manchester University Press.

Baumeister, Andrea (2021), 'Public Reason and the Burdens of Citizenship: A Case for Toleration', in Johannes Drerup and Gottfried Schweiger (eds), *Toleration and the Challenges to Liberalism*, 129–45, New York and Oxford: Routledge.

Beales, Derek (2000), 'Religion and Culture', in T. C. W. Blanning (ed.), *The Eighteenth Century*, 131–77, Oxford: Oxford University Press.

Becker, Carl L. ([1932]2003), *The Heavenly City of the Eighteenth-Century French Philosophers*, New Haven and London: Yale University Press.

Bejan, Teresa M. (2017), *Mere Civility: Disagreement and the Limits of Toleration*, Cambridge, MA: Harvard University Press.

Bell, Derrick (1989), *And We Are Not Saved: The Elusive Quest for Racial Justice*, New York: Basic Books.

Bentham, Jeremy ([1776]1948), *A Fragment on Government*, in Wilfred Harrison (ed.), *A Fragment on Government and an Introduction to the Principles of Morals and Legislation*, 1–112, Oxford: Basil Blackwell.

Berkowitz, Eric (2012), *Sex and Punishment: Four Thousand Years of Judging Desire*, Berkeley: Counterpoint.

Berkowitz, Eric (2021), *Dangerous Ideas: A Brief History of Censorship in the West, from the Ancients to Fake News*, Boston: Beacon Press.

Berlin, Isaiah (2014), *Freedom and Its Betrayal*, ed. Henry Hardy, 2nd edn, Princeton and Oxford: Princeton University Press.

Berman, Paul (2011), *The Flight of the Intellectuals*, New York: Melville House.

Berry, Jeffrey M., and Sarah Sobieraj (2014), *The Outrage Industry: Political Opinion Media and the New Incivility*, Oxford and New York: Oxford University Press.

Bhargava, Rajeev (2014), 'Beyond Toleration: Civility and Principled Coexistence in Ashokan Edicts', in Alfred Stepan and Charles Taylor (eds), *Boundaries of Toleration: Religion, Culture, and Public Life*, 173–202, New York: Columbia University Press.

Bird, Wendell (2020), *The Revolutions in Freedom of Press and Speech: From Blackstone to the First Amendment and Fox's Libel Act*, New York: Oxford University Press.

Black, Jeremy (2015), *The Cold War: A Military History*, London: Bloomsbury.

Blackford, Russell (2012), *Freedom of Religion and the Secular State*, Chichester: Wiley-Blackwell.

Blackford, Russell (2015), 'An Odor of Sanctimony: Responses to the Charlie Hebdo Murders', *Free Inquiry*, 35 (3): 8, 40–1.

Blackford, Russell (2019a), 'Bunge on Science and Ideology: A Re-analysis', in Michael R. Matthews (ed.), *Mario Bunge: A Centenary Festschrift*, 439–63, Cham: Springer.

Blackford, Russell (2019b), *The Tyranny of Opinion: Conformity and the Future of Liberalism*, London: Bloomsbury.

Blackford, Russell (2021), 'You Can't Please Everyone: The Secular State, the Liberal State, the Neutral State', in Jasper Doomen and Mirjam van Schaik (eds), *Religious Ideas in Liberal Democratic Societies*, 1–21, Lanham: Lexington Books.

Blackford, Russell, and Udo Schüklenk (2013), *50 Great Myths about Atheism*, Chichester: Wiley-Blackwell.

Blitt, Robert C. (2011), 'Defamation of Religion: Rumors of Its Death Are Greatly Exaggerated', *Case Western Law Review*, 62 (2): 347–98.

Blum, Carol (1986), *Rousseau and the Republic of Virtue: The Language of Politics in the French Revolution*, Ithaca and London: Cornell University Press.

Brown, Callum G. (2009), *The Death of Christian Britain: Understanding Secularisation 1800–2000*, 2nd edn, London and New York: Routledge.

Brown, Callum G. (2017), *Becoming Atheist: Humanism and the Secular West*, London and New York: Bloomsbury.

Bruckner, Pascal (2018), *An Imaginary Racism: Islamophobia and Guilt*, trans. Steven Rendall and Lisa Neal, Cambridge: Polity Press.

Cavanaugh, William T. (2009), *The Myth of Religious Violence: Secular Ideology and the Roots of Modern Conflict*, Oxford: Oxford University Press.

Centeno, Miguel A., and Elaine Enriquez (2016), *War and Society*, Cambridge: Polity Press.

Chesser, Eustace (1960), *Is Chastity Outmoded?*, London: Heinemann.

Cliteur, Paul (2019), *Theoterrorism vs. Freedom of Speech: From Incident to Precedent*, Amsterdam: Amsterdam University Press.

Cliteur, Paul (2021a), 'Islamism, Islam, and the Need for Critique', *Perichoresis*, 19 (3): 69–87.

Cliteur, Paul (2021b), 'Militant Democracy and the Clash of Ideologies', in Afshin Ellian and Paul Cliteur (eds), *The Open Society and Its Closed Communities*, 109–46, The Hague: Eleven.

Cohen, Andrew Jason (2018), *Toleration and Freedom from Harm: Liberalism Reconceived*, London and New York: Routledge.

Cohen, Mark R. (2008), *Under Crescent and Cross: The Jews in the Middle Ages*, Princeton: Princeton University Press.

Combahee River Collective (1979), 'A Black Feminist Statement', in Zillah R. Eisenstein (ed.), *Capitalist Patriarchy and the Case for Socialist Feminism*, 362–72, New York: Monthly Review Press.

Constant, Benjamin ([1820]1988), 'The Liberty of the Ancients Compared with that of the Moderns', in Biancamaria Fontana (trans. and ed.), *Constant: Political Writings*, 307–28, Cambridge: Cambridge University Press.

Courtland, Shane D., Gerald Gaus, and David Schmidtz (2022), 'Liberalism', *Stanford Encyclopedia of Philosophy*, spring 2022 edn. Available online: https://plato.stanford.edu/archives/spr2022/entries/liberalism/ (accessed 15 December 2022).

Crane, Tim (2017), *The Meaning of Belief: Religion from an Atheist's Point of View*, Cambridge, MA, and London: Harvard University Press.

Devlin, Patrick (1965), *The Enforcement of Morals*, London: Oxford University Press.

DiAngelo, Robin (2019), *White Fragility: Why It's So Hard for White People to Talk about Racism*, London: Penguin.

Doomen, Jasper (2018), 'A Veiled Threat: Belcacemi and Oussar v. Belgium', *Ecclesiastical Law Journal*, 20 (2): 190–200.

Dreger, Alice (2015), *Galileo's Middle Finger: Heretics, Activists, and the Search for Justice in Science*, New York: Penguin.

Duncan, Robert (2013), *Pubs and Patriots: The Drink Crisis in Britain during World War One*, Liverpool: Liverpool University Press.

Durkheim, Émile (1915), *The Elementary Forms of the Religious Life*, trans. Joseph Ward. Swain, London: George Allen & Unwin.

Ellis, John M. (2020), *The Breakdown of Higher Education: How It Happened, the Damage It Does, and What Can Be Done*, New York and London: Encounter Books.

Engels, David (2013), *Holocaust: The Third Reich and the Jews*, 2nd edn, Oxford and New York: Routledge.

Fawcett, Edmund (2018), *Liberalism: The Life of an Idea*, 2nd edn, Princeton and Oxford: Princeton University Press.

Faye, Shon (2021), *The Transgender Issue: An Argument for Justice*, London: Allen Lane.

Field, Clive D. (2017), *Secularization in the Long 1960s: Numerating Religion in Britain*, Oxford and New York: Oxford University Press.

Fiss, Owen M. (1996a), *Liberalism Divided: Freedom of Speech and the Many Uses of State Power*, Boulder and London: Westview Press.

Fiss, Owen M. (1996b), *The Irony of Free Speech*, Cambridge, MA, and London: Harvard University Press.

Forst, Rainer (2016), *Toleration in Conflict: Past and Present*, trans. Ciaran Cronin, Cambridge: Cambridge University Press.

Forst, Rainer (2017), 'Toleration', *Stanford Encyclopedia of Philosophy*, fall 2017 edn. Available online: https://plato.stanford.edu/entries/toleration (accessed 15 December 2022).

Foucault, Michel (1980), *Power/Knowledge: Selected Interviews and Other Writings, 1972–1977*, ed. Colin Gordon, Brighton: Harvester Press.

Freeman, Charles (2005), *The Closing of the Western Mind: The Rise of Faith and the Fall of Reason*, New York: Vintage.

Freeman, Charles (2008), *A.D. 381: Heretics, Pagans, and the Dawn of the Monotheistic State*, New York: Overlook Press.

Gaddis, John Lewis (2005), *The Cold War: A New History*, New York: Penguin.

Gaddis, Michael (2005), *There Is No Crime For Those Who Have Christ: Religious Violence in the Roman Empire*, Berkeley: University of California Press.

Gaus, Gerald F. (2003), *Contemporary Theories of Liberalism: Public Reason as a Post-Enlightenment Project*, London: Sage.

Geary, Daniel (2013), 'Children of The Lonely Crowd: David Riesman, the Young Radicals, and the Splitting of Liberalism in the 1960s', *Modern Intellectual History*, 10 (3): 603–33.

Gitlin, Todd (1973), 'The Future of a Effusion: How Young Activists Will Get to 1984', in Robert Paul Wolff (ed.), *1984 Revisited: Prospects for American Politics*, 11–39, New York: Alfred A. Knopf.

Glendon, Mary Ann (2001), *A World Made New: Eleanor Roosevelt and the Declaration of Human Rights*, New York: Random House.

Gray, John (1996), *Post-Liberalism: Studies in Political Thought*, paperback edn, London and New York: Routledge.

Green, David (1987), *Shaping Political Consciousness: The Language of Politics in America from McKinley to Reagan*, Ithaca and London: Cornell University Press.

Greer, Steven (2023), *Falsely Accused of Islamophobia: My Struggle against Academic Cancellation*, Washington, DC: Academica Press.

Gutmann, Amy, ed. (1994), *Multiculturalism: Examining the Politics of Recognition*, Princeton: Princeton University Press.

Hamilton, Neil ([1995]2017), *Zealotry and Academic Freedom: A Legal and Historical Perspective*, London and New York: Routledge.

Hart, H. L. A. (1963), *Law, Liberty, and Morality*, Oxford: Oxford University Press.

Haslam, Nicholas (2016), 'Concept Creep: Psychology's Expanding Concepts of Harm and Pathology', *Psychological Inquiry*, 27 (1): 1–17.

Heyd, David (2021), 'The Mutual Independence of Liberalism and Toleration', in Johannes Drerup and Gottfried Schweiger (eds), *Toleration and the Challenges to Liberalism*, 79–96, New York and Oxford: Routledge.

Himmelfarb, Gertrude (2004), *The Roads to Modernity: The British, French, and American Enlightenments*, New York: Vintage.

Hixson, Richard F. (1996), *Pornography and the Justices: The Supreme Court and the Intractable Obscenity Problem*, Carbondale and Edwardsville: Southern Illinois University Press.

Honneth, Axel (1995), *The Struggle for Recognition: The Moral Grammar of Social Conflicts*, trans. Joel Anderson, Oxford: Polity Press.

Horkheimer, Max, and Theodor W. Adorno ([1947]1988), *Dialectic of Enlightenment*, New York: Continuum.

Humboldt, Wilhelm von ([1852]1969), *The Limits of State Action*, Cambridge: Cambridge University Press.

Jamal, Arif A. (2015), 'The Impact of Definitional Issues on the Right of Freedom of Religion and Belief', in Silvio Ferrari (ed.), *Routledge Handbook of Law and Religion*, 91–102, Oxford and New York: Routledge.

Johnson, Luke Timothy (2009), *Among the Gentiles: Greco-Roman Religion and Christianity*, New Haven and London: Yale University Press.

Kamen, Henry (1967), *The Rise of Toleration*, London: Weidenfeld and Nicolson.

Kant, Immanuel ([1784]1991), 'An Answer to the Question: "What Is Enlightenment?"' In Hans Reiss (ed.), H. B. Nisbet (trans.), *Kant: Political Writings*, 2nd edn, 54–60, Cambridge: Cambridge University Press.

Katz, Martin F. (1985), 'After the Deconstruction: Law in the Age of Post-Structuralism', *University of Western Ontario Law Review*, 24 (1): 51–66.

Kaviraj, Sudipta (2014), 'Modernity, State, and Toleration in Indian History: Exploring Accommodations and Partitions', in Alfred Stepan and Charles Taylor (eds), *Boundaries of Toleration: Religion, Culture, and Public Life*, 233–66, New York: Columbia University Press.

Kendi, Ibram X. (2019), *How to Be an Antiracist*, London: Bodley Head.

Kenez, Peter (2013), *The Coming of the Holocaust: From Antisemitism to Genocide*, New York: Cambridge University Press.

Kenez, Peter (2017), *A History of the Soviet Union: From the Beginning to Its Legacy*, 3rd edn, Cambridge: Cambridge University Press.

King, Preston (1976), *Toleration*, London: George Allen & Unwin.

Kipnis, Laura (2017), *Unwanted Advances: Sexual Paranoia Comes to Campus*, New York: HarperCollins.

Kirsch, Jonathan (2004), *God against the Gods: The History of the War between Monotheism and Polytheism*, New York: Penguin.

Knox, R. A. (1927), *The Belief of Catholics*, London: Ernest Benn.

Koestler, Arthur, et al. (1950), *The God That Failed: Six Studies in Communism*, introd. Richard Crossman, London: Hamish Hamilton.

Kuo, Cheng-tian (2017), 'Introduction: Religion, State, and Religious Nationalism in Chinese Societies', in Cheng-tian Kuo (ed.), *Religion and Nationalism in Chinese Societies*, 13–51, Amsterdam: Amsterdam University Press.

Kymlicka, Will (1989), *Liberalism, Community, and Culture*, Oxford: Clarendon Press.

Kymlicka, Will (1995), *Multicultural Citizenship: A Liberal Theory of Minority Rights*, Oxford and New York: Oxford University Press.

Lagerwey, John (2019), *Paradigm Shifts in Early and Modern Chinese Religion*, Leiden and Boston: Brill.

Laqueur, Thomas W. (2003), *Solitary Sex: A Cultural History of Masturbation*, New York: Zone Books.

Laqueur, Walter (2006), *The Changing Face of Antisemitism: From Ancient Times to the Present Day*, New York: Oxford University Press.

Levy, Leonard W. (1985), *Emergence of a Free Press*, New York and Oxford: Oxford University Press.

Levy, Leonard W. (1995), *Blasphemy: Verbal Offense against the Sacred, from Moses to Salman Rushdie*, Chapel Hill: University of North Carolina Press.

Levy, Leonard W. (2001), *Origins of the Bill of Rights*, New Haven and London: Yale University Press.

Liu, Xiaogan (2018), 'All-embracing: A Laozian Version of Toleration', in Vicki A. Spencer (ed.), *Toleration in Comparative Perspective*, 235–53, Lanham: Lexington Books.

Locke, John ([1689]1983), *A Letter Concerning Toleration*, Indianapolis: Hackett.

Loewenstein, Karl (1937a), 'Militant Democracy and Fundamental Rights, I', *American Political Science Review*, 31 (3): 417–32.

Loewenstein, Karl (1937b), 'Militant Democracy and Fundamental Rights, II', *American Political Science Review*, 31 (4): 638–58.

McAdam, Marika (2018), *Freedom from Religion and Human Rights Law: Strengthening the Right to Freedom of Religion and Belief for Non-Religious and Atheist Rights-Holders*, London and New York: Routledge.

McClelland, Charles E. (1980), *State, Society, and University in Germany, 1700–1914*, Cambridge: Cambridge University Press.

MacKinnon, Catharine A. (1996), *Only Words*, paperback edn, Cambridge, MA: Harvard University Press.

McWhorter, John (2021), *Woke Racism: How a New Religion Has Betrayed Black America*, New York: Portfolio/Penguin.

Malik, Kenan (2010), *From Fatwa to Jihad: The Rushdie Affair and Its Legacy*, paperback edn, London: Atlantic Books.

Manent, Pierre (1995), *An Intellectual History of Liberalism*, trans. Rebecca Balinski, Princeton: Princeton University Press.

Manvell, Roger (1976), *The Trial of Annie Besant and Charles Bradlaugh*, New York: Horizon.

Marcus, Kenneth L. (2015), *The Definition of Anti-Semitism*, New York: Oxford University Press.

Marcuse, Herbert (1969), 'Repressive Tolerance', in Robert Paul Wolff, Barrington Moore, Jr., and Herbert Marcuse, *A Critique of Pure Tolerance*, 93–137, London: Jonathan Cape.

Mchangama, Jacob (2022), *Free Speech: A Global History from Socrates to Social Media*, London: Basic Books.

Mill, J. S. ([1859]1974), *On Liberty*, London: Penguin.

Millman, Brock (2005), 'HMG and the War against Dissent, 1914–18', *Journal of Contemporary History*, 40 (3): 413–40.

Montesquieu, Baron de ([1748]1989), *The Spirit of the Laws*, trans and ed. Anne M. Cohler, Basia Carolyn Miller, and Harold Samuel Stone, New York: Cambridge University Press.

Morris, Ian (2015), *War. What Is It Good For? The Role of Conflict in Civilisation, from Primates to Robots*, paperback edn, London: Profile Books.

Munck, Thomas (2000), *The Enlightenment: A Comparative Social History 1721–1794*, London: Arnold.

Nash, David (2007), *Blasphemy in the Christian World: A History*, Oxford: Oxford University Press.

Newman, Jay (1982), *Foundations of Religious Tolerance*, Toronto: University of Toronto Press.

Nixey, Catherine (2019), *The Darkening Age: The Christian Destruction of the Classical World*, New York: Mariner Books.

Nozick, Robert (1974), *Anarchy, State, and Utopia*, New York: Basic Books.

Okin, Susan Moller, et al. (1999), *Is Multiculturalism Bad for Women?*, Princeton: Princeton University Press.

Oldstone-Moore, Jennifer (2015), 'Chinese Religion', in Willoughby Deming (ed.), *Understanding the Religions of the World: An Introduction*, 115–66, Chichester: John Wiley & Sons.

Oxford English Dictionary, 3rd edn (online version).

Pabst, Adrian (2017), 'Postliberalism: The New Centre Ground of British Politics', *Political Quarterly*, 88 (3): 500–9.

Payer, Pierre J. (1984), *Sex and the Penitentials: The Development of a Sexual Code 550–1150*, Toronto: University of Toronto Press.

Payer, Pierre J. (1993), *The Bridling of Desire: Views of Sex in the Later Middle Ages*, Toronto: University of Toronto Press.

Pinkney, Alphonso (1984), *The Myth of Black Progress*, Cambridge: Cambridge University Press.

Pluckrose, Helen, and James Lindsay (2020), *Cynical Theories: How Activist Scholarship Made Everything about Race, Gender, and Identity – and Why This Harms Everybody*, Durham, NC: Pitchstone Publishing.

Popper, Karl R. (1994), *The Myth of the Framework: In Defence of Science and Rationality*, ed. M. A. Notturno, London and New York: Routledge.

Popper, Karl ([1945]2011), *The Open Society and Its Enemies*, Oxford: Routledge.

Rawls, John (1971), *A Theory of Justice*, 1st edn, Cambridge, MA: Harvard University Press.

Rawls, John (1993), *Political Liberalism*, New York: Columbia University Press.

Riesman, David (1942a), 'Democracy and Defamation: Control of Group Libel', *Columbia Law Review*, 42 (5): 727–80.

Riesman, David (1942b), 'Democracy and Defamation: Fair Game and Fair Comment I', *Columbia Law Review*, 42 (7): 1085–1123.

Riesman, David (1942c), 'Democracy and Defamation: Fair Game and Fair Comment II.The United States', *Columbia Law Review*, 42 (8): 1282–1318.

Riesman, David (1951), 'The "Militant" Fight against Anti-Semitism', *Commentary*, 11 (1): 11–9.

Riesman, David ([1950–1969]2001), *The Lonely Crowd: A Study of the Changing American Character*, abridged edn, New Haven: Yale University Press.

Rohmann, Dirk (2016), *Christianity, Book-Burning, and Censorship in Late Antiquity*, Berlin and Boston: De Gruyter.

Rotunda, Ronald D. (1986), *The Politics of Language: Liberalism as Word and Symbol*, Iowa City: Iowa University Press.

Rousseau, Jean-Jacques ([1762]1968), *The Social Contract*, trans. Maurice Cranston, London: Penguin.

Rundle, Guy (2022), 'Necessity Has No Law: The New Cultural Politics and the Rise of the Knowledge Class', *Meanjin*, 22 (1): 22–37.

Rüpke, Jorg (2018), *Pantheon: A New History of Roman Religion*, trans. David M. B. Richardson, Princeton and Oxford: Princeton University Press.

Rushdie, Salman (2012), *Joseph Anton: A Memoir*, London: Jonathan Cape.

Ruthven, Malise (1990), *A Satanic Affair: Salman Rushdie and the Rage of Islam*, London: Chatto & Windus.

Sandel, Michael J. (1982), *Liberalism and the Limits of Justice*, New York: Cambridge University Press.

Sauer, Eberhard (2003), *The Archeology of Religious Hatred in the Roman and Early Medieval World*, Stroud: Tempus Publishing.

Schonthal, Benjamin (2018), 'The Tolerations of Theravada Buddhism', in Vicki A. Spencer (ed.), *Toleration in Comparative Perspective*, 179–96, Lanham: Lexington Books.

Segerstråle, Ullica (2000), *Defenders of the Truth: The Sociobiology Debate*, New York: Oxford University Press.

Shapiro, Michael J. (1984), 'Literary Production as a Politicizing Practice', in Michael J. Shapiro (ed.), *Language and Politics*, 215–53, New York: New York University Press.

Smith, William Cantwell (1963), *The Meaning and End of Religion: A New Approach to the Religious Traditions of Mankind*, New York: Macmillan.

Sociobiology Study Group of Science for the People (1976), 'Sociobiology – Another Biological Determinism', *BioScience*, 26 (3): 182, 184–6.

Spencer, Vicki A. (2018), 'Introduction', in Vicki A. Spencer (ed.), *Toleration in Comparative Perspective*, ix–xxii, Lanham: Lexington Books.

Stock, Kathleen (2021), *Material Girls: Why Reality Matters for Feminism*, London: Fleet.

Stone, Adrienne (2007), 'How to Think about the Problem of Hate Speech: Understanding a Comparative Debate', in Katharine Gelber and Adrienne Stone (eds), *Hate Speech and Freedom of Speech in Australia*, 59–80, Sydney: Federation Press.

Swann, Julian (2000), 'Politics and the State in Eighteenth-Century Europe', in T. C. W. Blanning (ed.), *The Eighteenth Century*, 11–51, Oxford: Oxford University Press.

Taylor, Charles (1989), 'The Rushdie Controversy', *Public Culture*, 2 (1): 118–22.

Taylor, Charles (1994), 'The Politics of Recognition', in Amy Gutmann (ed.), *Multiculturalism: Examining the Politics of Recognition*, 25–73, Princeton: Princeton University Press.

Taylor, Charles (2007), *A Secular Age*, Cambridge, MA: Harvard University Press.

Tocqueville, Alexis de ([1856]2011), *The Ancien Régime and the French Revolution*, trans. Arthur Goldhammer, Cambridge: Cambridge University Press.

Tocqueville, Alexis de ([1835–1840]2012), *Democracy in America*, trans. James T. Schleifer, Indianapolis: Liberty Fund.

Tribe, Laurence H. (1992), *Abortion: The Clash of Absolutes*, paperback edn, New York and London: W. W. Norton.

van Schaik, Mirjam (2016), 'Religious Freedom and Blasphemy Law in a Global Context', in Paul Cliteur and Tom Herrenberg (eds), *The Fall and Rise of Blaphemy Law*, 177–207, Leiden: Leiden University Press.

Walker, Samuel (1994), *Hate Speech: The History of an American Controversy*, Lincoln, NE: University of Nebraska Press.

Warsi, Sayeeda (2017), 'Foreword', in Farah Elahi and Omar Khan, *Islamophobia: Still a Challenge for Us All*, v, London: Runnymede Trust.

Whitmarsh, Tim (2016), *Battling the Gods: Atheism in the Ancient World*, New York: Vintage.

Whittington, Keith E. (2018), *Speak Freely: Why Universities Must Defend Free Speech*, Princeton and Oxford: Princeton University Press.

Wilson, Edward O. (1976), 'Academic Vigilantism and the Political Significance of Sociobiology', *BioScience*, 26 (3): 183, 187–90.

Wilson, Edward O. ([1975]2000), *Sociobiology: The New Synthesis*, 25th anniversary edn, Cambridge, MA, and London: Harvard University Press.

Wokler, Robert (2012), *Rousseau, the Age of Enlightenment, and Their Legacies*, ed. Bryan Garsten, Princeton and Oxford: Princeton University Press.

Young, Iris Marion (1990), *Justice and the Politics of Difference*, Princeton: Princeton University Press.

Young, Iris Marion (2000), *Inclusion and Democracy*, Oxford: Oxford University Press.

Yu, Kam-por (2018), 'Two Conceptions of Tolerating in Confucian Thought', in Vicki A. Spencer (ed.), *Toleration in Comparative Perspective*, 217–33, Lanham: Lexington Books.

Zagorin, Perez (2003), *How the Idea of Religious Toleration Came to the West*, Princeton: Princeton University Press.

INDEX

Hinduism. *See* Indian civilization/
 religion
history, study of 10–11
Hitler, Adolf 119–20
Hobbes, Thomas 47, 171
Hobhouse, L. T. 98
Holbach, Baron d' 61–2
Holmes, Oliver Wendell, Jr. 111–12,
 222
Holocaust 9, 127, 136
Holyoake, George 87
homosexuality 40–1, 62, 89, 108 n. 2,
 133–8, 142, 194–5, 200, 220–1
Hone, William 86
Honneth, Axel 172 n. 5
Hoover, Herbert 105, 162
House Un-American Activities
 Committee 114–15
Huguenots 45–6, 64–5
Humboldt, Wilhelm von 94, 97, 153,
 171
Humboldtian model. *See under*
 universities
Hungarian Revolution 117
Hunt, Tim 206–7
Hus, Jan 43–4, 157
Hyrcanus, John 35

I Am Curious (Yellow) 146
identity politics 6, 9, 162–3, 165–92,
 193–5, 233
 early development 166–8
 stages 191–2
ideology
 concept 21
 distinguished from religion 21–7
inclusion 172, 182, 191–2, 198–201,
 209, 223
Index Librorum Prohibitorum 52, 60
Indian civilization/religion 8, 27, 30–3
Industrial Revolution(s) 79, 106
international human rights law 18,
 127–30, 176, 189–90, 209
Iranian Revolution 190
Islam 18, 27, 32–3. *See also dhimma*
 system, Muhammad

Islamism 14, 190–1, 230–5
Islamophobia 193–4, 197, 200,
 207, 209, 235

Jansen, Cornelius/Jansenists 57
Jaucourt, Louis de 60, 62
Jazz Age. *See* prohibitionism/
 Prohibition era
Jefferson, Thomas 47, 69, 71, 82–3
Jehovah's Witnesses 113–14
Jesus of Nazareth 32, 39, 73, 178, 181
Jews/Judaism 18, 35, 60. *See also*
 antisemitism, Zionist
 movement
 historical Christian attitudes
 38–40, 44, 46, 187–8, 194
 Islamic attitudes 32–3, 187–8
 in Nazi racial theory 119–20
 unsympathetic portrayals in
 media 124
jihadis 234–5
Jim Crow laws 81, 136, 168
Joyce, James 100
 Ulysses 110

Kant, Immanuel 77, 89, 100, 143,
 169
 interpretation of Enlightenment
 58–9
Katz, Martin F. 169–70
Kendi, Ibram X. 194, 214–17, 224
Khomeini, Ayatollah Ruhollah
 184–5, 190
King, Martin Luther 135
King, Preston 13
*Kingsley International Pictures Corp.
 v. Regents of the University of
 New York* 145
Kipnis, Laura 204–6
Kirkup, James 178, 182
knowledge class 182 n. 10, 196–8,
 225, 237
Knowlton, Charles 90–1
Knox, R. A. 219–20
Korean War 125
Krushchev, Nikita 117